FRANCE IN WORLD POLITICS

FRANCE IN
WORLD POLITICS

Edited by
ROBERT ALDRICH

and

JOHN CONNELL

ROUTLEDGE
London and New York

First published 1989
by Routledge
11 New Fetter Lane, London EC4P 4EE
29 West 35th Street, New York, NY 10001

© 1989 Robert Aldrich and John Connell

Printed and bound in Great Britain by
Mackays of Chatham PLC, Chatham, Kent

British Library Cataloguing in Publication Data

France in world politics.
1. France. Foreign relations
I. Aldrich, Robert, *1954-* II. Connell, John,
1946-
327.44

ISBN 0-415-03506-6

Library of Congress Cataloging in Publication Data

France in world politics / edited by Robert Aldrich and John Connell.
p. cm.
Includes index.
ISBN 0-415-03506-6
1. France — Foreign relations — 1969–1981. 2. France — Foreign
relations — 1981- 3. France — Foreign relations — Philosophy.
I. Aldrich, Robert, 1954-   II. Connell, John.
DC422.F73 1989

327.44–dc19   88-29384
                                                   CIP

CONTENTS

CONTRIBUTORS

Dr Robert Aldrich
Department of Economic History
University of Sydney
Sydney NSW 2006
Australia

Dr John Connell
Department of Geography
University of Sydney
Sydney NSW 2006
Australia

Dr Howard Evans
Department of French Studies
University of Leeds
Leeds LS2 9JT
England

Dr Mark B. Hayne
Department of History
University of New England
Armidale NSW 2350
Australia

Professor Jolyon Howorth
Department of French Civilisation
University of Bath
Bath BA2 7AY
England

Dr Guy Martin
Diplomacy Training Programme
University of Nairobi
PO Box 30197
Nairobi
Kenya

Dr Max Silverman
Department of French Studies
University of Leeds
Leeds LS2 9JT
England

Dr Mark Wise
Department of Geographical Sciences
Plymouth Polytechnic
Plymouth PL4 8AA
Devon
England

PREFACE

This book examines various aspects of France's
presence in the world. We have intentionally
chosen authors from outside France. Furthermore,
our contributors include not only political scientists but historians, geographers and specialists
in French civilisation. We hope that this gives a
different view to the themes than would otherwise
be possible. Each author bears responsibility for
his views, and we have made no effort to choose
writers who necessarily agree either with each
other or with us. The book is not comprehensive
though we have tried to look at what appear to us
to be some of the vital and distinguishing characteristics of France's foreign relations.

We are grateful to the various contributors,
some of whom we have never met since they are
spread over three continents, and most of whom responded to our ever-changing deadline with pa-
tience and alacrity. We would also like to thank
Kay Foster and Julie Manley for wrestling with
both our demands and the intricacies of word-
processing and laser printing.

Robert Aldrich and John Connell
Sydney
March 1988

Chapter One

BEYOND THE HEXAGON: FRANCE IN WORLD POLITICS

Robert Aldrich and John Connell

France rightly perceives itself as a nation with
influences and activities extending far beyond the
Hexagon, or la France métropolitaine, the European
territory of the country. In fact, most observers,
French as well as foreign, see France as having a
global presence. As a permanent member of the
United Nations Security Council, the fifth largest
economy in the world, the proprietor of the
world's third largest maritime zone, the former
administrator of the world's second largest colonial empire, the mother country of a language
spoken by over 1 million people, one of the five
nuclear powers, the third largest arms vendor in
the world and a founding member of the European
Community (EC), France can justifiably claim to
have an international presence, even if its might
does not equal that of the superpowers. Within
France it is not unusual for it to be described as
'the third superpower', which it is in terms of
nuclear capacity, or at least as a puissance
moyenne, a mid-range power. No other European nation has the same combination of military, political, economic and cultural power as France, and
few outside Europe enjoy the international influence of France, even when that power is often
seriously challenged. Recent events in such far-
flung areas as Chad and New Caledonia demonstrate
the commitment of France's policy-makers to maintaining that international presence.[1]
France maintains 150 diplomatic missions abroad,
and Paris, with a greater number of embassies than
anywhere else in Europe, is a crossroads for
chiefs of state, prime ministers and other officials, but France's international presence, like
that of any country, is more than just diplomatic
relations. France's overseas presence is also a
question of economic and technical aid, trade and
overseas investment, political links and treaties,
military bases and a cultural programme. In exceptional cases, one can even take the place of another, keeping an unofficial French stake in a

1

region where France's diplomatic presence is contested or rejected. Public and private concerns
intertwine to compose France's activities in
Europe, Africa, Asia, the Americas and the Pacific. Despite decolonisation and unwillingness to
participate in certain international organisations
and treaties, France has been able to keep a toe-
hold in every region of the world and, in Europe
and Africa, to play a major role during the past
several decades. Moreover, even with the changes
in French policy from Gaullism to post-Gaullism,
then socialism, and most recently the 'cohabitation' of a socialist president and a conservative prime minister, French external policy
has displayed a great continuity of ideology and
action. France's international role has not been
without its failures, contradictions and ambiguities, but it has been notably successful in maintaining a French presence when France's economy,
politics and culture have been buffeted by attacks
from France's rivals.

Various commentators have tried to discover the
structural features and guiding continuities in
France's external activities. Jean-Baptiste
Duroselle, an historian, chooses to look at
France's activities overseas in the context of the
longue durée and isolates several invariants in
that policy. First is geography, the natural pat-
rimony of France, which has given the nation a
mosaic of territories and populations inside the
Hexagon, but also the advantages and dangers of
having a continental frontier and coasts on both
the Atlantic and the Mediterranean. France has
thus been constantly in search of security, an effort pursued by arms, appeasement and alliances.
France, torn between a continental and a maritime
outlook, through most of history has preferred
continental ambitions. Duroselle also finds in
France's foreign activities a strand of invention,
discovery and creativity, and he emphasises the
'will power' of the country. This willpower has
four aspects: the will to be a nation (and the reality of a nation with a long history and a centralising heritage), the will to make the nation
part of an international movement (whether that be
Christianity, the Enlightenment, revolutionary
universalism, an empire or Europe), the will to
promote pity and tolerance and the will to be
democratic.[2]

Such a Braudelian perspective is certainly revealing about the centuries-long continuity in

French policy, and certain particular features of that policy which echo over long periods could be signalled: the uneasy relations between France and England dating from the Middle Ages; the French presence in the Americas, Africa and Asia, which goes back to the fifteenth century, the cultural vocation that was a key for the philosophes; the notion of the grandeur of the state, no better manifested than in the reign of the Sun King. Yet such generalisations, spanning centuries and continents, can only be hazardous, and they overlook the changes in French policy and the lack of coherence of some French actions. They also do not go very far in addressing the central question posed by historians of diplomacy and foreign policy in recent decades: is a nation's foreign policy an autonomous realm or does it depend largely on domestic constraints and strategies? If the prime component is domestic, is the deciding voice in foreign policy cast by the political elite or by pressure groups which exercise a dominant influence with politicians and statesmen? An ancillary question is whether there is a philosophical and ideological logic to foreign activities or whether they are simply a question of Realpolitik.[3]

Historians and political scientists are generally not so foolhardy as to offer brief answers to such questions which could sum up French foreign policy with a neat equation valid for an ancien régime, two restored monarchies, two empires and five republics. But most point to a continuity in French foreign policy at least over the past thirty years, that is, since the inauguration of the Fifth Republic. They credit General de Gaulle as the father, or at least the midwife, of contemporary foreign policy, the man who framed France's international presence (just as he formulated the constitution which gave him and his successors the tools with which to craft that policy) in the image of his own 'certain idea of France'. But there were several aspects to de Gaulle's vision: the call of 18 June 1940 and the Resistance against Nazi barbarism, the de Gaulle of 1944, collaborating with the Left in a campaign for the modernisation of France, the de Gaulle of 1958 facing decolonisation and unrest, and the de Gaulle of the late 1960s, provocative and reactionary. And the international situation changed dramatically: when de Gaulle returned to power, there were only a handful of independent countries in Africa, China

3

was in the midst of an isolationist and doctri-
naire period, the Berlin wall had not yet been
built, Vietnam rested in the lull between the
French and the American wars, the treaty establishing a common market of six European nations
was just coming into force. By the time de Gaulle
retired the world had been transformed.

Yet the strength of de Gaulle's vision is evi-
denced by the willingness of his successors to
adopt his views. Even François Mitterrand, whose
septennat was inaugurated with hopes of pursuing a
more 'socialist' policy, has rallied to the General. For example, a recent writer has spoken of
Mitterrand's speech at the Cancun conference of
1981, calling for a fairer deal for the Third
World, as 'the pendant, on the economic and financial level, of what was, on the strategic and military level, the famous speech of General de
Gaulle in Phnom Penh in 1968', a speech in which
de Gaulle overtly criticised the imperialist policy of the United States and its closest allies.
Jean Daniel speaks about the 'convergence' between
'a theme of the Gaullist Right and a project of
the social-democratic Left which contitutes a
consensual legacy that the President of cohabitation wants to make an irreversible policy'.[4]

Certain lines have hence remained constant in
French foreign policy. Stanley Hoffmann stresses
France's demand for independence and its activism.
Independence, argues Hoffmann, means for France a
desire to maintain rank with the major powers, to
preserve an equilibrium among the blocs and to
pursue a policy of political and economic modernisation. This general approach, continues Hoffmann,
is not without ambiguities, but the Gaullist vision was elastic enough to make progressive adjustments, a fluidity necessary to the fulfillment
of its goals.[5] Alfred Grosser, the most distin-
guished commentator on foreign policy in France,
stresses that 'for a whole group of reasons, independence is a key reference in the French political game'. He adds that the heritage of de Gaulle
has survived the general: 'This "certain idea of
France" has not been fundamentally different from
one president to the other'.[6]

Furthermore, commentators agree that the deciding element in French foreign policy in the Fifth
Republic has been the president himself. In
Grosser's words, 'external policy, including military policy, since 1958 has never ceased being the
prerogative of the chief of state', his domaine

réservé.[7] Although the government consists of a variety of departments and analysts - the vast Ministry of Foreign Affairs, the Ministries of Defence, Finance and Co-operation, various study centres and institutes - the President of the Republic signs and seals France's foreign policy. The vision of the president, the grandeur dear to de Gaulle, Giscard d'Estaing's rayonnement, the stress on solidarity of Mitterrand's early presidency moulds foreign policy, and it is the president who, constitutionally, bears final responsibility for French foreign policy. The tacit agreement of Prime Minister Chirac and President Mitterrand that the Elysée had the lead in foreign affairs in the post-March 1986 cohabitation, and, for example, Mitterrand's ability to impose his own views over a French acceptance of Soviet President Gorbachev's 'double zero option' reinforce this interpretation.

If national independence, safeguarded and managed by the President of the Republic, is the basis of foreign policy in the Fifth Republic, more specific traits to France's overseas presence are evident. President Mitterrand himself says that France's foreign relations are organised 'around several simple ideas: national independence, the equilibrium of military blocs in the world, the right of peoples to decide their future themselves, the development of poor countries'.[8] Those sentiments - which would not be disavowed by de Gaulle, Pompidou or Giscard - find expression in several policies. The first is reliance on France's independent nuclear deterrent force as the guarantee of the nation's independence. Although France has never used its nuclear weapons, it upholds its right to an arsenal of nuclear powered warheads and affirms its right to test nuclear devices. France refused to sign the Nuclear Test Ban Treaty, the Nuclear Non-Proliferation Treaty and, most recently, the South Pacific Nuclear-Free Zone Treaty. France withdrew its military forces from the combined NATO command to maintain independent direction and security over its nuclear deterrence force, and Paris says that French forces must not be considered in discussions between the USA and the Soviet Union on arms limitations in Western Europe. France also opposes the Strategic Defence Initiative of the Americans as a further curb on its strategic independence. France continues to test nuclear devices in French Polynesia, despite the opposition of many South

Pacific nations to the experiments. Some observers argue (or hope) that France's nuclear forces protect Western Europe in addition to the national territory of France. Alfred Grosser, along with others, argues that France's nuclear force is more of a diplomatic than a military weapon, guaranteeing Paris' stake in international affairs.[9] Only minority groups in France (several ecology organisations and small political parties) question or denounce France's nuclear policy. Pacifism is not considered a credible stand in France.[10] France backs up its nuclear force by sizeable conventional forces and armaments (notably the Exocet missiles). French troops are stationed in French overseas territories and, by treaty arrangements, in six African states; national service for Frenchmen gives the country a large army, and the country disposes of a special rapid deployment force and anti-terrorism squads as well, of course, as the Foreign Legion.

A corollary to this strategic independence has been France's determination to keep its distance from the superpowers and in particular from the USA and the Atlantic Alliance. The withdrawal from the command structure of NATO, unwillingness to allow American missiles to be based in France, criticism of American policy in Vietnam in the 1960s and in Central America in the 1980s, refusal to allow American planes to fly in French airspace on their way to bomb Libya, all point to France's desire to keep out of the military quarrels in which Americans have seemed anxious to engage themselves and, also, to keep away from domination by the big brother across the Atlantic. Some of these French policies have angered Washington and disconcerted more submissive allies of the USA, but France has always argued its right to disagree with the USA and to criticise its ally. However, Paris also implies - and political scientists confirm - that an independent stance is not a neutralist one; in a crisis France's loyalties are undoubted. France's attitude towards the Soviet Union has been an effort to keep lines of dialogue open, particularly when the USA has seemed to see its Soviet policy in terms of the 'red peril'. France has always prided itself on its cordial relations with the Soviet Union, a relationship which predates the 1917 Revolution; this has not kept Paris from occasionally expelling Soviet diplomats and from attacking the Soviet Union on such occasions as the invasions of Czechoslovakia

and Afghanistan. But by refusing the mantle of the
USA, France has tried to pose as a sympathetic ear
for Moscow in the West and an intermediary between
the superpowers.

While manoeuvring between Moscow and Washington,
Paris has developed two main axes for its foreign
presence: with Europe and with Africa. The movement for European integration is largely a French
invention, and the European Community traces its
history back to the pioneering work in the 1950s
of two Frenchmen, Jean Monnet and Robert Schuman.
France was an original signatory of the Treaty of
Rome in 1957 and has remained one of the leaders
of the EC. Although de Gaulle vetoed the admission
of UK to the Common Market, his successors have
approved the enlargement of the organisation to
twelve members. With acceptance of the Single European Act by the French Parliament in 1987, Paris
agreed to a further unification of Europe in 1992,
a decision which surmounted previous hesitations
and fears about loss of sovereignty. France's be-
haviour inside the EC has sometimes been contested, and France has been criticised from inside
and outside, in particular for the Common Agricultural Policy, which is seen primarily to benefit
French farmers. Moreover, French support for projects like the European Airbus is seen by some to
violate all the canons of the liberal world trading system. But, increasingly, France perceives
itself to be, and acts as, part of the suprana-
tional EC and is so perceived by the outside
world. Some have even suggested that if France's
voice still counts on the world stage, it is because of the muscle France can flex as a member of
the European Community, particularly in trade relations.[11] Even if French influence in the EC has
passed its peak, French commitment to the EC and
European economic integration has continued to
grow, despite France's protectionism, motivated by
anxieties over the long-term competitiveness of
French industry. Certainly, since the EC constitutes the second largest trade bloc in the world,
France's influence within it extends beyond the
country's own trade and political power. As the EC
has multiplied the number of its initiatives
(notably the Lomé conventions for aid to the
world's poorest countries and various projects
which have extended to non-EC states), France's
role in a common European policy has taken on a
different meaning. Since 1958, France has thus
played a European card, and in the last several

years has made the EC the focus of its policy.

Particularly important inside Europe have been the rapprochement between France and West Germany engineered by de Gaulle and the relations between Paris and Bonn which form one of the closest connections in French policy. The annual summits between the two countries, their open borders, and the 1987 decision to co-ordinate defence and eventually put a small contingent under joint command underline political ties. In commercial relations, the Federal Republic is France's most important trading partner, though France sees itself as under threat from German economic success and the more vibrant German economy. In short, there exists a Paris-Bonn axis, which has remained in place and been strengthened by such odd couples as de Gaulle and Adenauer, Giscard and Schmidt, and Mitterrand and Kohl. This co-operation combines the joint forces of Western Europe's two largest countries and major economies; it also reverses the Franco-German animosity that was a constant of European history from 1870 to 1945.

The other focus for France's overseas activity has been the relation between France and Africa, both the Maghreb and sub-Saharan Africa. Colonialism coloured this relationship and in the early years of de Gaulle's presidency embittered it. But one of the successes of France's policy has been to guard close links with its former colonies and protectorates in Africa. In North Africa, France enjoys particularly cordial political and commercial relations with Morocco and Tunisia. The relationship between France and Algeria is still fraught with problems a quarter of a century after Algerian independence, though it has gradually improved. In French-speaking black Africa, France is the largest supplier of aid, the major trade partner, a military presence and a cultural sponsor - wide-ranging relations which have been labelled neo-colonial. France stations troops in Chad, the Central African Republic, Djibouti, Gabon, the Ivory Coast and Senegal; 10,000 French coopérants work in Africa; more French citizens live in black Africa now than before decolonisation. France has not hesitated to intervene in African affairs; in addition to playing a role in various coups d'état in Africa, Paris sent parachutists to Kolwezi (in Zaïre) in 1978 and is the main supporter of Chad in its war against Libya. France has also expanded its influence in the former Spanish and Portuguese colonies of Africa, symbolised by the integration

8

of Equatorial Guinea into the French African franc zone and the inclusion of non-French-speaking states in the annual Franco-African summits.

It has also been suggested that because of France's role in sub-Saharan Africa Paris can still count as a small superpower.[12] France's connections with Africa have seemed stronger than those of the former colonial powers and the superpowers, even if those nations (and such third countries as Cuba) have found entrées into Africa. Even when Paris has disengaged itself from other arenas, as with the withdrawal of French troops from the UN peacekeeping forces in Lebanon, France shows no sign of reducing its role in Africa, nor of changing the direction of its African policy. Attempts by the government to promote more democratic rule and to move away from neo-colonial treatment of the African states have not caused a deviation in its approach.

France's relations with Africa point to two other aspects of French policy. One is the specific problem of immigration into France of foreign workers, the largest number of whom come from North Africa or Francophone black Africa. Immigration is a most volatile question in French domestic politics but also one with international repercussions. De Gaulle and his successors encouraged the large-scale migration of Africans when France was short of labour in the boom years of the 1960s. With the permanent migration of many Africans to France, coupled with the economic problems of the 1980s, the presence of those migrants has provoked controversy. Giscard promoted the repatriation of migrants, Mitterrand attempted to improve the lot of migrants inside France, and Chirac has clamped down on illegal migrants. (The expulsion of 101 Malians, a handful of Mauritians and the aborted new code of French citizenship testify to Chirac's policy.) The overtly racist National Front has created a growing political movement out of hostility to the non-Europeans in France, particularly towards Maghrebins. On the other side, such organisations as SOS-Racisme have reacted against increased racism, and the community of second generation migrants is experiencing a cultural awakening. The presence of three million Moslems in France, including North Africans and black Africans, remains one factor in France's foreign policy which shows the connection between domestic and international questions.

The French relationship with Africa also points

to a special characteristic of French policy, the ties between France and French-speaking countries. The regular Francophone summits highlight these connections, but more important are the amounts of economic, political and cultural assistance which Paris directs to the Francophone countries. This may be seen as an attempt to preserve French culture, another aspect of French neo-colonialism, or an effort to limit Anglo-Saxon (and particularly American) influence. Some French actions have been provocative, from de Gaulle's 'Vive le Québec libre!' of 1967 to allegations in 1987 that France was providing funding for the Francophone opposition in Vanuatu. Cultural and scientific relations can also be used temporarily to replace political ties when official relations are strained; such was the case when Francophone technical organisations maintained semi-official ties between France and the Comoros Islands, when that nation cut diplomatic relations with France.

Through aid and through Francophone connections, France pursues involvement in the Third World. French policy towards the developing countries has been activist and contributory. Tiers-mondisme, although seen from different perspectives by the Left and Right and recently under attack, has been a staple of French policy. France, in fact, has imagined itself as a privileged interlocutor of the Third World, an intermediary between Europe and Africa, between the Christian world and Islam, between the West and the Marxist states of the developing world. The petroleum crises of the 1970s, terrorism in the 1980s, and the tendency of some Third World states to turn for support to the superpowers rather than to France may bring into question the success of this policy; France has also lost some friends in attempts to win others - notably the alienation of Israel after the 1967 war through France's sympathetic stance towards the Arabs and the difficulties with Iran because of friendship with Iraq. But France has generally outdistanced the United States because of its more subtle and sympathetic policy towards the developing world and in particular because of its willingness not to see issues of independence, development and political ideology in a simplistic 'us' versus 'them' formula.

A final distinguishing characteristic of the French presence overseas is the phenomenon of France's overseas territories and departments. These ten remnants of empire - some of which have

been French possessions since the 1600s - are
strategically scattered in the Caribbean and the
Pacific and Indian Oceans. They afford France the
bases for a space station and a nuclear testing
site. In addition, they give France the third
largest maritime zone in the world in their territorial waters. They provide windows on the regions
in which they lie, bases for political and economic influence. The overseas zones are part of
France; their residents are French citizens.
Strictly, therefore, they should not be considered
an element of foreign policy. Yet they form a component in France's international presence.

In sum, France's overseas presence is a combination of various activities directed towards many
regions. Moreover, France's policy is substantially different from that of other European
states because of its nuclear deterrence, independence from the USA, favoured position with Africa
and its overseas territories. Above all, there is
France's self-appropriation of a global role. Alfred Grosser quotes the programme of the Conseil
national de la Résistance's claim that post-war
governments must 'defend the political and economic independence of the nation, reestablish
France in its power, in its grandeur and in its
universal mission'. Grosser then rhetorically asks
which political party would deny this statement
and adds 'it would suffice for the reader to replace "France" by "Spain" or "Germany" to understand how audacious and different is France's perception of its role'.[13] This constellation of features is not replicated elsewhere in the world.
They do not ensure the success of French foreign
policy, nor do they mean that France is everywhere
present in an active and coherent fashion. Several
examples prove the point.

In the Middle East, France's influence has waned
though France long retained the myth that it had a
'special role' in Francophone Lebanon and Syria.
Frenchmen have been taken hostage and killed in
Lebanon, and Paris' power to effect their release
- much less to sort out the chaos of Lebanon - has
been as severely limited as that of other powers.
France's influence with other states in the region
is similarly constrained. In South America, France
does not play a particularly important role, despite amicable and significant connections. Argentina used French missiles in the Falklands War,
and France has supported the Sandinistas against
the contras in Nicaragua, but this involvement has

been episodic and involved different considerations: in the first case, commercial, ideological in the latter. In Asia, with the exception of Japan and China, France possesses limited influence. Particularly in Southeast Asia, France is a bystander, even with the residual relations with the countries which made up French Indochina. French relations with the Indian subcontinent are not prominent, despite a growing presence in the Indian Ocean region. In the South Pacific, France is largely regarded as an interloper as Australia, New Zealand and the micro-states of Oceania excoriate Paris for nuclear testing in Polynesia and for continued control over New Caledonia.[14]

French policy is, therefore, less global than some would like to believe. But compared to Japan, Germany and even the UK, France enjoys an international stature that is a reflection of the theory and practice of French foreign policy since de Gaulle. Changes in governments have not substantially altered that position, and, domestically, there is little opposition to the basic lines of French policy. Lobby groups may castigate French lack of action in their own areas of interests; certain leftists ritually criticise the neo-colonialism of French policy. What is remarkable, however, is the relative continuity and consensus.

Several changes in recent years may force an evolution of French policy. The glasnost pursued by Gorbachev may change the Soviet Union's relations with the West; France may have to reduce its arsenal if arms and troop reduction occurs in Europe. The enlargement of the EC may weaken Paris' voice, or the Paris-Bonn axis could be lengthened to include London, Rome or even Madrid. At the end of 1987 Mitterrand invited Italy to join France and West Germany in defence co-operation. It is in this arena that there are signs of the declining strength of French commitment to independence, symbolised also in proposals for greater co-operation over nuclear issues between France and the UK, joint Franco-German military exercises and joint defence purchasing with European partners. Each of these has been influenced by changing American-Soviet relations putting more pressure on Europe to fend for itself. Islamic fundamentalism has already affected France's relations with the Moslem world, and repercussions could occur inside the Moslem community in France. Perhaps most dramatically, and certainly most dangerously, international terrorism has spread to French soil. A wave of deadly bombings in the autumn of 1986 was traced to Iran. Regularly caches of arms owned by Basque guerrillas are discovered by police. In 1987, a ship containing arms destined for the Irish Republican Army was captured by French customs officers. Colonel Ghaddafi occasionally threatens to retaliate against French support for Chad. Frenchmen have been taken hostage in Lebanon and Ethiopia and imprisoned in South Africa.

The problem for France lies not with the superpowers, its European partners or the countries with which it had maintained clientelistic relations (in the Maghreb and black Africa). French relations in these areas seem secure. Rather problems may occur with other countries outside the EC, Atlantic Alliance and Francophone ambit. De Gaulle predicted that the Islamic crescent from North Africa to the Middle East would be the region for future conflicts, and he seems to have been proven right. Neither the might of France nor that of the USA seems able to establish 'order' in this region. Iran and Iraq continue to fight, Lebanon remains close to anarchy, the Arab-Israeli problem festers, the Palestinians still lack a state, Islamic fundamentalism becomes stronger, Libya menaces French interests in Europe, Africa and the Pacific. The question for French policymakers has increasingly become France's role in this global tinderbox, rather than its more established relations with European powers.

Every nation hopes that its foreign policy will live up to a variety of criteria: that it will be independent, coherent, aimed at peace, development and democracy and that it will be effective. Few, if any, nations live up to these ideals. On balance, France does relatively well. France has steered clear of big-power confrontations and has itself kept out of war since 1962. France has largely maintained good relations with its former colonies and cemented strong ties with its European partners. It has retained an international voice. On the other side of the ledger, Paris has been associated with a number of undemocratic and brutal regimes, especially that of the President-Emperor Bokassa in the Central African Republic. France's aid has undoubtedly helped its client states, few of which are models of either democracy or development, though France is not alone amongst aid donors. French policy has not been devoid of ambiguities and contradictions. Rhetoric -

from de Gaulle's 'grandeur' to Mitterrand's 'rupture with capitalism' - has sometimes taken precedence over action. Some of France's gestures have been unworthy, such as the sinking of the Greenpeace ship, the Rainbow Warrior, in the waters of New Zealand in 1985. But, as an Italian diplomat has pointed out, France is the only country that wants to express its foreign policy in universal, logical terms.[15] It is also one of the few nations to aspire to a global role. Its successes and failures must be judged against those ambitions.

NOTES AND REFERENCES

1.   See, for example, François de Preuil, La Troisième super-puissance (Seuil, Paris, 1980). General issues of French foreign policy have been recently reviewed by Peter Morris and Stuart Williams (eds), France in the World (Association for the Study of Modern and Contemporary France, Nottingham, 1985), the special issue of Politique étrangère, No. 51 (1986) ('50 ans de politique étrangère de la France') and Patrick Wajsman and François Joyaux, Pour une nouvelle politique étrangère (La Table ronde, Paris, 1986). (The special issue of Politique étrangère includes a chronology and a lengthy bibliography.) The essential work is Alfred Grosser, Affaires extérieures. La Politique de la France, 1944-1984 (Flammarion, Paris, 1984). See also Elie Barnavi and Saul Friedländer (eds), La Politique étrangère du Général de Gaulle (Institut universitaire de hautes études internationales, Geneva, 1985); Samy Cohen and Marie-Claude Smouts (eds), La Politique extérieure de Valéry Giscard d'Estaing (FNSP, Paris, 1985) and François Mitterrand, Réflexions sur la politique extérieure de la France (Fayard, Paris, 1986). Le Monde Diplomatique provides the best regular periodical coverage.
2.   Jean-Baptiste Duroselle, 'Les "Invariants" de la politique étrangère de la France', Politique étrangère, Vol. 51 (1986), pp. 13-23.
3.   Gordon A. Craig, 'The Historian and the Study of International Relations', American Historical Review, Vol. 88 (1983), pp. 1-11.
4.   Jean Daniel, Les Religions d'un président. Regards sur les aventures du mitterrandisme (Bernard Grasset, Paris, 1988), pp. 202, 204. Catherine Nay, in Les Sept Mitterrand ou les métamorphoses d'un septennat (Grasset, Paris, 1988), argues that Mitterrand became almost entirely Gaullist in his foreign relations; see chapter IV, 'François-Charles de Gaulle', especially pp. 173-86. Another concurring opinion is that of Stanley Hoffmann, 'Mitterrand's Foreign Policy,

or Gaullism by any Other Name', in George Ross, Stanley Hoffmann and Sylvia Malzacher (eds), The Mitterrand Experiment (Polity Press, Cambridge, 1987), pp. 294-305.

5.Stanley Hoffman, 'La France face à son image', Politique étrangère, Vol. 51 (1986), pp. 25-53.

6. Alfred Grosser, '1958-1985: quatre présidents, une seule politique?', in Wajsman and Joyaux, pp. 62-80.

7. Ibid.

8. Mitterrand, Réflexions sur la politique extérieure, p. 7.

9. Alfred Grosser, Affaires extérieures, p. 195.

10. Jolyon Howorth, France: The Politics of Peace (Merlin Press, London, 1984); Diana Johnstone, 'How the French Left Learned to Love the Bomb', New Left Review, Vol. 146 1984, pp. 5-36.

11. Marie-Claude Smouts, 'France and Europe', in Morris and Williams, p. 34.

12. Pascal Chaigneau, 'Afrique: de l'affectif au rationnel', in Wajsman and Joyaux, p. 340.

13. Alfred Grosser, Affaires extérieures, p. 11.

14. Robert Aldrich, France and the Pacific, in John Ravenhill (ed.), American Lake No Longer? Alliance Problems in the South Pacific (University of California Press, Berkeley, forthcoming.)

15. Sergio Romano, 'Le Regard de l'autre', Politique étrangère, Vol. 51 (1986), pp. 35-41.

Chapter Two

CONSENSUS AND MYTHOLOGY: SECURITY ALTERNATIVES IN
POST-GAULLIST FRANCE

Jolyon Howorth

For a generation, French men and women have
believed (or, rather, have chosen to believe) that
their age-old security dilemmas were definitively
resolved in the 1960s by de Gaulle's far-sighted
decision to develop an independent strategic nuclear capability. France, a large number of
strategists (amateur and professional) claimed,
was now safe both from the vulnerability of isolation and from the problematics and unpredictabil-
ity of alliances. The development of a land, sea
and air-based 'triad' of independent strategic and
tactical nuclear weapons would, it was widely believed, keep the Russians to the east of the Rhine
(even if they elected to cross the Elbe) and, at
the same time, allow Paris the luxury of non-in-
volvement in the consequences of any military adventures launched by Washington. 'Proportional
deterrence', or la dissuasion du faible au fort
created, at least in the popular imagination, an
invisible shield around the perimeter of the
Hexagon, a national sanctuary, the guarantee of
eternal peace. So compelling was this vision that,
by 1977, both the Socialist Party and the Communist Party had abandoned fifteen years of opposition to what they had disparagingly called la
bombinette and, in an effort to make electoral hay
while the nuclear sun still shone, embraced the
Gaullist 'consensus' with all the fervour of neo-
phytes.[1] Opposition to this unanimity was
marginalised by the media, dismissed, pejora-
tively, as pacifist or condemned, more sinisterly,
as pro-Soviet.[2]
The 'consensus', seemingly cast in granite,
lasted barely five years. Indeed, by 1977, when
the Left-wing parties decided to step into line,
the pedestal was already beginning to crack and
sections of the superstructure were suffering seriously from the erosion of time and change. The
defence establishment and the media did their ut-
most to conceal these defects from the public gaze

and the edifice was solemnly declared, on every
official occasion, to be as pristine and resilient
as ever. But no amount of wishful thinking (or
window dressing) could conceal forever the fundamental fissures in the Gaullist monument. By the
mid-1980s these were beginning to burst forth.[3]
    In one sense, of course, the 'consensus' had
never existed other than as mythology. One logical
consequence   of   de   Gaulle's   pretence   of
'impartiality' between the superpowers was the
short-lived episode of omni-directional targeting
(défense tous azimuts) which theoretically brought
Washington as well as Moscow into France's nuclear
sights, but probably had no tangible effect (some
allege) other than to lead to the premature death
of its main protagonist - the chief of the general
staff, General Ailleret.[4] The 'impartial' line was
rapidly abandoned, as was the theology of 'all or
nothing strategic deterrence'. Tactical nuclear
missiles were introduced in 1974, not, it was
hastily asserted, as a battlefield system (NATO's
'flexible response'), but as an ultimate warning
shot across the bows of the advancing enemy lines,
summoning the potential aggressor to stop in his
tracks or risk strategic incineration. But this
overly theological approach to ANT (armes nucléaires tactiques) never carried much credibility
(being regarded by the Germans as tantamount to
fratricide) and eventually constituted a major
thin end in the wedge of strategic choices which
was to split open the granite of consensus. Technological development, diplomatic shifts and the
vast consequences of historical evolution have all
conspired to render France's defence 'consensus'
vulnerable to major revision. The various strands
of the revision process are difficult to disentan-
gle, but an attempt will be made to analyse them
one by one.

TECHNOLOGICAL PROGRESS AND STRATEGIC REVISION

For the first twenty-five years of France's status
as a 'nuclear capable' power, the small matter of
the technical credibility of its strategic arsenal
played a poor second fiddle to the diplomatic
prestige and posturing which was associated with
its existence. In the late 1960s, few serious
strategic analysts would have given France's
thirty or so Mirage IVA nuclear bombers more than
a slim chance of penetrating far inside Soviet

air-space, assuming they ever managed to get airborne. With the deployment of the first ballistic
missiles, land-based SSBS (Sol-Sol balistique
stratégique) units on the Plateau d'Albion and
sea-based Mls on the first nuclear submarine
(Sous-marin nucléaire lanceur d'engins, SNLE) in
1971, the technical credibility of the nuclear deterrent was enhanced, although its political credibility remained as problematic as ever. At one
level, with every new launch of a nuclear submarine and each new installation of a missile silo
in Provence, France's 'credibility' became a
greater headache for the Kremlin. Nevertheless,
despite these quantitative increases, one of the
most authoritative studies of French nuclear potential, describes its ability, as late as 1985,
to inflict 'unacceptable damage' on the Soviet
Union's 'vital centres' (the declared strategic
purpose) as 'minimal'.[5]

The problem was not simply one of France's targeting or 'attacking' posture or its ability to
inflict unacceptable damage. Leaving aside the
enormous question of its dependence on US satellite technology for targeting and guidance facilities, there was also the increasingly serious matter of Soviet first-strike or counter-force capability. The more accurate Soviet missiles such as
the SS-18, the SS-19 and the SS-20, first deployed
in the late 1970s and early 1980s and credited
with a Circular Error Probable (CEP)[6] of between
200 and 400 metres, came to pose a massive threat
against all of France's nuclear facilities, with
the exception, of course, of submarines out on pa-
trol. Yet even these allegedly 'invisible', unde-
tectable nuclear systems, lurking in the depths
of the oceans, were increasingly vulnerable to
Soviet advances in submarine detection, not to
mention the political incredibility or futility of
a hypothetical French nuclear submarine retalia-
tion after a Soviet nuclear counter-force strike.
The consequence of such an action would be to
leave France utterly defenceless against the massive remaining Soviet nuclear and conventional arsenal. The 'window of vulnerability' was not only
an US problem.

Given this residual and continuing vulnerability, it became clear to France's defence planners,
as early as the mid- to late-1980s, that
'modernisation' of the nuclear arsenal was an inevitable concomitant of the advent, in the
arsenals of the superpowers and especially in that

of the Soviet Union, of counterforce weapons. The vulnerability of the nuclear installations appeared to call for new developments such as silo-hardening, mobile missiles, multiple-warhead (if not actually MIRVed[7]) missiles and a new generation of nuclear submarines, quieter, faster and capable of much greater oceanic depth. By the late 1970s, in any case, the life expectancy of France's original 'triad' weapons was diminishing rapidly and a major political decision was imminent as to whether to repeat the original Gaullist 'gamble' and attempt to keep up, technologically, with the superpowers, or to reassess the global situation and cut the defence coat according to the cloth most appropriate to the present.

The debate about strategic alternatives ought logically to have taken place after 1976 under the presidency of Valéry Giscard d'Estaing. Giscard had always been far more of an 'Atlanticist' than his Gaullist coalition partners and, as such, was anxious to ensure that when the necessary reassessment of France's defence requirements came on to the political agenda, policies would be less geared to the rhetoric of national independence and more sensitive to the global requirements of the alliance, particularly in its European context. Given the shrinking resource base of the post-Yom Kippur world, when in the aftermath of the 1973 Arab-Israeli war the world was plunged into recession, Giscard's preference would instinctively have veered towards an upgrading of France's increasingly antiquated conventional forces and a moratorium on expensive nuclear technology.[8] However, Jacques Chirac (who might even have agreed with him) was, at that time, preoccupied with building up his domestic political base in the RPR, and Gaullist responses to the new Giscardian heresies were left in the hands of traditional 'barons' such as Pierre Messmer and Michel Debré. These orthodox Gaullists noisily demanded a return to the classical notions of strategic nuclear deterrence and Giscard was obliged (in order to safeguard his parliamentary majority) to reinstate the planned sixth nuclear submarine, which he had already cancelled, as well as to make noises in favour of various items of technological modernisation for which firm budgeting was in any case out of the question.[9]

Giscard's leanings in favour of greater conventional co-operation with the European allies were savaged not only by his Gaullist partners. The

Socialist Party and the Communist Party had just
'converted' to nuclear orthodoxy and, for a whole
range of reasons, sought to derive electoral and
political capital from a denunciation of Giscard's
sinful 'Atlanticism'. When François Mitterrand
took over from Giscard in 1981, there was an
abrupt reversion to the most orthodox Gaullist
positions, at least at the level of rhetoric.[10] In
terms of actual procurement, the Socialist defence
white paper of 1983 did little more than continue
with the programmes both the Left and the
Gaullists had imposed upon a reluctant Giscard
during the last years of his septennat. The 'will-
he-won't-he' situation of the sixth SNLE was resolved with firm budgetary backing and the new
vessel (L'Inflexible) was launched in 1985. The
missile silos on the Plateau d'Albion were hard-
ened and a new, mobile missile was touted as a
suitable replacement, although never budgeted for.
New ground-to-air (ASMP) medium range missiles
were deployed on the new generation of strategic
nuclear bombers (Mirage IVP and Mirage 2000). A
new longer range (350 km) tactical weapon (Hades)
was ordered to replace the existing Plutons.

All these developments represented a major budgetary swing in favour of the nuclear deterrent at
the expense of the conventional armed forces,
where drastic cuts were implemented. In 1974, Giscard had inherited a defence programme in which 37
per cent of expenditure was devoted to nuclear
systems. By 1981, he had, despite pressures from
the RPR and the Socialists, gradually reduced this
to 30 per cent. The savings went to upgrade
France's conventional forces.[11] Under Mitterrand,
the 'nuclear percentage' began to creep inexorably
upwards once again, reaching approximately 34 per
cent by 1986.[12] Behind the charts and graphs, however, there lies the nub of France's defence
dilemma. The tug-o'-war betweeen the different
budgetary heads of expenditure is conditioned by
the exponential increase in the cost of sophisticated new weaponry, both conventional and nuclear.
In a nutshell, France's 'urgent requirements' currently cost considerably more than limited resources allow.[13] The pace of technological advance
in every area of military hardware is fast out-
stripping the ability of a medium-sized nation
like France to foot the bill. 'Keeping up with the
superpower Joneses' in the field of nuclear missiles is a very different matter today than it was
in the early 1960s. France's efforts to modernise

its existing nuclear arsenal have recently been costed by the parliamentary defence commission. The country's total defence expenditure in 1986 has been estimated at around 158,000 m francs.[14] To put matters in perspective, the cost of equipping five SNLEs with the new M-4 multiple warheads is, alone, around 55,000 m francs. By 1991, the missile will be obsolete and plans are already under way to replace it with the M-5, a programme costed at 73,000 m. In addition, the new generation of SNLEs which will carry the M-5 are currently costed at around 70,000 m.[15] Thus, merely to keep its head below water in the field of nuclear submarines, funds have to be found well in excess of the entire defence expenditure for a twelve month period. That is even before the Minister begins to count the cost of all the other programmes such as the new mobile missile, the new generation of tactical missiles (land and air-based), the proposed military satellites (without which Paris will forever be dependent on Washington for guidance information). And these items by no means exhaust the list of essential nuclear or strategic systems.

But even in the area of conventional weaponry, the new generation of 'emerging technology' systems, the only ones considered to be capable of neutralising a major Soviet advance, carry an astronomical price-tag and, to date, France has not even attempted to move in any serious way into this field. In addition, France's determination to maintain a world role requires new aircraft carriers at an estimated 14,000 million francs apiece. One does not have to be a skilled accountant to recognise that painful choices are going to have to be made.

One final technological element looms menacingly over the entire panoply of France's nuclear deterrent. That is the issue of strategic defence (SDI or 'Star Wars'). There can be no doubt that the Soviet Union has made significant advances in this area and that, whatever the outcome of the current spate of arms control negotiations, both superpowers will funnel resources in this direction. Should the Soviet Union ever approach a strategic defensive capability with any credibility against an American attack, it goes without saying that France's phenomenally expensive new nuclear hardware would long have become more or less irrelevant. But the problem of the 'technology gap' between a medium-sized power and a superpower (and the associated problem of the financial cost of closing it) is only one of the issues currently urging France's defence planners to take a long hard look at its realistic requirements for the rest of this century. Other issues are diplomatic initiatives and the forward march of history.

DIPLOMACY AND ARMS CONTROL

Agreement has finally been reached between the superpowers on the so-called 'double-zero option'[16] for the elimination of all US and Soviet intermediate and short range nuclear missiles on the continent of Europe. The implications of this historic agreement for many aspects of France's strategic and tactical nuclear defence programmes are significant and far-reaching. Hitherto, the French (and the British) have succeeded in resisting constant Soviet pressures to include their 'national' nuclear arsenals in any superpower arms control discussions. The Soviet position, both in the earlier SALT talks and in the more recent START and INF discussions was that French nuclear weapons should be counted as part of the West's overall force levels.[17] The French have equally consistently resisted this argument, stressing several factors.[18] First, that there is a huge quantitative imbalance between the superpower arsenals and that of a nation like France: let the former first reduce their nuclear arsenals massively and then, perhaps, France will be more interested in talking. Second, France, and indeed NATO as a whole, has always rejected the implications of the Soviet position which would logically give the Soviets the right to a nuclear arsenal equal to that of all three nuclear nations in NATO put together. Third, France has always insisted that its nuclear weapons constitute a <u>national</u> deterrent disconnected from any American, Western European or NATO policies or objectives.

The Soviet position was maintained through various changes of leadership, and even Mikhail Gorbachev, as late as 15 January 1986, 'demanded', as his price for entering into general disarmament discussions, a halt to all modernisation or expansion of British and French nuclear systems.[19] However, at the Reykjavik summit in October 1986, this demand was dropped as part of Gorbachev's attempt to force a major breakthrough in his discussions with President Reagan.[20] When, in February

1987, Gorbachev formulated his ground-breaking proposals for a separate agreement on intermediate range nuclear weapons in Europe, which was to lead to the current 'double-zero option', he studiously avoided all mention of French or British weapons.[21]

The subtlety of this omission consisted precisely in the fact that the French and British weapons were, in a sense, more present through the absence of any mention than if they had somehow been included. For the consequence of the initial 'zero option' would be to remove all US and Soviet intermediate range weapons from European territory, thus leaving the French and the British systems all the more exposed in their isolation. Since February 1987 the cat has been out of the bag and French spokespersons from all political quarters have been at pains to come to terms with the new situation. That new situation was in fact spelled out by Marshal Akhromeyev, the chief of the Soviet general staff, in a press conference organised following the February 1987 Gorbachev initiative. The Marshal stressed that the logic of this initiative required that 'sooner or later' the problem of the French and British nuclear arsenals would have to be discussed. He would not be drawn on a timetable, but indicated that such discussions would have to involve the USA, the USSR and other nuclear powers.[22] How long can France withstand the various diplomatic pressures for disarmament to which it is already being subjected, and how have the political parties responded to Gorbachev's initiative?

The government's response had, in a general sense, already been formulated by François Mitterrand, in a speech to the General Assembly of the UN on 28 September 1983.[23] At that time, French resistance to inclusion in the INF talks was widely perceived as a major stumbling-block to a superpower agreement. Mitterrand, in an attempt to deflect some of the anti-French feeling, therefore laid out three conditions for any future French participation in disarmament negotiations. First, and most importantly, there would have to be a significant and verifiable reduction in the superpowers' own nuclear arsenals. Second, there must also be progress on conventional and chemical weapons reductions. Third, there should be no major advances in anti-ballistic missile defences. Suddenly, in 1987, Gorbachev put forward proposals in all these areas in a way which made it seem not

23

unlikely that, before too long, Mitterrand's list of conditions, which had seemed 'safe enough' in 1983, could actually be met.

Gorbachev's February proposals threw the French political class into disarray. First off the mark was the Quai d'Orsay with a highly negative reaction on 1 March 1987 stressing that the zero option would leave Europe 'terribly exposed'.[24] At a meeting of the Council of Ministers on 4 March, the fracture lines in the granite of consensus ran very deep, not only between the socialist President and his Right-wing government, but actually within the government itself. While Foreign Minister Raimond and Defence Minister Giraud denounced the Gorbachev proposals as a 'bluff' which, if implemented, would amount to a kind of nuclear 'Munich' for Western Europe, François Mitterrand, in cabinet, expressed his 'genuine interest' in the zero option, which he considered to be 'in accordance with France's interests and with the interests of peace'. His Prime Minister, Jacques Chirac, limited his own intervention to frequent comments, during Mitterrand's thirty minute exposé, to the effect that 'He is right, he is right', and was heard to reassure a perplexed Giscardian minister with the words: 'Don't worry, Giscard is in total agreement with Mitterrand and me'.[25] In reality, there has been little agreement anywhere. Partisans and opponents of the Gorbachev proposals have been found at the highest levels within each of the political parties.

The opponents of the zero option immediately mustered their forces around one major argument: a zero option on intermediate range missiles would leave the Soviet Union with a massive superiority in short-range nuclear systems.[26] This line was also enthusiastically embraced by sceptics and hawks in the other Western nations. Rare were the voices which pointed out that the West was potentially painting itself into a corner with this response, or that France in particular might find its own tactical weapons programme undermined by any general reductions in short-range weapons.[27] Gorbachev was not slow in spotting the chink in this particular piece of Western armour and, in a speech in Prague shortly after Margaret Thatcher's visit to Moscow, he formally proposed extending his zero option on INF to short-range nuclear systems (500 to 1,000 kilometres): the proposal now known as the 'double zero option'. Anticipating some potential Western reactions, Gorbachev backed up his proposal by an announcement that the Soviet Union was unilaterally ceasing to manufacture chemical weapons, and by new proposals on conventional arms reductions.[28] What Gorbachev was, in effect, proposing, was the virtual 'denuclearisation' of Europe, a suggestion which the peace movements were quick to remind everybody had been theirs for many decades.[29]

The French political class as a whole was badly shaken by the Gorbachev phenomenon and by these arms control developments. Irrespective of the detailed (and divergent) responses of the various political parties (or factions thereof),[30] the events of 1987 highlighted two generally applicable 'truths' which were already beginning to emerge for the other reasons examined in this chapter. Both developments indicate the demise of the old 'Gaullist' consensus, even though it is far too soon to detect with any precision the outlines of a clear new consensus. The first, which follows on logically from the disarmament agreements and from the new military situation in Europe emerging from them, is that there will have to be a radical rethink in France about the respective roles of nuclear and conventional weapons in that country's security policy. The second, which is a consequence of all the issues examined so far and of the historical factors to be examined in what follows, is that a new approach to European co-operation - not only confined to the Western nations, but embracing both halves of the divided continent - will be the inevitable corollary of the new security orientations implicit in recent events.

To conclude on the first development, before passing to an analysis of the second, it is clear that the potential 'denuclearisation' of Europe implicit in the double zero option cannot fail, sooner or later, to put the French and UK nuclear arsenals into the diplomatic and political firing line. From a purely quantitative perspective, first, it will be difficult for France to justify what amounts to a potential tenfold increase in its strategic nuclear warheads[31] at a time when the superpowers are scrapping their intermediate and short-range missiles and moving towards 50 per cent reductions in their strategic arsenals. Of course, French leaders, including François Mitterrand, deny that an INF agreement affects French missiles in any way. The official French (and UK) view is that, despite the removal of all Soviet

short and intermediate range missiles, Western
Europe still remains vulnerable to the interconti-
nental range Soviet SS-18s and SS-19s. Indeed, the
French and the UK argue that with the removal of
the American missiles from Europe, the importance
of Anglo-French missiles becomes all the greater.
Time alone will tell. A European opinion poll,
conducted before the Gorbachev proposals, revealed
a surprising level of public support for the complete dismantling of French and UK nuclear
weapons, especially in the non-nuclear nations of
Europe. While in the UK and France the figures
were 34 per cent and 32 per cent respectively, in
Germany and Italy, they were 57 per cent and 79
per cent. The 32 per cent figure for France is already a significant dent in the much heralded
'consensus', especially when taken in conjunction
with only 17 per cent wishing to develop the nuclear arsenal further and 11 per cent 'don't
knows'.[32] Indeed, despite necessary caution over
the validity of opinion polls, the cardinal feature of this first ever Europe-wide survey was
perhaps the fact that, whereas in Germany the percentage of 'don't knows' over an entire range of
questions was only 1 per cent or 2 per cent, in
France it often topped 20 per cent. The fact of
the matter is that the cosiness of the 'consensus'
has hitherto allowed most French people the luxury
of avoiding thinking about military or security
matters. As the debate heats up, the results become more and more unpredictable.

One of the consequences of the double zero option is universally perceived to be the inevitability of greater European co-operation on
defence and security policy. In France and the UK,
there is much talk of a Franco-British the UK
'umbrella' or of a European one replacing the
American one. Quite apart from the enormous technical, political and diplomatic problems involved,
the fact of the matter is that the 'other' European states, which are the presumed beneficiaries
of such a development, do not appear to want it.
The most revealing question in the European survey
asked whether a common Euro-defence should be nuclear or conventional. The results were as follows:

Q.   If there were to be a common Western European
     defence independent of the US and NATO, which
     of these three possibilities is in your
     opinion the most desirable?

	UK	France	Germany	Italy
Nuclear, Franco-British	13	8	12	3
Nuclear, All-Europe	35	35	14	14
Conventional	35	25	20	70
None of these	4	13	44	6
Don't know	13	18	2	7

Source: The Guardian, 16 February 1987, p. 9

Two features of these responses merit consideration. The first is the disparity between, on the
one hand, the UK and French levels of support for
a European nuclear 'deterrent' and the total lack
of enthusiasm for that notion elsewhere in Europe.
It should be noted that nowhere is there a majority for a nuclear solution, and in France only 43
per cent favour that course. It would seem that
any alternative to NATO and an American nuclear
umbrella would have to be based on something other
than a 'Euro-bomb'. The second feature of the responses is precisely the 44 per cent (by far the
biggest category) of Germans opting for that
'something other'. Implicit in that figure is undoubtedly the notion that the security of the continent is not solely, and perhaps not even primarily, a military matter.

HISTORY AND THE DEFENCE OF EUROPE: BROADENING THE DEFINITION OF SECURITY

Despite constantly reiterated reassurances from
Washington to the effect that a historic agreement
on the double-zero option would not constitute in
any sense an abandonment by the USA of its European allies,[33] many Europeans remain sceptical.[34]
How long, the sceptics ask, will the American people be prepared to deploy, in the European theatre, 300,000 GIs devoid of any clear nuclear
'protection'? The theology of US-European
'coupling' and 'decoupling' is as arcane as that
of nuclear deterrence itself. As Mitterrand himself put it in March 1987, coupling or decoupling
is something which exists mainly 'inside people's
heads'.[35] However, with the elimination of superpower intermediate and short range nuclear systems

from the European theatre, with mounting popular pressure in the USA to 'bring home the boys' (or some of them), with warning shots like the Nunn amendment,[36] and other 'signs of the times', many in Europe appear to tremble at the prospect of a historic new arrangement for the continent. Para-doxically, these West European uncertainties are the direct result of a new détente in which his-torical pressures and a new Soviet leadership are opening up relations between East and West in an unprecedented way. France appears to be the Euro-pean nation which is greeting the new situation with the greatest caution and misgivings.

Since 1945 France has enjoyed a security situa-tion more favourable than at any time in its his-tory. Surrounded entirely by friendly, eventually allied, neighbours, it has benefited from a 200-kilometre 'buffer-zone' between her eastern border and the nearest potential battlefield. Its great-est fear has been any uncontrolled change in that situation, especially German overtures to the East. And yet there can be no doubt that what Raymond Aron has called de Gaulle's 'Grand De-sign'[37] was based on a historic vision of the eventual inevitability of phasing out the blocs and facilitating the reconciliation of the two Germanies in a vast European unit stretching from the Atlantic to the Urals. Certainly the General believed that there could be no 'valid or solid' settlement in Europe short of the reconciliation, through mutual agreement, of the continent's East-ern and Western sections.[38] In answer to a ques-tion from the present author, François Mitterrand, in January 1987, said almost exactly the same thing: 'Europe will not be Europe until Eastern Europe and Western Europe devise the correct contract... Europe will not be Europe until she has recovered her geographical and historical unity'.[39]

'Gaullism', in this sense, has remained an im-portant reality in Europe, even though, paradoxi-cally, France, for the last ten years, has been the country where this 'original' conception of a historic solution to the division of the continent has found least favour.[40] From the beginnings of the current wave of peace demonstrations in Eu-rope, the aspirations of 'radicals', East and West, have been remarkably close to the original Gaullist vision: the assertion of the historical reality of a trans-European community, a call for the loosening of superpower hegemony, for the dis-

28

solution of the blocs and for the gradual reconciliation, at all levels, of the peoples of both
sides.[41] Why has France, with the exception of a
small but dedicated group of peace activists,[42]
proved so unresponsive to this spirit? The answers
are many and complex[43] but three points are worth
bearing in mind. First, there was the phenomenon
of the 'defence consensus' on the part of the major political parties, which effectively removed
the necessary space for an opposition movement to
produce any impact on public opinion. Second,
there was the development in France, from the mid-
1970s for about a decade, of a virulent wave of
'anti-totalitarianism' on the part of the
(formerly Stalinist) Left intelligentsia, a mood
which was nurtured and relayed by the media and
the entire 'political class'.[44] Third, there was
the strange evolution of the Left-wing parties,
the Communist Party swinging wildly from enthusiastic Eurocommunism (1976) to born-again Stalinism
(1978-9) to powerless ministerialism (1981) and to
increasing irrelevance; the Socialist Party living
through the traumas of unexpected electoral defeat
in 1978 and equally unexpected victory in 1981,
with the result that policy was reactive, conjunctural and unpredictable rather than proactive,
ideological and coherent.

In particular, French fears of 'neutralist
drift' in Germany, as the great peace movements of
the early 1980s rose to a crescendo, became so
widespread, not to say obsessive, that French security policy concentrated almost exclusively on
trying to guarantee that Bonn would remain firmly
wedded to the West. Thus, Mitterrand was led, in
January 1983, to intervene in the German general
elections with a speech before the Bundestag which
amounted to a disavowal of the SPD in favour of
Helmut Kohl's CDU.[45] The German Socialists were
believed to be infected with neutralism, whereas
the conservatives could be relied upon to stick to
the Atlanticist line. For all these reasons,
France has stood aloof from the new spirit of reconciliation which is abroad in Europe and has regarded the advent of Gorbachev with bemused
suspicion.

But the anti-totalitarian wave is already reced-
ing, the Socialists are now back in opposition,
the defence 'consensus' is crumbling rapidly and
an INF agreement has been reached. Exchanges of
all sorts with Eastern Europe are gathering pace
constantly: trade, technical co-operation and cul-

tural visits are increasing all the time. The aspirations of various constituencies in Eastern Europe towards greater independence from the Soviet Union are increasingly powerful.[46] The historical forces nudging Europe, East and West, in the direction of a new understanding are plainly visible across the continent. In this context, and given the inevitable reorientation of American policy towards Western Europe in the wake of the successful arms control treaties, is it not likely (to put it no stronger) that the native land of Gaullism will find a major role to play in redefining East-West relations and in discovering the outlines of a new 'security partnership'[47] for all the nations of the continent? France, after all, has more direct lines of communication, at every level from establishment to dissent, with the nations and peoples of Eastern Europe than any other European country. If there is to be a 'new deal' with the Soviet Union of Gorbachev, is it not far more likely that this will take the shape of enhanced détente and increased political trust, rather than of the forging of a new West European bloc, squaring off against the Soviet bloc with an endlessly problematic Franco-British (or even European) nuclear arsenal? It is this author's conviction that history is currently offering France a major new diplomatic role, one its leaders are still reluctant to assume but one which, for all the reasons outlined above, they cannot evade for much longer.

The fragmentation of the defence 'consensus' in France was quite recently driven home (perhaps unintentionally) by former Socialist Defence Minister Paul Quilès. In an article in Le Monde, he set out the areas of agreement and disagreement within the political class. Agreement exists, if Quilès is to be believed, around the celebrated notions of the 'three circles' first outlined in the 1972 defence white paper.[48] Yet this notion of a clear separation between the strategic interests of the Hexagon and those of her European allies has been eroded to the point of disappearance. The 'three circles' idea exists only as mythology, the abstract framework of a consensus from a bygone age. And Quilès himself makes that clear when, in the same article, he acknowledges that disagreement begins the moment implementation of any aspect of the 'three circles' strategy is discussed: how and when to use either strategic or tactical nuclear weapons? what to do about chemical weapons? how to

solve the chronic resource dilemma? and, most significantly of all, how to define a new European
defence?[49] If there is no agreement on any of
these matters in France today, it is not only because the world has changed in major ways since
1958. It is also because there has been virtually
no public debate on issues which, for too long,
have been regarded as belonging to the president's
reserved domain. In a very real sense, France had
no clear defence policy in 1987. There are, it is
widely recognised in knowledgeable circles in
Paris, fundamental differences between the major
political parties and their leaders on how to face
up to the Gorbachev world of the new détente.
Those different options range from actually phasing out the nuclear deterrent in favour of European conventional collaboration to putting even
more eggs into the nuclear basket. Yet, for the
moment, the vicious circle is being perpetuated.
For how much longer can it continue?

NOTES AND REFERENCES

1.   On the evolution of the Left wing parties, see
Pascal Krop, Les Socialistes et l'Armée, (PUF, Paris, 1983);
Yves Roucaute, Le PCF et l'Armée, (PUF, Paris, 1983; Jolyon
Howorth, 'Consensus of Silence: the French Socialist Party
and Defence Policy under François Mitterrand', International
Affairs, Vol. 60, 1984.
2.   Jolyon Howorth, France: the Politics of Peace
(Merlin, London, 1984).
3.   By June, 1985 an opinion poll was revealing that
57 per cent of respondents felt France should commit
herself automatically to the defence of West Germany and an
even larger majority felt that the reunification of Germany
was desirable (Le Monde, 28 June 1985).
4.   John Saul, in his book La Mort d'un Général,
(Seuil, Paris, 1977), argues that the mysterious death of
General Ailleret was the result of an American-organised
assassination plot in retribution against France's adoption
of omni-directional targeting.
5.   David S. Yost, France's Deterrent Posture and
Security in Europe. Part I Capabilities and Doctrine
(Adelphi Paper No. 194, IISS, London, 1984/5) p. 28.
6.   The CEP is the radius of an imaginary circle within
which 50 per cent of arriving warheads can be guaranteed to
fall.
7.   MIRV = Multiple, Independently-Targetable Re-entry
Vehicle. For a good discussion of this, see Patricia
Chilton, 'French Nuclear Weapons' in Jolyon Howorth and

Patricia Chilton (eds), <u>Defence and Dissent in Contemporary France</u> (Croom Helm, London, 1984), p. 143.

8. See Giscard's 1 June 1976 speech to the Institut des Hautes Etudes de Défense Nationale, in <u>Défense Nationale</u>, July 1976, and the equally revealing article by his Chief of the General Staff, General Méry, 'Une Armée pour quoi faire et comment?' in <u>Défense Nationale</u>, June 1976.

9. See Paul-Marie de la Gorce, 'Bilan d'un septennat: la politique extérieure française', <u>Politique étrangère</u>, Vol. 46, 1981.

10. In reality, as I have argued in a number of areas, there was little programmatic change. See my article, 'Resources and Strategic Choices: French Defence Policy at the Crossroads', <u>The World Today</u>, Vol. 42, May 1986, pp. 77-80. On this whole problem, see in particular, Robbin F. Laird (ed.), <u>French Security Policy</u> (Westview Press, Boulder, 1986).

11. UDF, <u>Redresser la Défense de la France</u> (UDF, Paris, 1985), Annexes, p. 17, Tableau 4.

12. Assemblée Nationale, <u>Rapport fait au nom de la Commission de la Défense Nationale et des forces armées</u>, No. 622, 2 April 1987, p. 54.

13. Jolyon Howorth, 'Of Budgets and Strategic Choices: Defence Policy under Mitterrand' in Stanley Hoffmann, <u>et al</u>. (eds), <u>The Mitterrand Experiment: Continuity and Change in Socialist France</u> (Polity Press, Cambridge, 1987).

14. Report cited in note 12, above, p. 51.

15. <u>Ibid</u>, pp. 158-9.

16. The 'double zero option' refers to the agreement to eliminate altogether two categories of nuclear missiles: short range weapons (500 to 1,000 kms) and intermediate range (1,000 to 5,000 kms) ones. [This chapter was completed in September 1987 and discusses strategic issues at that time.]

17. SALT = Strategic Arms Limitation Treaty (Salt 1, 1972: Salt 2, 1979). START = Strategic Arms Reductions Talks. INF = Intermediate Nuclear Forces.

18. For a good overview of this question, see Jonathan Alford, 'The Place of British and French Nuclear Weapons in Arms Control', <u>International Affairs</u>, Vol. 59 (1983), pp. 569-74. Also Yves Boyer, 'Illustration d'un monde en crise: 'Arms Control' et zone grise', <u>Stratégigne</u> No. 9, 1981. The best detailed study is David S. Yost, <u>France's Deterrent Posture and Security and Europe. Part II, Strategic and Arms Control Implications</u> (Adelphi Paper, No. 195, IISS, London, 1984/5).

19. See Hella Pick, 'Gorbachev Gives Arms Timetable', <u>The Guardian</u>, 14 October 1986, p. 6.

21. See <u>Le Monde</u>, 3 March 1987, p. 5.

22. <u>Le Monde</u>, 4 March 1987, p. 2; <u>The Guardian</u>, 3 March

1987, p. 8.

23. Speech printed in full in La Politique Etrangère de la France - Textes et Documents, September/October 1983, pp. 38-44.

24. Bernard Brigouleix, 'Les Embarras de Paris', Le Monde, 3 March 1987.

25. Le Monde, 6 March 1987, p. 6.

26. See, for example, Jacques Isnard, 'Une Europe prise au piège des déséquilibres nucléaires', Le Monde, 5-6 April 1987, and Pierre Lellouche, 'La France et l'option zéro: réflexions sur la position française', Politique Etrangère, Vol. 52, Spring 1987.

27. Editorial in Le Monde, 3 April 1987, 'Cohabitation exemplaire à Washington'.

28. See the article by Michel Tatu in Le Monde, 5-6 April 1987, and Le Monde, 12-13 April 1987, pp. 1-3.

29. Paul Anderson et al., 'Alliance in Crisis over INF Deal', END Journal, No. 27, May-June 1987.

30. Some early 1988 presidential contenders have all responded in different ways. See Michel Rocard, Le Monde, 11 July 1987; Jean-Pierre Chevènement, '1992 et le rendez-vous franco-allemand', La Lettre de la République Moderne, No. 13, June 1987; Raymond Barre, 'De la Sécurité en Europe', Faits et Arguments, Special Issue, April 1987, which was Barre's Alastair Buchan Memorial lecture to the IISS, also published, in English, in Survival, July/August 1987; Jacques Chirac, Le Monde, 8 July 1987. See also the document prepared for the UDF by the Groupe Renouveau Défense entitled L'Affaire de l'option zéro, 10 May 1987 (Paris, UDF). Laurent Fabius, 'Pour un couplage franco-allemand', Le Monde, 20 August 1987.

31. Prior to 'modernisation', France's five nuclear submarines carried a total of 80 nuclear warheads. After complete modernisation with the M-4 missile, France's SNLE fleet will carry 496 warheads. Plans for the M-5 involve even more multiple warheads which could push the total to nearer 800.

32. Libération, 16 February 1987.

33. Caspar Weinberger, 'Europe-Amérique: la sécurité indivisible', Le Monde, 11 September 1987, is only the most recent of many such reassurances.

34. Le Figaro, on 21 April 1987, published an opinion poll in which 45 per cent of respondents judged the zero option to be a Soviet 'trap' for Western Europe. Thirty-five per cent were in favour and 20 per cent had no opinion.

35. François Mitterrand on TF1: see Le Monde, 31 March 1987.

36. In June 1984 Senator Sam Nunn of Georgia introduced legislation to effect a reduction on the order of 100,000 US troops in Europe unless the allies did more for their own defence. See, on this, Phil Williams, US troops in Europe

(Chatham House Papers 25, Routledge and Kegan Paul, London, 1984).

37. Raymond Aron, 'Le Grand Dessein du Général', _Mémoires_ (Julliard, Paris, 1983) especially pp. 605-11.

38. See the long quote supplied by Aron, _ibid_., p. 608, and, on this entire question, Stanley Hoffmann, 'France's Relations with West Germany', _French Politics and Society_, March 1985.

39. 'Discours prononcé par le Président de la République', Chatham House, London, 15 January 1987. Text supplied by the Service de Presse of the Elysée, pp. 28-9.

40. Much of what follows has been examined in greater details in Jolyon Howorth, 'The Third Way', _Foreign Policy_, No. 65, Winter 1986/7.

41. For continuous reporting on this new European spirit, see the bimonthly journal _END Journal_, London, and the END Manifesto of April 1980.

42. The CODENE (Comité pour le désarmement nucléaire en Europe, 20 rue Chandron, 75020 Paris, France).

43. This point has been examined in much greater detail in Howorth, _France: the Politics of Peace_.

44. This was the movement spearheaded by the so-called 'new philosophers' of the late 1970s. Anti-totalitarian writers who posited a new spirit of nuclear resistance to the 'Soviet menace' included, notably, Cornelius Castoriadis, _Devant la Guerre_ (Grasset, Paris, 1983) and André Glucksmann, _La Force du Vertige_ (Grasset, Paris, 1983). But see also Admiral Antoine Sanguinetti's response to Glucksmann in _Le Vertige de la Force_ (Paris, La Decouverte, 1984).

45. See _Le Monde_, 22 January 1983.

46. See my article cited in footnote 40 above, pp. 124-6.

47. The concept comes from the German SPD and no doubt represents that 'something else' which 44 per cent of Germans said they hoped for, in response to the opinion poll cited above. See Chapter Three, 'East-West Partnership in the Pursuit of Security' of the SPD's document _Peace and Security_.

48. First devised by General Lucien Poirier, the 'three circles' idea is as follows. The first circle is France herself, to be defended by strategic and tactical nuclear weapons; the second is Europe, in whose defence France is prepared to play a part (unspecified and by no means automatic) with conventional weapons; the third is France's world interests, for which it needs a vast array of military hardware.

49. Paul Quilès, 'Du bon usage du consensus', _Le Monde_, 8 April 1987.

Chapter Three

FRANCE AND EUROPEAN UNITY

Mark Wise

'La France a toujours rêvé d'une Europe à la
française'.
(Philippe Moreau Desfarges, 1984)[1]

The relationship between France and European
political unity has a long history. Across the
centuries, Frenchmen have been prominent in devis-
ing schemes for European unity, creating a tradition which persists to the present day. Yet many
people are quick to associate France with a narrow
defence of national interests which frequently
spills over into chauvinism. It is instructive to
summarise some of the facts that can be assembled
to substantiate both of these images, not least
because an ideal of European union often provides
the conceptual framework within which many Frenchmen reconcile these apparently contradictory aspects of their political life.

FRANCE: A MAJOR SOURCE OF EUROPEAN UNITY

As far back as 1306 a certain Pierre Dubois argued
that the Catholic rulers of Europe should form a
Common Council designed to settle disputes between
them peacefully. Later, Sully, chief minister to
Henri IV (1620-35) proposed a similar association
of European monarchs within a General Council empowered to resolve inter-state conflicts. In 1712,
the Abbé de Saint-Pierre advocated a multi-state
organisation designed to preserve the peace of Europe within which each government would have one
vote. Jean-Jacques Rousseau, in the eighteenth
century, elaborated this tradition by imagining a
federal European League with the power to intervene in the internal affairs of member states. In
the wake of the Napoleonic Wars (1792-1815) Henri
de Saint-Simon wrote 'De la Réorganisation de la
société européenne' in which he suggested a single
European king with a single grand parlement having
very wide political powers including that of taxa-

35

tion. At the Universal Peace Congress of 1848, Victor Hugo proposed a United States of Europe. In the 1860s another Frenchman, Proudhon, urged that all European states become federations with 'Europe' evolving into a 'federation of federations'. Such ideals did nothing to check the growth of national rivalries in Europe which eventually ignited the First World War. This tragedy gave a new impetus to the European idea; the most prominent practising politician promoting it was Aristide Briand, the French Foreign Minister during the 1920s. However, his scheme for a 'European Union', put before the League of Nations in 1929, faded away as Europe sank into the Great Depression, saw the rise of fascism and was eventually subjected to the horrors of the Second World War.

In the aftermath of years of nationalistic destruction, Frenchmen again emerged as major initiators of renewed efforts to unite Europe by peaceful means. It was Jean Monnet, high-ranking French civil servant and founder of the Action Committee for the United States of Europe, who devised the strategies leading in 1951 to the European Coal and Steel Community (ECSC), which provided the model upon which to base the European Atomic Energy Community (Euratom) and the European Economic Community (EEC) in 1958. These separate entities are now controlled in common by a single set of supra-national institutions in the 'Monnet' mould, known as the European Communities or, increasingly, the European Community (EC). Robert Schuman, France's Foreign Minister, provided the political strength to turn Monnet's plans for an ECSC into a reality linking France, West Germany, Italy and the Benelux countries in the crucial first step towards the EC of today. It was also the French government which in 1950 proposed the creation of a European Defence Community, but this ambitious scheme ultimately foundered. Since these early days, the French tradition, unmatched elsewhere, of conceiving grand schemes of continental co-operation and taking related initiatives has continued.

French determination has led to the establishment of the EC's one truly common policy, that of agriculture. French President Giscard d'Estaing got his partners to agree to the creation of a European Council in 1974 (in which Common Market heads of government/state meet at regular intervals), thus adding to the Monnet-inspired institutions already in place. His Socialist successor, François Mitterrand, has become increasingly ambitious in his conception of 'Europe'. In 1981 he invited other EC member states to envisage the building of a 'European Social Area' to deal with issues like unemployment, harmonising social security systems, working weeks and the like, thus balancing a Community too pre-occupied, in his view, with narrow economic issues. This typically expansive French view of European unity also led Mitterrand to initiate the EUREKA project in 1985 with the aim of encouraging trans-frontier co-operation in research and development of new technologies so that Western Europe could compete with the USA and Japan. In a similar vein, the French President in the autumn of 1987 proposed a Common Defence Council between France and West Germany which could, in his view, become the noyau européen (the core) of a wider body of West European states concerned with their common security.

Such ambitious ideas for 'Europe' (as the French invariably refer to the EC and related moves towards West European unity) flourish in French political debate.[2] Moreover, French politicians are speaking to a receptive audience. The detailed opinion surveys carried out by the European Commission's 'Euro-barometre' programme invariably show the French public to be among the most solid supporters of the EC.[3] For example, over the period 1973-86 some 59 per cent of the French public on average maintained a favourable attitude towards the Community, with the figure rising as high as 68 per cent at times. In the UK, the average proportion of those favourably disposed towards the EC over the same period was a mere 34 per cent with the number never rising above 50 per cent. In 1986, only 30 per cent of the French population 'never' thought of themselves as 'citizens' of Europe, while the comparable proportion in the UK was 67 per cent; the EC average on this score was 41 per cent. The European flag fluttering alongside the national tricolour on buildings across France doubtless reflects the finding that 66 per cent (1985) of the French find this symbol 'a good thing', whereas a mere 38 per cent of Britons, for the most part utterly incapable of identifying it, shared this view.

FRANCE: DEFENDER OF ITS NATIONAL INTERESTS AND INDEPENDENCE

While it is easy to demonstrate the leading role of France in the construction of European unity, it is not difficult also to characterise the French as stubborn defenders of their national interests and independence. For example, while it was the French government which proposed the creation of a European Defence Community in 1950, it was the vigorous opposition of députés in France's parliament, determined to protect national sovereignty, which finally sunk the project in 1954. Since then France, for all the periodic speculation about 'European defence' that emanates from it, has resolutely developed a very independent system of national security outside the integrated military command structure of NATO and with its own nuclear deterrent. The determination of de Gaulle to preserve national sovereignty also checked progress towards the genuinely supra-national European institutions planned by Monnet and Schuman. In 1965, as the EEC prepared to adopt obligatory majority voting in the Council of Ministers, which lies at the heart of the Community's decision-making system, de Gaulle's government refused to accept this requirement of the Rome Treaty, and boycotted Community institutions for some six months in order to underline its refusal to accept anything reducing national sovereignty. This crisis of 'la chaise vide' (the empty chair) was eventually resolved to French satisfaction in the so-called 'Luxembourg Compromise' which in fact, if not in strict legal terms, gives member states the power of veto over anything that threatens ill-defined 'vital national interests'.

Nationalist attitudes survived the passing of de Gaulle. With its long tradition of central governmental intervention into the details of economic life, France has often found itself before the European Court of Justice (an EC institution) accused of contravening some regulation on freedom of competition and trade within the EC. However, France is not alone in this respect, and its citizens can be found among those challenging the 'European' legality of protectionist measures. For example, the Leclerc family, creators of one of France's largest supermarket chains, have used the European Court to challenge (often with success) national restrictions on car imports from other EC countries and government fixing of petrol and book prices to protect small French retailers.[4] France has, however, been a fertile ground for the generation of European schemes calling for closer 'political' co-operation on foreign policy issues. But, faced with a crisis, French governments have

often acted strictly according to the philosophy
of national independence. For example, when the
1973 Arab-Israeli war triggered off an enormous
increase in oil prices and saw one of France's EC
partners, the Netherlands, singled out by an Arab
oil embargo, the French Foreign Minister, Michel
Jobert, was reluctant to support a common Community stand to protect the interests of all the
member states.[5] France did not want to be associated with anything that gave the impression of
'ganging up' on the Arab world, with which it was
trying to develop a privileged relationship.[6] This
can be judged as intelligent diplomacy, but it did
little to advance French pretensions in the realm
of European political co-operation. To be fair,
another French government did get its EC partners
to adopt a joint declaration on the Arab-Israeli
conflict in 1980. But, with the arrival of the
Socialist government in 1981, France reverted to
taking independent national initiatives to this
dispute, notably in the Franco-Egyptian plan of
July 1982 (which had no more effect that its
'European' equivalents!).[7] The Mitterrand presidency of the early 1980s provided other examples
of this French readiness to 'go-it-alone' if its
partners are thought to be 'out-of-step'. Along
with the West Germans, the French had been a major
instigator of the European Monetary System (EMS)
in 1979. The success of this system, designed to
control exchange-rate fluctuations in the EC, depends on a convergence of the economic policies of
the member states. But the incoming Socialist government of 1981 decided, against the grain of de-
flationary policies being pursued elsewhere in the
Community, to implement reflationary strategies in
order to create jobs and finance an ambitious new
series of social measures. It would be wrong to
pretend that only the French are capable of such
independent action, but the resulting series of
EMS 're-alignments' (involving successive devalua-
tions of the French franc against the West German
mark) did little to strengthen French credibility
as a would-be leader of European monetary union.[8]

EUROPEAN UNITY: AN EXTENSION OF FRENCH NATIONAL INTERESTS

The oscillations of successive French governments
between visions of European unity and independent
pursuit of national interests are, in part, a man-
ifestation of different strands of political opin-

ion in a large and diverse country. Sometimes the federalist aspirations of a Jean Monnet lie behind some grand 'European' project, while at others the tradition of national independence embodied by de Gaulle has held sway. But it is significant that most political tendencies in France, Left and Right, have espoused some sort of 'European' ideal in the post-war years. Any contradiction this might engender in patriotic French minds is resolved by seeing the ideal of European unity as a means by which France's national interests can best be protected and her influence in the world promoted. This marriage of nationalism and Europeanism was succinctly expressed by France's Minister for European Affairs in the Chirac government (1987) when urging a substantial strengthening of the European Community:

> I believe that, today, the more one is
> nationalist, the more one is European.
> In tomorrow's world, there is no chance
> of being great, free and respected with-
> out working through Europe.[9]

Even the speeches of de Gaulle, that symbol of French national independence, are littered across the years with references to the need for some sort of European framework within which France could find security and influence world affairs. In 1948 he spoke of France's 'dignity' and 'duty' requiring it to be 'the centre and key' of a group of states 'having as its arteries the North Sea, the Rhine and the Mediterranean'.[10] This theme of France's destiny being irrevocably linked to that of European unity (primarily expressed by the EC) has been elaborated with increasing emphasis by French leaders of many political persuasions.[11] Few among France's elites would disagree with former socialist Prime Minister Laurent Fabius: 'We need for France a strong, therefore united, Europe'.[12]

The widespread conviction that France needs a successful EC to assure its future is allied to an equally strong belief that the Community needs France, one of its major states. This two-way relationship was forcibly expressed in a report produced for the Commissariat Général du Plan in 1983 which tried to define a 'European strategy for France during the 1980s':

> France's European strategy is not a

secondary element of its general policy,
but is to be found right at its heart.
France needs a dynamic and enterprising
Europe [the EC] in order to achieve its
own objectives. But Europe cannot do
without France, not only because our
country is linked geographically and
culturally to the continent and its
civilisation, but, above all, because
France, by its view of the world, its
way of approaching and dealing with the
problems of our region [Europe],
strengthens the building of European
unity.[13]

What characterises this French world view to which
the report refers? One feature is the French
propensity to think in large-scale geopolitical
terms with the world seen as an interrelated system in which all states struggle to dominate, remain independent or simply survive. Political discourse is full of references to global trends
(often seen as menacing to France), international
power relationships and 'wars' of a military, economic and cultural kind. Popular academic texts
invite the reader to envisage such things as the
USA unleashing a 'merciless economic and trade
war' on the EC.[14] In more measured terms the government report referred to above develops a macro-
level analysis of global trends to justify its argument that France should aim to create a strong
European Community:

An analysis of evolving power relationships in the world, the growing tensions, the increasing imbalance between
the powerful and the weak, as well as
the expectations many countries have of
Europe, all lead to the conclusion that
a Europe [the EC] capable of making decisions and taking action is absolutely
necessary.[15]

THE CHALLENGE OF THE USA (AND OTHER 'ANGLO-SAXONS')

In the 1960s, the prominent journalist-politician,
Jean-Jacques Servan-Schreiber published a best-
selling book entitled The American Challenge (Le
Défi americain)[16]. It was designed to alert the
French public to the danger of being dominated by

41

the USA in technological and economic terms. In so doing it was popularising a theme long-established in French political circles. More than any other EC country, France struggles to resist what it sees as excessive American influence in European affairs, be it related to military matters (US predominance within NATO), business (the power of American multi-national companies), finance (the influence of the US dollar), technology (the strengthening of American research and development) or culture (the ubiquitous presence of American films, television series and popular music in West European mass-media). This French fear of subjugation to the USA (which should not be equated with simple anti-Americanism) sometimes spills over into a more generalised resistance to being overwhelmed by 'les Anglo-Saxons' in general. This rather quaint term is used by the French to designate other English-speaking countries, notably the UK and its old imperial offshoots such as Canada, Australia and New Zealand. Suspicion of a continuing 'special relationship' between the USA and the UK has not disappeared as the UK continues to buy American nuclear weapons (the French develop their own), to allow USAF jets to take off from bases in the UK in order to bomb Libya (having to fly around French air space) and to do a higher proportion of its trade with the USA than any other EC country (some 14 per cent of imports and exports, about twice the French equivalent in 1985). Moreover, UK efforts to reform the EC's Common Agricultural Policy (CAP) in order to reduce surpluses of dairy products and meat often confront French criticisms of the UK's continuing insistence on importing butter and lamb from their 'kith and kin' in the Antipodes.

THE CHALLENGE OF JAPAN

Nowhere in Europe is the growing technological, economic and financial power of Japan perceived with greater apprehension than in France. However, little more than 2 per cent of French imports during the mid-1980s came from Japan (compared to some 4-5 per cent for the UK and West Germany). This situation owes not a little to the skill of the French in checking the inward flow of Japanese electrical goods and cars. In the early 1980s, all Japanese video-recorders imported into France had to be checked by a handful of customs officials in

the small provincial city of Poitiers, thus making
these much sought-after machines a much rarer and
more expensive commodity for the French than for
their EC neighbours. In the meantime, the French
government was making urgent and ultimately futile
efforts to get France's giant electronics company,
Thomson, to joint forces with Grundig of West Germany and Philips of the Netherlands to produce
'European' machines to counter the Japanese challenge.[17] The Japanese threat to more traditional
industries like car manufacture has been fended
off by simpler and more effective means: their
sales are limited to a mere 3 per cent of France's
national market. The French have little faith in
the sort of 'gentlemen's agreements' which aim to
keep Japan's car sales to around 10 per cent of
the British and West German markets and note with
alarm that the Japanese share of total EC car
sales rose from 3 per cent in 1973 to 12 per cent
in 1978.[18] French apprehension that Japanese financial and industrial strength could weaken or
even eliminate vital sectors of European manufacturing also leads them to be critical of countries
like the UK which allow Japanese car companies to
build assembly plants on their territory and thus
get inside the EC's common customs barrier. Even
French leaders committed to the idea of 'free market' competition have no difficulty in adopting a
protectionist strategy if they feel that some important element of the national or European economy is at risk from the Japanese challenge.

THE CHALLENGE OF THE USSR

While a fear (mixed with fascination) of North
American and Japanese economic prowess is a powerful force moulding French attitudes toward the
European Community, suspicion of the ultimate objectives of the Soviet Union remains very strong
in France - even among parts of the non-communist
Left - providing another motivation for promoting
unity among the countries of Western Europe. Although French determination not to be subservient
to the USA in security matters tends to be highlighted by public gestures of one sort or another,
fear of Soviet strength in conventional and nuclear weapons runs deep in France. As the possibility of a reduction in the American nuclear
guarantee to Western Europe become more real, the
expression of this sense of insecurity becomes

less muted and a French drive to ensure their national defence within some sort of united European framework more evident.[19]

THE CHALLENGE OF THE THIRD WORLD

The world of developing states as viewed from France is seen as posing a mixture of opportunity and threat. For example, the spread of militant Islamic fundamentalism around the Mediterranean basin is observed with some concern in France. Opponents of Arab immigration ask people to imagine what would happen if the fundamentalist movement took root among the 2.5 to 3 million Moslems living in France.[20] The perceived need for France and the EC to combat poverty in the poor countries is often linked to this view of potential menaces emanating from the Third World. Take, for example, the recent observations of someone with presidential aspirations, left-winger Jean-Pierre Chevènement:

> Underdevelopment provides fertile ground for the growth of Moslem fundamentalism. If, in the future, it becomes established at our gates in Egypt or in North Africa, you will see lots of 'boat people'! I leave you to imagine the reaction in France! It's time we take the measure of this challenge. And it is the concern of Europe [EC] as a whole to take a major initiative linking the two sides of the Mediterranean in an enormous effort of co-development.[21]

This statement also reveals the more positive side of French attitudes towards the Third World and the role the EC should play. A perception of economic opportunities to be seized there is particularly sharp with regard to Africa, where France retains extremely close cultural and political links with the Francophone countries of its former empire (now virtually all associated with the EC via the Lomé Convention). But most French politicians now tend to see the destiny of France as interlinked with that of the rest of the EC in developing countries; in the words of one of them:

> The European Community, more than the superpowers, depends to a large extent

on these countries. Europeans import,
mainly from the Third World, about half
of the energy they need. For numerous
commodities such as coffee, cocoa, copper, manganese, and many others, the
dependence of the Community on developing countries is around 90 per cent.
Finally, the Third World is not only the
leading supplier of the Community, but
also its major client, absorbing more
than a third of its exports.[22]

THE NEED FOR WEST EUROPEAN COOPERATION TO MEET THESE CHALLENGES

Faced with these formidable challenges, most leaders in France argue that their country can maintain its position in the world only through increasing West European co-operation, mainly, but
not necessarily, within the framework provided by
the EC. The apparent paradox of nationalism and
'Europeanism' co-existing within France is hereby
resolved. Individually, European states are seen
to be too small to maintain their political, economic, military and cultural independence in a
world dominated by the superpowers. Therefore,
they must unite to find the collective strength to
survive as unsubjugated nations. Exactly what form
this unity should take remains open to question,
but few in France seriously question the basic argument.
    This awareness of French limitations in a world
dominated by superpowers and destabilised by er-
ratic forces emanating from the poorer regions of
the globe is intensified by a fear that France,
like the rest of Western Europe, is entering a period of relative decline. The sense of lagging
ever further behind the USA, Japan and the USSR in
various ways is felt in countries other than
France. But the French elaborate this pessimistic
theme by re-formulating the old national fear of
demographic decline in more general European
terms.[23] Although in post-war years, the French
birth rate has declined less rapidly than those of
its major EC partners, the deep-rooted obsession
of France's leaders to prevent demographic stagna-
tion periodically surfaces. The worry is no longer
about a feebleness of French fecundity in relation
to its immediate neighbours, but with the decreas-
ing proportions that France and the rest of the EC

contribute to the global population. France has fallen from being one of the world's most populated nineteenth-century states to around sixteenth place in global rankings,[24] while the EC's share of humanity will slip from 6 per cent in 1982 to a mere 3.3 per cent in 2025. This trend, warns one writer, echoing a familiar French theme, 'will affect the ability of Europe [the EC] to maintain its influence and independence in the global arena'.[25] A vision of an 'ageing' France and Europe, beset with the problems of too few young to support too many elderly and trying to manage inexorable flows of immigrants from the youthful populations of North Africa and elsewhere, creates anxiety in not a few influential French minds, thus providing an additional incentive to seek national security within the context of the European Community.

THE IMPORTANCE OF THE FRANCO-GERMAN RELATIONSHIP FOR EUROPEAN UNITY

The 'challenge' posed by post-war West Germany also motivated French leaders to promote European co-operation in the 1950s. When it became clear that the economic renaissance and military rearmament of the newly created Federal Republic of Germany was inevitable, French politicians conceived the idea of controlling this revival within a supra-national 'European' framework. Thus fear of any further German aggression across the Rhine could be neutralised. In the words of Robert Schuman, when proposing the original European Coal and Steel Community in 1950: 'The gathering together of the European nations requires that the age-old opposition of France and Germany be eliminated: the action undertaken must primarily deal with France and Germany'.[26] In 1963, de Gaulle underlined this 'special relationship' by signing the Franco-German Treaty which established a regular system of consultation between the two countries and provided for co-operation across a wide range of activities from youth exchanges to security matters. Over the years, geopolitical circumstances have changed, but Germany remains central to France's European policy. There is no longer any fear of a German attack westwards into France, but some worry that West Germany might drift eastwards into a central European neutralism and closer relationships with East Germany. Such development would create all kinds of uncertainties for the security of France and other European countries. Thus, the prominent authors of a report to the French government urged that France give top priority to strengthening its trans-Rhine links in order to renew the attractiveness of the EC for West Germans:

> In our analysis of challenges confronting the [European] Community, we have attached great importance to the German problem.... One of the major uncertainties hanging over the future of Europe... resides in the choices made in the coming years by the Federal Republic [of Germany] and its people. The economic and political construction of the European entity has been made essentially around the Franco-German axis. Europe will not be reassured until the Federal Republic is convinced that its only possible future lies within a European Community aware of its identity and made confident by its economic and political dynamism.[27]

Such sentiments slip into public pronouncements across the political spectrum as, for example, in the comment of Jean-Pierre Chevènement regarding the major problems confronting the EC: 'Is it possible to meet these challenges? In order to do so it is not enough to make ritual invocations about European unity. The key will be whether France and [West] Germany have enough common political will'.[28] This French conviction that their relationship with West Germany is the 'keystone' of the European Community recurs as a constant theme.

FRANCE AND THE EC'S COMMON AGRICULTURAL POLICY (CAP)

The CAP is the most 'common' of all EC policies in that it is decided and financed almost completely by the supra-national institutions of the Community rather than national authorities. Although very complex in detail it is based on three fundamental principles: a single common market for agricultural produce, preference for Community produce over imports in this internal market, and Community financing of the common price support system and other agricultural expenditure. The

47

completion of this imposing edifice owes most to
French determination. Underlying the establishment
of the EEC in 1958 was a 'basic pact' between
France and West Germany which guaranteed the former a CAP tailored to its needs in order to coun-
terbalance the advantages the latter would gain
from the dismantling of industrial protection
within the common market.[29] Faced with problems of
modernising its manufacturing industry to meet increased West German competition, France needed to
perceive a clear advantage in the agricultural
field where it possesses enormous resources in relation to its EC partners.

In the immediate post-war period nearly a third
of the French labour force worked on the land,
producing about a quarter of the national GDP. By
1986, the comparable figures had dropped to some
7.6 per cent of the working population and just
4.7 per cent of GDP. But these figures still represent a large population (1,582,000) as well as a
substantial agro-industrial sector. (The comparable figures for the UK, which has a similar overall population of around 55 million, are 2.6 per
cent of the labour force - 620,000 people - a mere
1.7 per cent of GDP.)[30] Furthermore, even in the
much enlarged contemporary Community of twelve
states, France still has some 23.6 per cent of the
EC's utilised agricultural area. (The comparable
figures for the UK, Italy and West Germany are 14
per cent, 13 per cent and 9 per cent respectively.) With over 60 per cent of the land used
for agriculture and a relatively small population
living upon it, the French have sought to exploit
the export potential of their <u>pétrole vert</u>
(literally 'green oil') which compensates for
France's lack of the 'crude' variety. Their insistence upon a CAP which protected this agricultural
industry and offered it open access to the huge
urban populations of West Germany, Benelux and,
later, the UK is easy to understand.

In general, French food producers and processors
have grasped the opportunities opened up by the
CAP. France has become one of the world's major
food exporters and developed a large food-process-
ing industry employing around 610,000 persons -
which occupies second place in national occupa-
tional rankings as well as being the world's third
largest after the USA and the UK.[31] In 1985, 15.3
per cent of France's total exports were composed
of agricultural commodities, while the comparable
figures for the UK, Italy, West Germany and the

USA were 6.3 per cent, 7.1 per cent, 4.7 per cent and 10.2 per cent respectively. In fact, France is the world's largest exporter of food and related products after the USA. Nearly two-thirds of these exports go to France's EC partners. France is also a significant importer of agricultural products, but since 1970 and the completion of the CAP it has had an increasing balance-of-trade surplus in this sector (5,310 million ECU in 1985) and is determined to maintain this situation.

This enormous agricultural industry not only provides direct employment for some two million people in France, but also indirectly contributes to the living of many more in service industries. Although the number of farmers continues to diminish, the degree to which agriculture is integrated into the rest of French society should not be underestimated. Many French people no longer working on the land retain a real interest in the fortunes of farming folk, be it related to the plot of land they rent out or the fate of a relative still working the family farm. Any French politician in pursuit of power ignores agricultural interests at his or her peril, particularly in a country where elections are won or lost by relatively small margins.

Having created a CAP adapted to its interests (a task facilitated by the fact that the other five 'original' EC member states had traditionally pursued similar protective agricultural policies), the French have remained at the head of those protecting it against the attacks of 'Anglo-Saxon' countries with different interests and different systems of agricultural support. A major factor in de Gaulle's veto on UK entry into the EC during the 1960s was the justifiable fear that the British would try to undermine the establishment of a French-inspired CAP and replace it with a looser free-trade/deficiency payment system more suited to its interests. In the general French view, it was not possible for Britain 'to enter Europe and continue to buy from the Antipodes at the expense of a partner [France] whose agriculture vitally needs to export'.[32] This attitude also explains why France insisted, often in the face of opposition from its original EC partners, that the extremely comprehensive CAP system be completed before negotiations on British entry could begin in the early 1970s. This meant that the UK would have to accept the CAP as part of the non-negotiable <u>acquis communautaire</u> (established

EC policy and law). The rigour of French strategy in this regard - characteristic of their coherent approach to EC matters as a whole - can be illustrated by noting that one of the last pieces of the enormous CAP jigsaw (a common policy for fisheries) was being put in place just hours before enlargement negotiations with the UK, Norway, Denmark and Ireland were opened.[33]

Once in the EC and confronted with the difficulties of adaptation foreseen by de Gaulle, the British have indeed striven to reform the CAP and related elements of the Community budget. Others in the 'Anglo-Saxon' camp have assisted in what the French perceive as an attempt to undermine the CAP. Australia and New Zealand have been severely affected by the loss of British markets as Community preferences keep their products out of the EC. For example, of the countries making up the EC, nine states took between 50 per cent and 70 per cent of Australian exports of meat, dairy products, sugar and wheat in 1958; by 1980 the proportions were virtually nil.[34] Moreover the CAP's system of subsidising exports of surplus produce amounts to dumping and reduces their ability to find alternative markets. Similar arguments, denouncing the CAP's protectionism and advocating 'free trade' on the global market, have emanated forcibly from the USA, the world's major food exporter.

Faced with these onslaughts from English-speaking countries,[35] the French, often acting as a 'front' for most of their EC partners, justify the CAP by adopting contrasting perspectives and selecting sets of statistics which differ from those of their opponents.[36] They remind their partners that the CAP remains the one truly 'common' policy of the EC which must be preserved as the base upon which further unity can be built; after all, it 'has been a success... in that it has achieved, indeed surpassed, most of its objectives'.[37] With their penchant for geopolitical thinking, the French also point out how the CAP has 'guaranteed the security of food supplies to 270 million European consumers... on a world market where shortages and tensions exist'.[38] Critics are invited to remember such things as the American embargo on soya exports in 1973 (threatening EC livestock farmers), the shortages of wheat on the world market between 1972-74 and similar turbulence in the global sugar trade in 1974-80. The security enjoyed by the European consumer is attributed to the greatly increased degree of self-sufficiency generated by the CAP's system of Community preference and price support. For example, the EC of six states in the late 1950s produced only about 85-90 per cent of its wheat and barley requirements, whereas the enlarged Community of ten (despite the incorporation of a major cereal importer in the UK) enjoyed a self-sufficiency rate of around 110-115 per cent by the mid-1980s and was exporting these commodities. A similar evolution has affected other basic foodstuffs. In response to criticisms that this high level of self-sufficiency is achieved at excessive cost, the Gallic response is predictable: 'Security has a price and... excessive dependence on overseas supplies is a cause of weakness. [Therefore]... preservation of the CAP is a strategic necessity'.[39] A French member of the European Parliament has elaborated the theme; after recognising that the UK desire for cheaper non-EC food imports has 'on first sight some seductive aspects', she found that 'it loses its strength when faced with the fact that Europe, already so heavily dependent on imports, notably in the field of energy, would again have to increase its dependence in the area of food supplies where it has the means to satisfy its needs'.[40]

On the crucial issue of the CAP's cost the French often adopt offence as the best form of defence. Whereas the British, in general, endlessly complain that EC butter costs some four to five times its New Zealand counterpart, that agriculture absorbs about two-thirds of the Community budget, that, on average, each common market farmer gets over US$3,000 per annum from EC taxpayers,[41] the French defence of farmers takes a different tack. Is it really excessive that the equivalent of less than 0.5 per cent of the EC's GDP is used to support agriculture? Is it really such a burden that less than 3 per cent of European consumers' expenditure on food goes to finance the CAP? Is it really so abnormal that the CAP consumes the larger part of EC spending when it is the only policy primarily supported by the Community budget? (Other policies are overwhelmingly financed by national resources.) Dismissing 'Anglo-Saxon' pretensions to be champions of 'free trade' on a 'competitive world market' as simplistic, if not fraudulent, a standard French defence of the CAP stresses that all major farming coun-

tries, not least the USA, provide financial support for their food producers in one form or another, along with a whole host of other protective
measures. The guaranteed price support system of
the CAP is unique, it is argued, mainly in that it
is simpler and more transparent than measures
adopted elsewhere which are just as costly.[42]

French defenders of the CAP also deny that it is
excessively protectionist. They point out that the
EC is the world's largest importer of agricultural
goods with purchases representing around 25 per
cent of global trade in these commodities. Furthermore:

> This astonishing dependence on outside
> supplies does not signify that Europe
> [the EC] is obliged to import large
> quantities of things which it cannot
> produce itself or for which it has no
> substitute. Just the opposite. For the
> most part, its imports concern products
> covered by [trade] concessions freely
> granted.[43]

More specifically they counter US hostility by
pointing out that the Community's growth in agricultural self-sufficiency has been achieved
largely at the expense of Third World sugar-pro-
ducing countries rather than the USA. Thanks to
liberal common market policies (such as the zero
tariff on soya imports) the USA has more or less
maintained its share of the EC market in recent
years at around 10-12 per cent, which represents
about 20 per cent of total US agricultural exports. The agricultural balance of trade between
the USA and the EC has also been evolving in
favour of the former during the operation of the
CAP.[44]

French attitudes to the CAP are not bogged down
in the pricing details of butter, beans and so on,
but rise to confront what it is often seen as another element of the US will to dominate in world
politics. The tone adopted by the vice-president
of France's Assemblée Permanente des Chambres
d'Agriculture is not untypical:

> And since we are being accused, we
> wish... to defend ourselves and reveal
> with the utmost clarity that those [in
> the USA] who would judge us have abso-
> lutely no right to do so. That is why we

expose several poorly understood aspects
of American agriculture and the real
causes of its progress towards the con-
quest of the world.[45]

A top-ranking French civil servant working in the
EC institutions echoes these sentiments when wishing to see 'the end of the passive acceptance by
Europeans of the international order that the
Americans presently impose in the domain of agricultural trade'.[46] France's desire to emulate, as
well as resist, the USA also finds expression in
these analyses of the CAP. Noting the great expansion of US agricultural exports during recent
decades and the diplomatic muscle thus achieved, a
French politician calls upon the EC to do like-
wise: 'We will thus have at our disposal a master
card in the game of international trade which will
allow us to conserve our place in the world'.[47]

France's defence of the CAP does not reside
purely on such international considerations. Apart
from the obvious electoral imperative of protecting farming interests, there is a genuine concern
to preserve a vigorous rural society in France despite, or because of, the enthusiastic drive to
urban-industrial modernity which characterises
post-war French society. Thus the CAP often takes
on the additional dimension of being an instrument
of rural social policy in French eyes. The perception of farmers as 'guardians of nature' has
influenced farm policy discussions for a decade or
more. Farmers should be viewed as more than mere
producers of food, but as those who preserve and
maintain access to attractive countryside, an increasingly important recreational resource for Europe's massive urban population. The CAP which,
despite its protective aspects, has not prevented
an enormous 'rural exodus' should, it is argued,
be unequivocal about giving 'financial aid to
farmers who provide the Community with a free service in preserving its natural heritage'.[48]

An example of how the CAP should, in French
eyes, be based on social considerations extending
beyond a concern with 'cheap food' relates to imports of New Zealand lamb into the EC via Britain.
In the early 1980s a series of so-called 'lamb
wars' broke out when French farmers blocked shipments of sheepmeat from the UK by a series of
illegal actions such as lorry hijackings. These
actions flew in the face of Community regulations
requiring internal free trade but French farmers,

not without government support, mobilised a number of sophisticated arguments in defence of their rather less subtle physical actions. They argued against continued imports, despite the principle of Community preference, of cheap New Zealand lamb into the UK which, it was maintained, allowed the British to 'flood' the French market with their own production, thus threatening the livelihoods of France's sheep farmers who generally eked out a modest existence in some of the country's poorest regions. The bankrupting of small French farmers was, according to many in France, socially intolerable, particularly as the major beneficiaries of this situation were perceived to be the seven or so UK multinational companies who control the lamb trade.[49] Faced with this protest in the context of the CAP, French agricultural ministers have sought to compromise, but remain adamant that the social issue of 'small producers' versus 'large producers' cannot be swept aside in a single-minded pursuit of food produced at the lowest possible cost, especially when unemployment throughout the Community is around the 12 to 13 million mark.

Despite their dogged defence of the CAP, it would be wrong to suggest that French leaders reject any reform. As the surpluses of certain products have grown - notably butter (147 per cent self-sufficient in 1983-84), sugar (123 per cent) and wheat (116 per cent) - agricultural support costs have escalated, thus generating negative attitudes to the CAP as a whole as well as the Community in general. But while recognising the need to tackle these problems, the French remain attached to the basic principles of the CAP and think in terms of amendments to the policy instead of the radical restructuring, sometimes amounting to demolition, proposed from the other side of the English Channel. Thus they have been able to accept such things as production quotas and 'co-responsibility schemes' (designed to make farmers bear more of the costs of dealing with surpluses they create), but remain reluctant to envisage a reduction in overall output. In the words of Edgard Pisani, a former French Minister of Agriculture, 'the errors of the CAP are errors of orientation, not errors of over-production'.[50] Dismissing the misconception that there are massive surpluses of all agricultural products (the 'butter mountains' are exceptional and the 'wine lakes' a drunken vision), he developed a common French argument that some of the resources presently generating unsaleable excesses should be switched to producing animal feedstuffs which European farmers now import in large quantities from the USA. After this reference to the omnipresent 'American dimension', Pisani weaves another constant strand of French policy-making into his thesis, that of the opportunities offered by the Third World. While recognising the danger that food aid to developing countries can lead to an unhealthy dependency, he insists that 'the CAP must not be reformed to produce less on a world market dominated by demand, but rather to produce other things at a cheaper price'.[51] Like it or not, the need to import food into the poorer countries will inevitably go on rising in the foreseeable future and any gap left by the EC in satisfying this demand will be filled by the 'Anglo-Saxon' nations of the USA, Canada, Australia, New Zealand and by other food producers.

FRANCE AND THE ECONOMIC CHALLENGES FACING THE EUROPEAN COMMUNITY

In 1973, President Pompidou, along with UK Prime Minister Heath and West German Chancellor Brandt, issued a joint statement calling upon Community countries to co-operate closely in the development of new technologies or run the risk of being dominated by the USA and Japan in a rapidly evolving world economy. Ten years later a report to the French government reiterated this need for European co-operation: 'Without such an approach, there is every reason to fear that, in the future, the Community will no longer be an actor in, but a mere spectator of the competition between Americans and Japanese on its own [common] market'.[52] Acts to follow such words have been slow in coming, but France has taken a leading role in what steps have been taken to close the perceived 'technological gap' opening up between the EC and its main competitors, as Europe trails in the 'third industrial revolution'. The shift of the EC from being a net exporter of advanced technologies in the early 1960s to a net importer in the 1980s has followed American and Japanese dominance of the electronics industry. For example, the USA and Japan had built up an impressive lead in the production of industrial robots: a French working group reported with alarm that in 1981 the Japanese made 11,000, the Americans made 8,130 while the EC countries managed a combined total of 4,017.[53] Such statistics fuel the fear that a growing dependence on imported technology will eliminate jobs in Europe while new ones are created elsewhere.

Faced with technological challenges, a common reaction is to maintain that the combined expenditure per head in EC countries on research and education is lower than in its major challengers. However, while the USA invariably tops any statistical chart on this subject, comparisons with Japan are not conclusively detrimental to the EC. Laurent Fabius, when French Minister of Industry and Research, pointed out that in the first half of the 1980s, 'the different countries of the EEC spent, in chaotic fashion without co-operation or co-ordination, twice as much as Japan on microprocessors; over the same period Japan has succeeded in controlling 40 per cent of the world market while the EC share is just 10 per cent'.[54] He went on to make a crucial point, which recurs frequently in conventional French wisdom on this issue. European research and developent is lagging because the EC, despite the so-called common market, is still essentially divided into separate national economies. Governments and their related bureaucracies (the French not least among them, whatever the 'European' rhetoric) continue to protect 'national' industries, to guard their public monopolies, to perpetuate very closed national systems of education and so on. A mass of different national health and safety regulations, varying taxes, etc., still leads to hold-ups and substantial administrative costs at the borders between EC member states. All this makes trans-frontier European co-operation in industrial research and development very difficult to establish. For example, separate national postal organisations adopt different, often incompatible telecommunications systems based on nationally developed technologies or those imported from outside Europe. Railways devise different high-speed train technologies in France, West Germany and the UK at a time when new land linkages such as the cross-Channel tunnel are being planned. One former French state planner calculated that the cost of this continuing 'fragmentation' of the EC (or 'non-Europe' as he called it) amounted to at least the equivalent of 2 per cent of the Community's GDP in the mid-1980s.[55]

Such analyses lead inexorably to the conclusion

that the French and their neighbours must overcome
this national parochialism and turn the EC into a
genuine 'domestic' common market to be comparable
to their American and Japanese competitors. If
they do not, the danger of economic subjugation
will become very real. In the words of a report to
the French government:

> Faced with this situation, the European
> countries will gain nothing by trying to
> negotiate separately their integration
> into a world market dominated by the
> confrontation between states which are
> more powerful (the USA), more coherent
> (Japan) or more youthful (the newly in-
> dustrialising countries). European re-
> sponses, reinforcing national policies
> struggling against the collective de-
> cline of the countries of the Old Conti-
> nent, are imperative.[56]

Such perceptions are not unique to France. But the
fear of technological domination by others - with
all the implications this has for economic, cultural and political subordination - is particularly noticeable among French elites. It explains
why they have been so prominent in initiating what
action has been taken to formulate a European reply to the economic challenges from across the
Atlantic and the Pacific Rim. This reply has taken
a variety of forms - inside or outside EC structures - according to the French concept of a
Europe à géométrie variable (a Europe of different
shapes). While the goal of harnessing Western Europe's combined capacities to meet external
threats remains the same, the precise form of this
co-operation can vary according to circumstances.
    The fact that a few Franco-British supersonic
Concorde airliners were eventually put into service owes a great deal to French determination to
possess a tangible symbol of the Old World's technological expertise at a time when the USA and the
USSR were advancing spectacularly into space exploration. Similarly, French drive and financial
commitment have been crucial in the development of
the European Airbus Industrie programme to a point
where it can compete with American giants like
Boeing on world markets. The French have a 38 per
cent share in this project, equal to that of West
Germany, their pivotal EC partner, while the UK
(20 per cent) and Spain (4 per cent) have smaller

stakes. The European Space Agency with some 13 member states (not all in the EC)[57] is dominated by France, which, since 1973, has provided 59.25 per cent of its funds. Other countries have played supporting roles, with West Germany contributing 20 per cent and Belgium 4 per cent. After a difficult start, the ESA's Ariane rocket now regularly launches half the world's satellites into orbit from its base in Guyane. Following this success, the French proposed an ambitious expansion of this space programme with the clearly stated aim of developing European 'independence' in this domain. This proposal involved the construction of a much larger rocket (Ariane-5) to 'strengthen Europe's position in the market for launching services and resist the ambitions of the Americans, as well as those of the Soviets, Chinese or Japanese'; a manned European space laboratory (Columbus) to be attached to the American space station in the mid-1990s; and finally a European space shuttle (Hermes) which would be launched by Ariane-5 and glide back to earth in similar fashion to the existing American counterpart.[58] Once again France would assume the leading financial responsibility, assuring 45 per cent of the costs of the most ambitious aspects of the overall package, namely Ariane-5 and Hermes. West Germany (38 per cent) and Italy (25 per cent) would finance the bulk of the Columbus scheme, with France providing 15 per cent. But, in general, the French remain firmly at the head, ready to pay for some 36 per cent of the whole programme, while the West Germans and Italians would play the leading supporting roles.

However, this space programme, enthusiastically promoted by France, where it enjoys near-unanimous support, hit up against familiar reservations in other countries. With a general public much less susceptible to appeals about 'Europe', 'new frontiers', 'independence' and the like, the West German government found itself torn between the hesitations of its very earthbound financial and scientific communities (which, in general, see space exploration as a poor investment diverting resources from more useful pursuits) and the desire to keep a 'foothold' in an area of endeavour where German science and industry has always had a presence. Meanwhile, the British government, sceptical of French-inspired designs for European 'grandeur' and heavily influenced by 'Thatcherite' conceptions of 'value for money', found the whole programme 'far too ambitious', a sort of 'despotic

dream' which in fact was only trying to 'imitate
the Americans' twenty or thirty years too late.
Indeed, the UK minister responsible for space policy making these dismissive comments, Kenneth
Clarke, was reported to favour UK withdrawal from
the ESA.[59] The whole episode encapsulates differ-
ing national attitudes to European unity with remarkable neatness. Eventually, in November 1987,
twelve of the thirteen ESA member states decided
to support the French proposal to press ahead with
all three elements of the overall plan.[60] Enthusiasm was, however, kept in check by the necessity
to review the progress of the project after three
years before confirming further financing. This
element of financial control did nothing to change
the view of the UK minister, whose performance at
the ESA meeting drew universal if somewhat re-
signed criticism from a French mass-media always
ready to fall back on terms such as 'insularity',
'Atlanticism', and 'perfidious Albion' when de-
scribing attitudes to European unity. The UK refused to contribute to Ariane-5 and Hermes and reserved its position about a possible, and
relatively minuscule, contribution to Columbus.
Their extremely economic 'profit and loss' approach to European affairs is in stark contrast to
that of the French, who see the space programme in
very comprehensive terms and place it in the wider
context of movement towards integration. Thus, the
aventure spatiale is valued for its symbolic potential as a generator of support for Europe among
the general public, for the stimulus it will provide for European industry and science in new
technologies, as well as for the capacity it will
furnish France to lead its neighbours towards a
more independent West European defence policy.[61]
In the words of Alain Madelin, the French Minister
of Industry: 'There is no question of imagining a
situation where we [the Europeans] can only travel
in space in the year 2000 either with an American
or a Soviet passport'.[62] This attraction to vi-
sionary 'Euro-projects' exemplifies a persistent,
distinctive French characteristic. With their long
tradition of government intervention in large-
scale, long-term projects (colbertisme) they find
it normal to propose European industrial policies
which advocate public investment to help meet economic challenges from outside the EC. This approach often contrasts with the more liberal economic traditions found among ruling circles in the
UK and West Germany, where scepticism about heavy

public investment in schemes which do not promise profits in some foreseeable future runs deep.[63] Furthermore, many French, true to a tradition of national economic protectionism not completely dissipated within the common market, do not hesitate to advocate European measures to shelter nascent EC industries based on new technologies. Thus, while supporting the elimination of economic barriers within the EC to create a genuine single market, a French government working group concluded:

> This large market must be as effectively defended as those of its competitors. The common policy for commerce and trade must also permit the 'sun-rise' industries of Europe to develop: from now on it must not limit itself just to the defence of traditional industries in crisis.[64]

To encourage the growth of these new industries a variety of EC programmes have been implemented including: ESPRIT (information technology), INSIS (information systems), RACE (telecommunications), BRITE (basic research in new industrial technologies). France obviously supports such schemes, but, ever determined to maintain its leadership role in movements to West European unity, has launched its own separate initiatives which sometimes extend beyond the strict confines of the EC. For example, in 1985, President Mitterrand promoted the EUREKA scheme which presently groups the EC and European Free Trade Association (EFTA) countries. The aim of this organisation, with some 500 million pounds at its disposal in 1987 (much of it from EC funds), is to facilitate collaborative projects in advanced technology across European borders, especially those which give early promise of commercial applications.

Encouraged by the success of this initiative, President Mitterrand, in September 1987, called for an additional EUREKA à l'audiovisuel. Echoing a concern frequently expressed in France's establishment, he feared that unless such a scheme was devised to encourage the mass production of TV programmes 'the imagination of Europeans... would... be conquered' by a flood of imported American and Japanese materials, and, 'We would lose an essential pillar of our independence'.[65] A recent French study[66] showed that the USA and

Canada supplied about 79 per cent of world exports
in the audio-visual field with the UK being the
most prominent European producer. More than 40 per
cent of international trade in this area is made
up of European purchases of American programmes.
While the destiny of characters in such American
serials as 'Dallas' and 'Dynasty' (dubbed in the
appropriate language) grips millions of European
viewers (the French not least among them), those
of their Gallic equivalents rarely break out of
France's national borders. The answer to this
'cultural invasion' that springs to the minds of
French ministers of culture, be they on the Left
(Jack Lang) or the Right (François Léotard), is
once again to be found in co-operation with their
neighbours where 'there is a gigantic effort to be
made in the realm of European co-production'.[67] In
a similar vein, the director of the French organisation Communication Média Technique has reminded
his compatriots that these would-be 'European'
programmes might well be watched on new-generation
high-definition TV screens imported from Japan and
the USA unless the EC countries co-operate and
catch up with the substantial lead established by
their competitors. In fact, three EC companies,
the giant French electrical company, Thomson,
Philips of the Netherlands and Bosch-Fernseh of
West Germany, have joined forces within a EUREKA
project in an attempt to do so.[68]
One of the barriers hindering cross-border co-
ordination is the persistence of separate national
currencies which are subject to fluctuating exchange rates. Such financial instability also disturbs ordinary trading relationships which now
bind all Community countries. It was the perceived
need to provide a more stable framework for these
commercial exchanges that led France, once again
in conjunction with West Germany, to propose the
European Monetary System (EMS) in 1978. Most EC
countries accepted the idea - the British being a
notable but predictable exception - and the EMS,
despite some severe strains in the central Franco-
German axis, has contributed to nearly a decade of
greater stability among the exchange rates of member states. In many French eyes, however, the EMS
has a role which extends beyond EC boundaries; it
is seen as a potential instrument to use in the
struggle to achieve a more balanced relationship
with the USA and the dollar. French frustration
with the way in which the US dollar, as the
world's major reserve currency, dominates world

trade is frequently articulated. In a section typically entitled 'a dollar which disturbs Europe', the authors of a recent book on the EC explain: 'Because the dollar is at one and the same time the US currency and the near-exclusive means of transacting international trade, Europe is permanently subjected to the vicissitudes of monetary control on the other side of the Atlantic'.[69] The French alone cannot hope to release themselves from this subordinate role but, so the argument continues, the EC offers a way towards greater equality in the world's financial affairs. Thus a sound EMS is presented as 'an essential condition if we are not to live, in the coming decades, under the reign of the dollar-standard'.[70] The need to consolidate the EMS and thus 'constitute a united front in face of the United States' is perceived across the political spectrum. For example, former Prime Minister Raymond Barre picked the absence of a 'common policy regarding the dollar' as the most worrying weakness of the EMS,[71] while Jean-Pierre Chevènement saw the system as part of 'a global strategy... to permit Europeans to become actors in control of their destiny and to tear themselves away from colonisation and unemployment'.[72] Again the familiar French argument recurs that a fragmented Western Europe lacks the co-operative will rather than the material means to match the power of the dollar (and increasingly the Japanese yen). As Michel Alibert points out:

> The countries of the Community might well hold a third of the world's foreign exchange reserves and nearly a half of its gold reserves, but the fact remains that in monetary matters they constitute nothing other than a 'non-Europe', thus wasting some of their most valuable assets.[73]

Of course similar arguments are heard throughout the Community, but they are made with particular force in France. The West Germans, with a strong Deutschmark, feel less vulnerable than their EMS partners. Indeed, part of French motivation to secure the EMS stems from the belief that it is 'the last rampart against the establishment of a privileged relationship between the West German mark and the US dollar'.[74] Successive Labour and Conservative governments in the UK have so far refused to place the pound sterling in the EMS, thus confirming Gallic suspicions about Britain's lack of commitment to European unity and its lingering 'special relationship' with the USA.

FRANCE, EUROPEAN UNITY AND NATIONAL SECURITY

The previous discussion of the CAP and economic challenges to Western Europe relates to matters where the EC has clear competence to act, even though France and others have sometimes found it easier to work within different, but often related, organisations on particular problems. However, in French debates about European unity another far more sensitive issue invariably emerges, albeit in a rather speculative way. In the words of one French commentator specifically discussing the future of the EC: 'The defence theme recurs in the debate about Europe at more or less regular intervals, and always in an ambiguous fashion'.[75] One of these ambiguities relates to the role, if any, that the EC might play in the future. At present it is hard to imagine a body that includes states firmly committed to the trans-Atlantic NATO (such as the UK and West Germany), states within the Atlantic Alliance but outside NATO's integrated military command (notably France) and a neutral country (the Irish Republic) playing any coherent role. But the strategic certainties of the post-war world are losing their solidity and the question of whether the EC states can develop some sort of common defence policy has surfaced again in French public debate. In this context, it is worth reflecting on the crucial role security considerations played in France's original initiatives which have led to today's Community.

In May 1950 Robert Schuman proposed that a European Coal and Steel Community be formed within which national resources would be pooled and managed by unique supra-national institutions. The 'Schuman Plan' was primarily directed at the newly-created Federal Republic of Germany, but other West European countries, including Britain, were invited to join. In the event, France and the Federal Republic were joined by the Benelux countries and Italy, with Britain refusing to join an institution which threatened its national sovereignty. Although this vital first step towards today's EC was overtly 'economic' in character, France's primary motivation was its national security and that of Western Europe as a whole. As the anti-Nazi alliances disintegrated and the 'Cold War' between Communist 'East' and capitalist 'West' began, so the USA began to believe that the defence of its camp required the resurrection of a strong West German economy and society which could also make a military contribution towards the deterrence of a perceived Soviet threat. The resurgence of German strength was viewed with concern in France, hence the Schuman Plan was in large part devised as a means of integrating the basic elements (coal and steel) of a West German economic revival into a supra-national European entity where it could be supervised. In the words of Robert Schuman, first a German citizen in the Alsace-Lorraine of Bismarck's Reich but rising to prominence after 1919 as a French political leader:

> The French government proposes to place the whole of Franco-German coal and steel production under a common High Authority, in an organisation open to the participation of the other European countries. The pooling of coal and steel production will ensure immediately the establishment of a common basis for economic development - first step towards a European Federation - and change the destiny of these regions for so long dedicated to making the weapons of war of which they have been the most constant victims. The interdependence of production thus established will make all war between France and Germany not only unthinkable, but physically impossible.[76]

In June 1950 the Korean War broke out, intensifying American pressure to re-arm the West Germans as a bulwark against Communist expansionism. This triggered off another 'European' initiative from the French government of an even more ambitious kind. The Pleven Plan of October 1950 advocated the creation of a European Defence Community (and a related European Political Community to co-ordinate foreign policy) controlled by supra-national institutions similar to those of the ECSC and today's EC.[77] Once again France believed that the EDC would provide a way of placing the proposed new German Army under the controlling supervision of a European entity. A treaty was drawn up and was duly signed by the six original ECSC states. The UK, clinging to its 'great power' status, again stood aside, greatly irritating French sensibilities. The EDC (and EPC) eventually foundered in 1954 due to parliamentary opposition in France. With Gaullists (concerned about national sovereignty) and Communists (pro-Moscow) implacably opposed to the scheme, more or less supported by other députés torn between national and European concepts, the government headed by Mendès France eventually abandoned the project. West German rearmament thus took place within the US-dominated NATO organisation.

When de Gaulle became President of France in 1958, he inherited his country's membership of the European Communities (ECSC, EEC and EURATOM) whose supra-national characteristics he had opposed. While perceiving the advantages France could gain from these organisations, he tried to mould them more to his conception of a Europe des Etats, where independence was preserved rather than merged into a quasi-federal body. This led him to strive for a French-led system of institutionalised 'political' co-operation designed to co-ordinate foreign and defence policies of the EC states. True to Gaullist conceptions of European unity, this would be intergovernmental in character and not reduce national sovereignty in the manner provided for in existing supra-national EC institutions. It was the refusal of France's partners to accept this dilution of the European idea that led to the demise of this Gaullist design in 1962. This concept of closer inter-state co-operation did find limited expression in the Franco-German Treaty of 1963.[78] This treaty provided for a permanent system of co-operation on a wide variety of matters including defence, but little materialised in this sensitive sphere over the following two decades. France's withdrawal from the integrated military command structure of NATO in 1966 and its criticisms of West German and British suivisme (following the USA in foreign and defence policy) estranged the French still more from their European neighbours. Successive French presidents kept campaigning, however patiently, for a more independent foreign policy among EC states. Thus, the contemporary efforts of the Community to adopt common positions on such issues as the Middle East, South Africa and international terrorism owe not a little to persistent French diplomacy.

What some would see as the logical shift from

foreign policy co-ordination to defence co-operation within the EC is fraught with difficulties,
not least those posed by the French themselves.
Ideas of linking French and British nuclear forces
to form a 'European' deterrent face several obstacles, not least the incompatibility of Britain's
US-made systems and France's domestically produced
weapons. Another EC country, the Irish Republic,
is neutral. On the southern flank of Europe the
Greeks find it hard to align themselves with even
the most ineffectual EC foreign policy pronouncements let alone get involved in formulation of a
common defence policy. Such difficulties, plus internal French opposition to anything which threatens national independence on military matters, has
led the French government to fall back on a Europe
à géometrie variable and focus its efforts, once
again, on the Federal Republic of Germany. In the
late summer of 1987 some 22,000 French soldiers of
the Force d'Action Rapide (FAR) joined 55,000 West
German soldiers in a joint exercise in southern
Germany. For the first time, French troops, under
the 'operational control' of West German officers,
were given the clear task of reinforcing their
neighbour against a would-be attack from the East.
Subsequently, it was announced that a 'Common
Council of Security and Defence' was to be established between the two countries for the twenty-
fifth anniversary of the Franco-German Treaty in
January 1988. A mixed French/West German army
brigade would be created at the same time.[79] In
President Mitterrand's view, these initiatives
could form the core of efforts to construct a
wider West European defence policy.[80] In response,
the Italian government expressed a wish to be associated with such moves while agreeing with the
observation of France's President that 'European
defence is a desirable objective, but the ways to
it are complicated'.[81] This was followed by the
French and Spanish foreign ministers stating their
common accord on the need to strengthen the
'European pillar' of the Atlantic Alliance as well
as their wish to work towards a Europe de la
défense.[82] At the same time the French Senate,
with the participation of prominent politicians
from West Germany, the UK and Italy, was debating
the need to create a more self-reliant West European defence system.[83] Most of these French-inspired discussions think in terms of a 'more' independent European stance, rather than a breaking
of the Atlantic Alliance. But Chevènement appears

to take a more assertive line:

> It is time that Europe [the EC coun-
> tries] thought about ensuring by them-
> selves their own defence.... Today the
> objective must be to replace the
> 'American defence' of Europe with an au-
> tonomous European defence, based on the
> concept of deterrence rather than bat-
> tle.[84]

This latest resurgence of interest in a European
defence policy has been sparked off by the bilateral negotiations between the USA and the USSR
designed to remove intermediate range missiles
from Europe. These moves are viewed with suspicion
by many leading figures in France.[85] In simple
terms, they feel frustrated that, once again, they
are mere spectators of superpower actions deter-
mining their destiny and fear that Western Europe,
including France, will be less secure at the end
of this disarmament process. But whether this perception of external danger will push EC states
into common action to reinforce their defences remains very doubtful. Even in the critical Franco-
German relationship the obstacles remain
formidable. The fact that many of the nuclear missiles designed to protect France's 'national sanctuary' can only reach German territory does not go
unnoticed on the eastern side of the Rhine. France
would have to give much more unambiguous substance
to its speculative European defence proposals before the Germans and others are convinced of its
merits. The fear, openly articulated in France,
that West Germans might eventually drift into some
kind of 'nuclear-free', neutralised central European zone where they could rebuild relations with
their 'fellow-nationals' in the German Democratic
Republic may eventually motivate such clarifica-
tions from Paris. France's political strategists,
who, more than most of their EC partners, think in
long-term comprehensive terms about European
unity, would expect any French effort to guarantee
West German security to be met by reciprocal measures in other fields of common endeavour. As one
assessment of recent French diplomacy in the European arena put it:

> If France is ready to make a decisive
> contribution to the security of Europe,
> if need be by modifying its own defen-

sive doctrines and organisation, its
West German ally will have to make a
comparable effort in showing itself more
supportive in political, economic and
monetary areas.[86]

But all this remains extremely speculative. The
European Defence Community is not about to be re-
suscitated.

CONCLUSION: WHAT SORT OF 'EUROPE' FOR FRANCE?

The leading role of France in pursuit of European
unity is beyond dispute. But what form is this
unity to take? Frenchmen have advocated a variety
of models from the loosest form of inter-state co-
operation to a fully-fledged European federation.
Jean Monnet clearly envisaged a 'United States of
Europe' involving a major transfer of sovereignty
from nation-states to institutions of a federal
character. The various supra-national institutions
of the EC were designed with this in mind. Robert
Schuman described the ECSC as 'the first solid
foundations of a European Federation indispensable
for the preservation of peace'.[87] But such visions
have always met vigorous opponents in France, notably among the Communists and the original
Gaullists. When de Gaulle inherited the Monnet-inspired structures of the EC he tried, with some
success, to mould them into his concept of a
'Europe of States' where independent national governments would seek to co-operate rather than integrate into systems diluting their sovereignty.
This clash of concepts culminated in the inevitable conflict of la chaise vide and the unanimity requirements of the 'Luxembourg Compromise'. De Gaulle's successors have frequently used
the concept of a confederation to describe the
sort of European union they seek. This notion con-
jures up, in conveniently ill-defined manner, the
image of something more integrated than de
Gaulle's 'concert of states' but stops well short
of federation according to the USA model. For example, in 1978 Giscard d'Estaing envisaged 'an organisation of Europe which is confederal... in
which no one can impose his will on anyone'.[88]
Such a view led him to propose, with success, the
creation of a European Council in 1974. This vital
institution requires regular meetings of EC heads
of government (or state) in order to make major

Community decisions and define general strategies.
It is outside the supra-national framework of the
other EC institutions, thus having no problems
with majority voting; hence it can be seen as a
partial victory for the Gaullist concept of European unity.

The loosening of Monnet's original plans can
also be found in other French initiatives in the
European sphere. A realisation that not all aspects of the drive towards unity can be contained
within the precise geographical and institutional
limits of the EC has led French leaders to devise
the notions of a Europe à géometrie variable and a
Europe à plusieurs vitesses. It is clear that
progress on all possible aspects of European integration cannot be achieved in parallel fashion by
all twelve very diverse EC member states. Therefore, French leaders have, along with their partners, proved very pragmatic about pressing ahead
with co-operative schemes involving different col-
lections of West European states advancing at different speeds. For example, France has been at the
forefront of the effort to develop an effective
EMS within the EC despite the UK's refusal to join
this Franco-German creation. France has struggled
to keep West Europe in the 'space race' by leading
a group of countries, not all of which are in the
EC. Similarly, its EUREKA project, while enjoying
EC support, extends to the member states of the
EFTA as well. At present, it is striving to encourage some kind of common 'European' defence
policy by strengthening military links with West
Germany and inviting other countries to think
along similar lines.

The EC remains central to French efforts to construct the unity of what they invariably, if somewhat imprecisely, refer to as 'Europe'. French
governments of the late 1980s, Socialist and conservative, have willingly accepted the Single European Act (SEA) designed to reinforce the Community in a number of ways by removing internal
frontiers to create a genuine common market by
1992, strengthening EC policies to alleviate socio-economic inequalities among member states and
extending majority voting in the Council of Ministers in order to attain these objectives.[89] True,
some 'old-school' Gaullists and others have had to
be reassured - with appropriate doses of ambiguity
- that the unanimity requirement of the Luxembourg
Compromise is not dead. But the fact remains that
the French Parliament approved this significant

step forward to greater union by 498 votes to 35. In stark contrast to the situation on the other side of the English Channel, the challenges and opportunities of this 'Europe without frontiers' by 1992 are enthusiastically discussed by France's politicians, businessmen and journalists in the widest public forums. Meanwhile, the French remain resolute defenders of the acquis communautaire, particularly when a national interest, such as defence of the CAP, is at stake. Here, UK talk of managing agriculture in a less monolithic manner, yet according to the French concept of a 'Europe' of variable geographical configurations, is firmly rejected by France.

This ability to alternate between lofty rhetoric replete with grand plans for European unity and fierce defence of narrowly defined national interests can irritate the UK, with which Franch shares a relationship of mutual suspicion in the EC. But to an extent far greater than their 'Anglo-Saxon' neighbour, the French can quite happily marry the pursuit of national interests with the quest for greater West European integration. This convergence of nationalism and Europeanism in France will probably ensure that the French will remain at the head of the movement towards the greater union of the states of 'Europe'. Whether the French in general can follow this lead any more effectively than other European nations remains, somewhat paradoxically, open to question.

NOTES AND REFERENCES

1. P. Moreau Desfarges, 'L'Europe à reformuler: la Communauté au lendemain de la clarification d'Athènes', Politique Etrangère, Vol. 49 (1984), p. 21.

2. See, for example, the declarations of various French political leaders in 'Pourquoi nous voulons l'Europe, L'Express, 27 February 1987, pp. 34-96.

3. Commission of the European Communities, Eurobaromètre, No. 26 (Official Publications of the European Communities, Luxembourg, 1986).

4. L'Express, 27 February 1987, p. 47.

5. M. Jobert, Vive l'Europe libre (Ramsey, Paris, 1984), pp. 1-207.

6. R. Formesyn, 'Europeanisation and the Pursuit of National Interests' in V. Wright (ed.), Continuity and Change in France (Allen and Unwin, London, 1984), pp. 219-43, and W.J. Feld, The European Community in World Affairs (Westview Press, Boulder, 1983), pp. 282-92.

7. P. Moreau Desfarges, 'L'Europe à reformuler', p. 29.

8. R. Barre, 'Le Système monétaire européen après cinq ans', Politique Etrangère, Vol. 49, (1984), pp. 41-8, and R. Formesyn, 'Europeanisation and the Pursuit of National Interests', pp. 238-9.

9. B. Bosson, quoted L'Express, 27 February 1987, p. 59.

10. R. Massip, De Gaulle et l'Europe (Flammarion, Paris, 1963), p. 153.

11. See, for example, the statements of J. Chirac, S. Veil, M. Rocard and L. Fabius in L'Express, 27 February 1987, pp. 55-7.

12. L. Fabius, ibid., p. 55.

13. Secrétariat d'Etat auprès du Premier Ministre, Commissariat Général du Plan, Quelle stratégie européenne pour la France dans les années 80? (La Documentation Française, Paris, 1983) p. 16.

14. J. Léonard, C. Hen, B. Dréano, L'Europe (Editions La Découverte, Paris, 1987), p. 34.

15. Secrétariat d'Etat, Quelle stratégie, p. 18.

16. J.J. Servan-Schreiber, Le Défi américain, published in English as The American Challenge (Atheneum, New York, 1968).

17. M. Alibert, Un Pari pour l'Europe (Seuil, Paris, 1983), p. 103.

18. Léonard et al., L'Europe, p. 98.

19. See, for example, the series of articles under the general heading 'L'Europe sans défense' in L'Express, 25 September 1987, pp. 40-56; and A. Besançon, 'L'Autre Gorbatchev', L'Express, 9 October 1987, p. 37.

20. See G. Kepel, Les Banlieues de l'Islam (Seuil, Paris, 1987) for a recent study of Moslem immigrants in France.

21. Le Monde, 24 September 1987, p. 3.

22. C. Scrivener, L'Europe: une bataille pour l'avenir (Plon, Paris, 1984), p. 108. See also Secrétariat d'Etat, Quelle stratégie, pp. 191-226.

23. A. Sauvy, L'Europe submergée (Dunod, Paris, 1987).

24. J.L. Mathieu and A. Mesplier, Géographie de la France (Hachette, Paris, 1986), p. 113.

25. Léonard, et al., L'Europe, p. 76.

26. Schuman Declaration, 9 May 1950, concerning the establishment of a European Coal and Steel Community; reproduced in G. Moreau, La CEE (Sirey, Paris, 1987), p. 18.

27. Secrétariat d'Etat, Quelle stratégie, p. 17.

28. Le Monde, 24 September 1987, p. 3: see also M. Jobert, Par trente-six chemins (Albin Michel, Paris, 1984), p. 210

29. J.F. Deniau, L' Europe interdite (Seuil, Paris, 1977), p. 122.

30. All the statistics in this section come from Eurostat, <u>Basic Statistics of the Community</u>, 24th ed. (Official Publications of the European Communities, Luxembourg, 1987) unless otherwise stated.

31. Mathieu <u>et al.</u>, <u>France</u>, pp. 185-6.

32. A. Philip, <u>Le Monde</u>, 31 January 1963.

33. M. Wise, <u>The Common Fisheries Policy of the European Community</u> (Methuen, London, 1984), pp. 107-8.

34. B. Hill, <u>The Common Agriculture Policy: Past, Present and Future</u> (Methuen, London, 1984), p. 113.

35. See, for example, R. Cottrell, <u>The Sacred Cow</u> (Grafton Books, London, 1987); and 'Beyond Mountains and Lakes', <u>The Economist</u>, 3 October 1987, pp. 18-9.

36. See, for example, J. Raux (ed.), <u>Politique agricole commune et construction communautaire</u> (Economica, Paris, 1984); and Scrivener, <u>L'Europe</u>, pp. 92-106.

37. Secrétariat d'Etat, <u>Quelle stratégie</u>, p. 56.

38. Scrivener, <u>L'Europe</u>, p. 104.

39. Secrétariat d'Etat, <u>Quelle stratégie</u>, p. 65.

40. Scrivener, <u>L'Europe</u>, p. 103.

41. <u>The Economist</u>, 3 October 1987, p. 18.

42. G. Caffarelli, J.C. Clavel, D. Buhagiar, D. Bigou, 'L'Agriculture et le défi américain', <u>Chambres d'Agriculture</u>, supplément au numéro 689, November 1982, pp. 1-31; and Raux, <u>Politique agricole</u>, p. 483.

43. Secrétariat d'Etat, <u>Quelle stratégie</u>, p. 61.

44. Raux, <u>Politique agricole</u>, pp. 244-5.

45. Caffarelli, 'L'Agriculture et le défi américain', p. 2.

46. P. Lelong in Raux, <u>Politique agricole</u>, p. 483.

47. Scrivener, <u>L'Europe</u>, p. 105.

48. Secrétariat d'Etat, <u>Quelle stratégie</u>, p. 69.

49. M. Geoffroy in Faux, <u>Politique agricole</u>, pp. LV-LVIII.

50. E. Pisani, <u>ibid.</u>, p. LX111.

51. <u>Ibid</u>.

52. Secrétariat d'Etat, <u>Quelle stratégie</u>, p. 34.

53. Alibert, <u>L'Europe</u>, pp. 47-52 and pp. 102-20; and Secrétariat d'Etat, <u>Quelle stratégie</u>, pp. 133-62.

54. L. Fabius, 'Pour un espace européen scientifique, industriel et social', <u>Politique Etrangère</u>, Vol. 49, No. 1 (1984), p. 51.

55. Alibert, <u>L'Europe</u>, p. 109.

56. Secrétariat d'Etat, <u>Quelle strategie</u>, p. 39.

57. The ESA members are, in order of their future financial contributions to the organisation, France, West Germany, Italy, Belgium, Spain, the Netherlands, Switzerland, Sweden, Denmark, Austria, Norway, Ireland and (?) the UK.

58. <u>Le Monde</u>, 23 October 1987, pp. 1 and 4 and 10 November 1987, p. 15.

59. For elaboration on these contrasting attitudes see:

The Economist, 7 November 1987, pp. 95-8; L'Express, 6 November 1987, pp. 61-4; The Independent, 22 October 1987, pp. 1-2.

60. Le Monde, 12 November 1987, p. 9.

61. For elaboration on the defence connection see P. Boniface and F. Heisbourg, La Puce, les hommes et la bombe: L'Europe face aux défis technologiques et militaires (Hachette, Paris, 1986).

62. Le Monde, 12 November 1987, p. 9.

63. P. Moreau Desfarges, 'L'Europe industrielle: la tapisserie de Pénélope?', Politique Etrangère, Vol. 49 (1984), p. 55.

64. Secrétariat d'Etat, Quelle stratégie, p. 40.

65. Le Monde, 1 October 1987, p. 26.

66. Bureau d'Informations et de Prévisions Economiques (BIPE); reported in Le Monde, 1 October 1987, p. 26.

67. L'Express, 27 February 1987, p. 59.

68. E. Lambert, 'Télévision: les marchés de la haute définition', Le Monde Diplomatique, September 1987, p. 23.

69. Léonard et al., L'Europe, p. 71.

70. T. de Montbrial, 'La Communauté en crise', Politique Etrangère, editorial, Vol. 49, No. 1 (1984), p. 5.

71. Barre, 'Le Système monétaire européen après cinq ans', p. 44.

72. Le Monde, 24 September 1987, p. 3.

73. Alibert, L'Europe, p. 100.

74. Secrétariat d'Etat, Quelle stratégie, p. 37.

75. P. Moreau Desfarges, 'L'Europe à reformuler', p. 35.

76. Schuman Declaration.

77. M. Delarue, '1954, vie et mort d'une armée européene', Le Monde, 24 September 1987, p. 2.

78. D. Pickles, The Government and Politics of France, Vol. 2 (Methuen, London, 1973), p. 235.

79. Le Monde, 15/16 November 1987, p. 4.

80. Le Monde, 27/28 September 1987, p. 3.

81. Le Monde, 4/5 October 1987, p. 3.

82. Le Monde, 20 October 1987, p. 3.

83. Le Monde, 17 October 1987, p. 4.

84. Le Monde, 24 September 1987, p. 3.

85. See, for example, P. Lellouche in 'Double zéro, double péril', Le Monde, 1 October 1987, pp. 1-2.

86. J. Isnard, 'Les Avances de M. Giraud à une Europe orpheline', Le Monde, 20 October 1987, p. 4.

87. Schuman Declaration.

88. Formesyn, 'Europeanisation and the Pursuit of National Interests', p. 227.

89. Commission of the European Communities, 'The Single Act: a New Frontier for Europe', Bulletin of the European Communities, Supplement 1, 1987 (Official Publications of the European Communities, Luxembourg, 1987).

Chapter Four

TRAVAILLEURS IMMIGRES AND INTERNATIONAL RELATIONS

Max Silverman

Questions of immigration, race and national identity have rarely been out of the news during the
1980s. The flurry of laws, decrees, <u>arrêtés</u> and
circulars between 1981 and 1984 represented an attempt by the Socialists to extend the legislative
framework defining, notably, the right of entry
into France, the rights of immigrants legally established in the country and action to be taken to
deal with illegal entry. The increased support for
Jean-Marie Le Pen's Front National in municipal,
EC and parliamentary elections, together with the
growing number of attacks on North African immigrants, are signs of a hardening of racist attitudes, whilst the publication of an increased number of official documents and the appearance of
books and special issues of magazines devoted to
the subject bears witness to the importance of the
debate in the public domain.

A new phenomenon? Not entirely. The influx of
foreigners into France in the 1920s took the estimated immigrant population to over three million
by 1931. As a percentage of the total population,
these figures are roughly equivalent to the situation in the 1980s (6.8 per cent in 1982 compared
to 6.6 per cent in 1931). Then, as now, a dramatic
increase in immigration was due to the demand for
increased labour created by an economic boom;
then, as now, measures were introduced by government (including repatriation schemes) to try to
control the flow of immigration once economic recession and mounting unemployment had followed the
boom. Then, as now, a virulent racism and xenophobia were propagated by the extreme Right and found
tacit approval amongst wider sections of the population.

This comparison serves as a reminder that the
response of government and society in the 1980s to
a perceived 'problem' of immigration is ominously
familiar. Yet the comparison, spanning fifty
years, can only be valid on a very general level.
The largely European immigration of the inter-war

years gave way to the predominantly African immigration of the post-war period. The earlier influx, which saw the arrival of large numbers of
Poles, Slavs, Czechs, Italians and Spaniards, was
accompanied by a process of assimilation into
French society, whereas in the 1980s the very word
assimilation is redolent of the centralising ethos
of the colonial era. Furthermore, following the
post-war increase in immigration from North
Africa, French perceptions of racial difference
and national identity have become dependent upon
images of the Arab and the world of Islam. This
recent phase of immigration must therefore be situated in the context of decolonisation and the
subsequent relations between France and her former
colonies. In addition to this, the creation of the
European Community and the increased effort towards state control and surveillance of the population have also ensured, in their different ways,
that certain fundamental aspects of the situation
in the 1980s do not find their equivalents in the
early 1930s. This chapter examines the context,
nature and effects of immigration in France in the
1980s through a discussion of the background to
the present situation, the major aspects of policy
regarding immigrant workers and the wider context
of immigration and international relations.

RECENT HISTORY AND THE PRESENCE ETRANGERE IN FRANCE

The Commissariat au Plan, set up in 1946 to create
a programme for the economic reconstruction of
France after the war, saw the necessity for a substantial increase in foreign labour. With this expansion in mind, the government had created the
Office National d'Immigration (ONI) the previous
year to oversee the planned increase in numbers of
immigrant workers. However, despite the needs of
economic growth, the number of immigrants actually
fell over the next ten years, totalling 1,553,000
or 3.6 per cent of the population in 1954 compared
to 1,743,000 or 4.2 per cent of the population in
1946 (excluding immigration from Algeria). The
only significant increase in this period was in
the number of Algerian workers entering France.
   The real post-war boom in immigration occurred
after 1955 and especially in the 1960s. The modernisation of industry, the opening-up of the
hitherto heavily-protected French economy and the
consequent effects of international competition,

coupled with the new markets opened up within the recently-established EC, all created the need for a new workforce. The eighth Plan clearly defines the new worker required to meet the demands of industry:

> The new worker no longer needs to possess a specialist knowledge acquired by long apprenticeship. Nor does he even need to have skills in writing or speaking French. He is required to perform duties of a repetitive nature, fixed in advance and regulated by others. The ideal labour force is one that can be easily redeployed, needing only the barest training to be fully productive.[1]

There is little doubt that, in the eyes of planners and government alike, the worker best suited to fill this role was the immigrant. During his time as head of the section Population et Migrations at the Ministry of Employment (1962-8), Michel Massenet made this quite clear. Speaking of the young Algerians entering France at this time, he praised them for having 'the "merit" of being mobile, where the use of French nationals would risk creating "rigidities": for example, with regard to increases in salary and the problems of redundancies in the event of restructuring'.[2]

By contrast to the increase in Moroccan immigration between 1955-61, the number of Algerian workers entering France actually fell to 11,300 per year, largely due to the effects on immigration of the Algerian war (1954-62). The end of the war marked not only a large increase in Algerian immigration (111,000 between 1962-65) but also the return of the pieds noirs and the military. The parallel development of Tunisian and Moroccan immigration during the 1960s established the presence of the North African communities in France in modern times. Yet the phenomenon of North African immigration during this period often overshadows the fact that the largest immigrant community had become the Portuguese, whose numbers increased dramatically after a Franco-Portuguese agreement of 1963. From an estimated 20,000 at the time of the 1954 census, the number of Portuguese immigrants rose to 758,000 by 1975. The economic boom of the 1960s thus attracted North Africans and poor Europeans and was also responsible for the beginnings of emigration to France from such French-speaking African states as Mali, Senegal and Mauritania.[3]

Overall, the period between 1962-68 saw a steady influx of more than 100,000 foreign workers each year. At this time of economic expansion for the major producing countries in the West, France relied heavily on imported labour to meet the demands of the new age. In response to those who make the charge that immigrant labour was responsible for slowing down the rate of technological progress, there is ample proof to show, on the contrary, that without this new workforce France would not have been able to press ahead with the modernisation programme so urgently required.[4] Indeed, the success of France's economic enterprise in the post-colonial era depended as much on the recruitment (and exploitation) of workers from former colonies as did the era of colonialism itself. In this sense, then, decolonisation continued to benefit France economically, for governments took full advantage of the links established with former colonies to propel the country into the modern technological age.

One of the effects of the recruitment of foreign workers to run the machines was the loss of state control over the number of immigrants entering the country. Immigrant labour was functioning according to the law of supply and demand, thus bypassing the ONI, which was powerless to regulate the influx. Consequently, the change in the economic climate at the end of the decade brought with it a renewed effort at state intervention and control. Certain measures introduced from 1968 (notably the Marcellin and Fontanet circulars of 24 January and 23 February 1972) aimed at restraining the practice of _régularisation_ by which foreigners who had entered the country ostensibly as tourists could easily obtain a work permit and thus legalise their situation. As the economic recession deepened in the 1970s, controls on immigration were considered more necessary. This process culminated in July 1974 in the suspension of primary immigration (a policy which has been maintained ever since).

The major principles underlying immigration policy during the presidency of Valéry Giscard d'Estaing (1974-81) were, firstly, to stop all new immigration into France and, secondly, to reduce the number of foreigners already in the country. Thus, during the 1970s, France (like the UK) embarked on a path of harsh, often repressive state measures to deal with the 'problem' of immigration, a path from which succeeding governments have deviated very little. Ironically, this policy proved unsuccessful judged not only according to the criteria of respect for human rights but also according to the policy aims outlined above. It is true that the number of foreigners entering the country was severely reduced during Giscard's presidency compared to the previous seven years,[5] but the ban on primary immigration had the effect of accelerating the process of family reunification (réunification familiale), whereby families which had hitherto remained in the country of origin would come to France to rejoin their spouse/parent already resident in the country. This phenomenon took place in spite of the suppression of family reunification in 1974 (a measure which was declared unconstitutional by the Conseil d'Etat) and its reintroduction in April 1976 under extremely severe conditions. It had the effect of producing a more sedentary foreign population and, in so doing, altered people's perceptions of immigration. Having previously been regarded as a temporary phenomenon, during which foreign workers would do the jobs that often the French did not want to do, before returning to their countries of origin, immigration was now deemed to be responsible for the implantation of a permanent community settled in France and whose children were born on French soil.

Two measures in particular highlight the effort by government at this time to control immigration and reduce the number of foreigners in the country. On 30 May 1977, the Secretary of State responsible for immigrants, Lionel Stoléru, instituted a scheme of financial aid for repatriation (the aide au retour scheme) which offered 10,000 francs to each applicant. Known familiarly as the million Stoléru after the Secretary of State's declared aim to remove one million foreigners from French soil in five years, the measure proved to be a dramatic failure. Only 57,953 workers took up the offer (most of whom were Spanish and Portuguese workers who had already decided to return to their countries of origin) before its eventual suppression by the Socialist government on 31 December 1981. The second measure, the loi Bonnet of 10 January 1980, introduced a stricter regime defining the right of entry and stay in France and was specifically designed to combat illegal immigration (immigration clandestine).

The failure to reduce the number of foreigners and control illegal immigration was matched by the government's failure to meet its declared aim of improving the conditions of foreigners in the country.[6] In his assessment of the government's record on immigration, Stanislav Mangin presents a scathing criticism of Giscard's term of office, pointing up numerous illegalities, state infringements of human rights, the harshness of controls and expulsions and the clear racist thrust of many of the measures introduced:

> The conditions of immigrants, claimed the government, would be improved: they have deteriorated. The number of immigrants would be reduced: it has not changed. Illegal immigrants would be expelled: there are now more than ever before.... In fact, what successive governments really wanted was to expel the non-Europeans. To this end, they were willing to resort to any means, even illegal measures, the use of violence and the creation of fear and anxiety: they did not succeed.[7]

Poor housing conditions, ghettoisation and racism - all of which were often accentuated by government policy - were familiar problems for immigrant communities during this period.

The persistence of these problems and the ambiguities of government policy since 1981 will be discussed in the following sections. However, a brief outline of some of the principal characteristics of the foreign population in France today reveals the effect of developments in the 1970s. For example, the demographic trend between 1975 and 1982 (the inter-census period) has been continued since 1982, namely a very slight increase in the size of the immigrant population due to births and family reunification. It is difficult to be exact for, between censuses, one must rely on figures provided by the Ministry of the Interior which tend to overestimate the real number.[8] Since the most recent figures from the Ministry suggest that the number of foreigners in the country now stands at about 4.5 million, it is probably safe to assume that the real number is about 500,000 less.[9] The other significant feature confirms the major post-war trend in immigration in France: apart from the dramatic increase in Portuguese immigration, the European communities in France (mainly Spanish and Italian) which constitute an older immigration have been in decline, whereas immigration from Africa has increased. The 1982 census figures showed that 42 per cent of the foreign population in 1982 was African compared to 20 per cent in 1962. The Algerians (795,920 or 21.6 per cent of the foreign population) are now slightly ahead of the Portuguese (764,860 or 20.8 per cent of the foreign population) in terms of the largest foreign community in France, with the Moroccans now the third largest community (numbering 431,120 or 11.7 per cent of the foreign population).

The dramatic decrease in the number of foreign workers entering France in the 1970s and 1980s has been accompanied by a decline in percentage terms of the number of foreigners in employment (42.3 per cent in 1982 compared to 50.4 per cent in 1962). This is partly due to the change from the single male worker immigration of the period before 1974 to the family immigration after that date, producing a greater number of immigrants not available for work (the young, women at home). The other reason is that foreign workers have suffered more from unemployment than French nationals. This is due not only to the larger number of redundancies in industries in which many foreign workers had found employment (building, automobiles, textiles) but also to racism. It is a worrying fact that the proportion of foreigners in work is lower than the proportion for the population as a whole.

The proportion of foreigners to French nationals varies greatly according to region, with almost 60 per cent of the foreign population concentrated in three regions - Ile-de-France (36 per cent), Rhône-Alpes (12.5 per cent) and Provence-Alpes-Côte-d'Azur (9 per cent). This uneven distribution means that immigrants are concentrated largely within and around the cities of Paris, Lyon and Marseille.[10] Clearly the changing pattern of immigration in the 1970s has led, in the 1980s, to the presence of permanent communities (ethnic minorities) in these areas. It is also responsible for a shift in focus by government agencies, political parties and the media on the position of these communities in society. It was the visibility of North African women and children in French cities which largely contributed, during the 1970s, to the sense of a threat to Frenchness and the subsequent move towards a more xenophobic and racist perspective. This trend has intensified in the 1980s through the impact of the Front National, the increase in racist attacks and the rightward move of the RPR.[11] However, the 1980s have also witnessed a struggle by second generation immigrants from the Maghreb (commonly known as 'Beurs') to find a voice and space within French society. The newspaper Sans Frontières, the radio station Radio-Beurs, the rock group Carte de Séjour, and the magazine Baraka reflect the emergence of a Beur culture in the 1980s.[12] More recently, attention has been focused on the wider and more populist anti-racist movement SOS-Racisme (with its slogan 'Touche pas à mon pote') under the leadership of Harlem Désir. If racism has become more explicit in the 1980s, then so has the struggle to create particular forms of opposition to this racism which affirm different types of cultural practice. We must now look in more detail at the period covered by the presidency of François Mitterrand to locate more specifically these tensions in French society.

MAITRISE, INSERTION ET REINSERTION

In February 1986 the Ministry of Social Affairs published a booklet entitled 1981-1986: Une nouvelle politique de l'immigration which outlines the measures taken by the Socialist government between these years. The title is only partly true for the Socialist programme was both new - and, as such, a challenge to the policy of the preceding administration - and a continuation of past policy. It was a continuation in that it maintained the ban on primary immigration introduced in 1974 and was dedicated to a strict control of the right of entry and stay in France; but a challenge, too, in that there was a genuine effort - at least in the first few years - to improve the lives of foreigners in the country through measures designed to aid the integration of immigrants into French society. What was perhaps particularly new was the attempt to establish a coherent programme on immigration rather than a random series of measures taken in response to conjunctural requirements; a programme, therefore, that would consider all aspects of the question, from the problems faced by young immigrants at school to the wider considerations of migration and international co-operation.

The two poles upon which this programme was based - those of controls and integration (maîtrise and insertion) - were conceived as mutually-reinforcing and constituted an integrated approach to the question of immigration. However, despite this concept of a 'vision globale de l'immigration', contradictions in approach and racial tensions were not eradicated. The bi-polar policy led to the two poles frequently pulling in different directions - not unlike the programme in the UK in the 1970s, composed of harsh immigration controls coupled with a race relations policy.

The shortcomings of the new policy were perhaps exaggerated by the inability of the government to live up to the expectations raised by the election triumphs of 1981. These dramatic victories for the Socialists held out the prospect of a real break with the past in the area of economic and social reform, and the immigrant population was particularly hopeful that a change in policy would improve their rights after years of neglect and abuse.[13] Indeed, the first statements on the immigration question from the new government did nothing to dampen these hopes, with talk of putting an end to 'the insecurity of immigrant workers' and the need to 'improve the situation inherited from past governments'. Four early measures introduced in 1981 were in keeping with these aims and augured well for the future. Firstly, the circulars of 6 July and 7 August announced a temporary suspension of all expulsions of foreigners born in France or having entered France before their tenth birthday. Subsequently, a circular of 11 August, which announced the régularisation exceptionelle of all foreign workers who had entered France illegally before 1 January 1981, introduced a sort of amnesty for many illegal immigrants in the country and led to the position of some 130,000 sans-papiers being legalised. Shortly after this, the law of 9 October made the right of association legal for foreigners, hence bringing into line in this domain the rights of foreigners and French nationals.[14] Finally, the notorious voluntary repatriation scheme introduced under Giscard was withdrawn on 25 November.

The one subsequent measure which was welcomed as a genuine advance towards the improvement of the rights and conditions of foreigners and which had long been a demand of the immigrant population was the introduction, through the law of 17 July 1984, of a single residence and work permit known as the

carte unique 'séjour-travail'. Prior to this measure, immigrants had to be holders of both a residence and a work permit, each card being valid for
either one, three or ten years. The iniquities and
illogicalities of this system are explained in Une
nouvelle politique de l'immigration as follows:
'The two permits were not necessarily of the same
duration. The foreigner was therefore obliged to
take numerous steps - the outcome of which was
never certain - to ensure that both residence and
work permits were always in order'. The new law
rationalised the previous system by stipulating
that all foreigners over the age of sixteen residing in France must be the holders of either a
carte de résident - valid for ten years and automatically renewable - or a carte de séjour tempo-
raire - valid for one year but renewable there-
after. Such a system certainly went a long way towards removing the precarious situation of many
foreigners residing in France and allowed, at
least in theory, the possibility of an accelera-
tion of the process of integration of immigrants
into French society.[15]
Other measures with the same end in view were
less publicised than the new residence and work
permit but, nevertheless, constituted an attempt
to deal with some of the major problems affecting
immigrants in their home and work environments.
The Fonds d'Action Sociale was reformed by a decree of 18 January 1983 to extend its powers of
aid to immigrant communities. Representatives of
these communities were now incorporated into its
enlarged conseil d'administration and a new re-
gion-based policy established. Another decree (of
17 July 1984) set up the Conseil National des Populations Immigrées which could be consulted on all
matters concerning the immigrant population, especially within the areas of housing, work, education and culture. Much was done too in the areas
of education, formation and insertion professionnelle to improve the opportunities of immigrants
at school and in employment.
These measures of integration and ethnocultural
accommodation were a welcome improvement on the
poor record of the previous administration in this
domain. For some, they were seen to be part of a
more general move away from a 'monolithic cultural
centralism' towards a more decentralised approach
based on ethnocultural pluralism.[16] Yet the notion
that government policy was alone effecting such a
transformation would seem to ignore the more fun-

damental problem of a nation-state whose very
structures, fabric and apparatuses - laws, institutions, ideologies, discourses - were deeply per-
meated by the colonial experience and representations of other peoples.[17] However, even on the
level of government policy itself, disquiet was
soon being felt when it became clear, shortly after the Socialists' accession to power, that the
right of immigrants to vote in municipal elections
- included in Mitterrand's 110 pledges in the
presidential election campaign - was no longer
seen as a priority.[18] More worrying still for the
immigrant population was the severity with which
the new government intended to pursue the other
aspect of its bi-polar policy on immigration,
known as maîtrise des flux migratoires. Repressive
measures soon convinced some that the new government's approach contained 'more elements of continuity than of rupture with regard to previous measures introduced'.[19]

A closer consideration of the Socialists' controls on immigration certainly seems to corrobo-
rate this claim since they were based, on the one
hand, on a stricter definition of the right of entry and stay and, on the other, on what had become
known during the 1970s as the lutte contre le travail clandestin, the twin concerns of the previous
administration. As regards the former, the law of
29 October 1981 redefined the documentation needed
for the right of entry into France, the conditions
under which this could be refused and the punish-
ment for infringement of this code. It also modi-
fied the existing law on the conditions for expulsion from the country and thus replaced the loi
Bonnet as the major text defining this area of
law. A further law on expulsion (10 June 1983) effectively denied the right of appeal of all those
deemed to be illegal immigrants.

As the Socialists maintained the ban on primary
immigration, the only legal way of entering the
country continued to be through the right of family immigration. Here Socialist policy manifested
the same hypocrisy as was shown by Giscard's governments. Whilst affirming the automatic right of
families to join their spouse or parent residing
in France, the government not only reaffirmed the
strict process of vetting laid down in the decree
of April 1976, but added a new rigour. The decree
of 4 December 1984 imposed fresh conditions to be
fulfilled for the right to become a reality -
amongst which the worker already residing in

France had to prove that his finances were sufficient to maintain his dependent(s) - and, furthermore, stipulated that these formalities should be
carried out before departure in the country of
origin rather than, as before, on French soil.

The severity of these measures aimed at a more
effective control of illegal entry led, in some
quarters, to charges of racism and infringement of
human rights. They were clearly designed specifically to deter illegal entry from non-European
countries since the EC operates a policy of free
movement between member states. Those who suffer
the rigours of control are therefore predominantly
North African. The supposed automatic right of
family immigration remains only theoretical since
the rigorous nature of control means that a number
of genuine applicants are refused right of entry.

The attempt to stamp out the practice whereby
unscrupulous employers would secretly employ illegal immigrants, thus obtaining cheap, undeclared
labour whilst conniving with the illegal entry of
foreigners into France, has also had harmful consequences for the immigrant population as a whole,
largely due to the connotations inspired by the
coupling of the words immigration and clandes-
tin(e). Ironically, the practice of clandestinité
was openly encouraged by Jeanneney, the Minister
of Social Affairs in the mid-1960s, at a time of
economic expansion and demand for a new type of
worker.[20] Indeed, at that time the term itself was
a complete misnomer, as it was not illegal to enter the country with or without a passport. It
merely sufficed for an employer to declare the employment of the worker for the latter's position
to become legalised. However, the official legiti-
macy bestowed on the term immigration clandestine
and the use of other equally emotive words in association with immigration (sauvage, for example)
were then instrumental in the construction of a
particular image of immigrants. As Cordeiro points
out, these associations reinforce the concept developed by those on the Right of the illegality of
this immigration.[21]

Between 1974 and 1981 government rhetoric de-
ploring illegal immigration and the non-declared
employment of foreign workers was not matched by
an eradication of the practices themselves. The
effect was merely to reinforce a stereotype without solving the problem. To a certain extent, the
Socialist administration continued this trend between 1981 and 1986. The rhetoric was certainly

unceasing. Nearly all official statements on immigration emphasised the declared aim of stamping
out the illegal employment of immigrants, a number
of communiqués of the Conseil des Ministres were
devoted to the same end (23 July 1981, 2 September
1981, 28 April 1982, 10 October 1984) and a pro-
liferation of official reports treated the
topic.[22] Action taken to curb the practice
(accompanying the stricter border controls men-
tioned above) was based principally on the imposi-
tion of more punitive sanctions against employers
of illegal immigrants (the law of 17 October
1981, the decree of 5 March 1984, which quadrupled
the amount payable to the ONI by employers of illegal immigrants, and the law of 26 July 1985
which extended the sanctions covering the whole
area of non-declared foreign labour). In addition
to this, the powers of the Mission de Liaison Inter-Ministérielle pour la Lutte contre les Trafics
de Main-d'Oeuvre (established by an interministe-
rial arrêté of 10 August 1976) were extended, especially since the decision taken at the Conseil
des Ministres of 31 August 1983 to introduce more
inspectors into more regions and with greater powers of search for evidence of employment of illegal immigrants.

These measures succeeded in curtailing the number of immigrant workers employed illegally but
did not eradicate the practice. Many immigrants,
predominantly from North Africa and the French-
speaking African states, who have either entered
France illegally or have extended their stay illegally, continue to work for salaries far below the
minimum wage (the SMIC) and live in conditions far
below the standard of average accommodation in
France. (Clearly it is impossible to know the exact numbers because of the clandestine nature of
their lives in France.) Indeed, as a world-wide
phenomenon the practice can never be fully controlled by the authorities.[23] The most recent
French governments, however, have tended to exag-
gerate the scale of the problem to such a degree
that, once again, pernicious stereotypes of the
total immigrant population have been reinforced
(whether inadvertently or not), racial tension has
been exacerbated and prejudice and xenophobia have
been fuelled, thus accentuating the insecurity
felt by immigrant communities rather than putting
an end to it, as the new Socialist government had
promised in 1981.

For those on the far right, however, the steps

taken to stamp out illegal immigration, to redefine the right of entry and stay and to control
the frontiers were hardly sufficient to combat
what they saw as the menace to France of the growing number of immigrants. One of their principal
demands continued to be the introduction of a
scheme of repatriation. On the other hand, for immigrant associations and other sympathisers, the
government's measures were often repressive and
insensitive to the real needs of the immigrant
population. The government's reaction to the
events of 1983 and the reintroduction of a voluntary repatriation scheme through the decree of 27
April 1984 seemed to mark a realignment of policy
so as to reveal more clearly to the French public
the iron fist beneath the velvet glove. The aide
au retour scheme introduced in 1977 was considered
by the new government in 1981 to be a barely-dis-
guised attempt to make foreigners scapegoats at a
time of economic recession and rising unemployment
and was duly suppressed in November 1981. However,
by the middle of 1983 unemployment was still rising and there was also a mounting tide of anti-immigrant feeling which was manifested not only in
violent attacks on immigrants but also in the increased support for the Front National in the municipal elections of March of that year. The government response was largely reactionary. During
the election campaign the Minister of the Interior
and Mayor of Marseille, Gaston Defferre, had
prided himself on being ideally placed to expel
immigrants and fight against delinquency (thus
suggesting and reinforcing the association between
the two),[24] whilst the day before the elections
the Prime Minister, Pierre Mauroy, more or less
blamed the immigrant question for the loss of
votes to the extreme Right, rather than condemning
the wave of xenophobia aimed at the immigrant communities.

One must take this context into account when ap-
praising the reasons for, and timing of, the introduction of the new scheme of repatriation, for
officially this background was conspicuous by its
absence. The communiqué for the Conseil des Ministres of 31 August 1983 - where proposals for the
new scheme were put forward for the first time -
merely states that 'the accent will be put on
training, so as to aid the process of reintegration of those foreign workers who wish to return
to their country of origin', whilst the communiqué
for the Conseil des Ministres of 4 April 1984

maintains that the scheme is merely a response to a request from immigrant workers suffering from unemployment.[25] The other official reason for the introduction of a new scheme of voluntary repatriation was the prospect of the expiry of the Franco-Algerian agreement on 31 December 1983 and the need to redefine a new régime de retour. This agreement had been concluded through an exchange of letters between the two countries on 18 September 1980 but was redefined by the Socialist government in the summer of 1981 to change the orientation from a simple programme of financial aid for voluntary repatriation to a consideration of the difficulties involved in the process of reintegration, both for foreign workers and their countries of origin.[26]

The government's new scheme would therefore be a general one (not only confined to Algerian workers) and would also differ from the previous programme of voluntary repatriation according to the new orientation outlined above. The scheme was named aide à la réinsertion and was founded on the twin notions of negotiation and agreement with the countries of emigration (taking into account their own economic problems) and a financial commitment to the worker's reintegration within his/her country of origin. In theory, therefore, the principles underlying the government's policy of control and integration in a domestic context would also apply in an international context. However, in practice the scheme was thwarted from the very outset by the refusal of the countries of emigration to negotiate accords de réinsertion. They showed little enthusiasm for a project which encouraged a mass return of their own citizens at a time of economic hardship. This meant that the programme was effected unilaterally by the French government without the hoped-for consultation, negotiation and agreement with the countries of emigration. Coupled with the fact that, from its introduction, there were relatively few takers for any aspects of the scheme, this gave the impression that the programme was little more than a device for reducing the numbers of immigrants in France at a time of high unemployment and growing anti-immigrant feeling (the very reasons given by the Socialists in 1981 for suppressing Giscard's repatriation scheme).

The problems encountered by the Socialist government with regard to their programme of aide à la réinsertion were perhaps indicative of some of the problems of their bipolar policy as a whole. What was continually packaged as a 'vision globale de l'immigration' seemed to critics of varying political persuasions to be an unsuccessful attempt to marry humanitarian and authoritarian principles, to appease both the liberal and anti-immigrant lobbies.[27] The attempt to incorporate the need for international co-operation, however praiseworthy in theory, also foundered on the complex issues underlying migration and international relations. A closer consideration of France's recent immigration policy within the international arena highlights the nature of some of the problems involved.

IMMIGRATION AND INTERNATIONAL RELATIONS

According to the review of Socialist immigration policy between 1981 and 1986, Une nouvelle politique de l'immigration, governments were prompted by the desire, on an international level, to establish 'a continual dialogue and increased cooperation both with the authorities of the countries of origin of foreign workers and, on a multilateral level, with the authorities of other countries of immigration and emigration'. We have already seen how, in the context of the government's scheme of réinsertion, the type of dialogue referred to here - in particular conversations held, since 1982, with Senegal, Mali, Morocco, Tunisia, Portugal and Turkey - did not produce the required co-operation from the countries of emigration, a fact which the report describes euphemistically as 'a certain reticence on the part of the countries of emigration', leading to unilateral action by the French government rather than multilateral accord. This pattern was indicative of a fundamental flaw in the government's immigration policy viewed in an international context. Although the government's intention was to situate immigration policy within the wider sphere of international relations - which was itself an aspect of the desire to forge new links with Third World countries[28] - the measures introduced were frequently accomplished without consultation with the countries of emigration and often aroused their displeasure. In the context of the government's policy of immigration controls, the repressive nature of the decrees of May 1982 concerning the right of entry into France led to such a large number of foreigners being

refused entry that President Chadli of Algeria
lodged a formal protest. (President Mitterrand was
subsequently obliged to put an end to these excessively severe measures.) The agreements signed
with the three Maghreb countries in August and
November 1983 regarding a more effective control
of immigration produced no significant reduction
in the numbers wishing to enter France, whilst the
rigorous formalities regarding the right of family
reunification and the stipulation that these be
carried out in the country of origin led to re-
sentment from many North Africans and long queues
and delays outside consulates in the countries of
the Maghreb.

The harsh immigration controls undermined the
government's attempt to work in harmony with the
countries of emigration. It was perhaps rather
naive to expect these countries to collaborate
with France in the implementation of measures
which were against the interests of many of their
citizens; but it was also wishful thinking to believe that patterns of immigration could be controlled effectively in this way. Finally, and most
importantly, it was hypocritical, to say the
least, to believe that severe immigration controls
were compatible with a commitment to human rights
and equality between foreigners and French nationals. Even measures aimed at improving the conditions of foreigners in France frequently failed to
eradicate fundamental injustices and therefore ran
counter to the spirit of human rights. For example, although the introduction in 1984 of the single residence and work permit went a long way towards increasing the security of foreigners in the
country, each applicant was nevertheless obliged
to prove that he had sufficient resources to maintain himself and his family, and was also bound to
observe the vague notion of 'public order'. A
failure to meet either of these criteria would
lead to expulsion within four weeks. The first of
these obligations was a constant reminder to the
immigrant that, unlike French nationals, the sole
reason for his presence in France was that of
work; the second obligation could inhibit him from
engaging in any activity which might be inter-
preted as a threat to public order.

Discrimination was therefore built in to the
very fabric of the law, a fact which clearly contradicted the Socialists' declared aim to situate
its immigration policy within 'a judicial framework defining the status of the migrant, founded

on the principles of human rights and equality of treatment between foreigners and "nationals"'.[29] However well-intentioned this aim was, we must note the discrepancy between the theory and what actually took place in practice. Hence, the ratification by a number of the member states of the Council of Europe of the <u>Convention relative au statut juridique du travailleur migrant</u>, which took effect in France on 1 January 1984, promised a greater respect for the rights of immigrants than was often forthcoming. Once again there was a basic contradiction between the government's policy at an international and domestic level: the rhetoric and measures aimed at improving the conditions of immigrants were often totally at odds with, and frequently undermined by, the repressive and discriminatory nature of controls.

However, the Janus face of recent French immigration policy is understandable (though hardly excusable) when seen in the wider context of European development in the post-colonial era. The break-up of empire had been succeeded by a redefinition of alliances and markets within the framework of the EC. To set about this recreation of Europe in the post-colonial period, West European states had initially welcomed immigrants from former colonies, then closed their doors to them during the economic recession of the 1970s. Since then immigrants have been conceived of as a 'problem' and, frequently, deemed to be responsible for the 'problems' of the economy. After the first oil-shock of 1973-74 the general thrust of policy has increasingly become the movement towards the creation of a barrier-free zone comprising the member states of the EC whilst maintaining a strict control over the entry of foreigners from elsewhere. Given this basic aim, it has become difficult for Europeans to hide the racist aspect of their immigration policy. Although immigration controls are in theory the same for everybody, they are in practice aimed specifically at controlling immigration from the former colonies (predominantly from North Africa for France, predominantly from the West Indies, India and Pakistan for the UK) and from Turkey in the case of West Germany. The real contradiction appears when this policy, guided by economic imperatives and those of race, is coupled with the rhetoric produced by the EC and the Council of Europe concerning human rights and equality, or with statements of support for the Third World. Like other EC partners (notably the UK), France has found itself caught between the traditional image of a <u>pays d'exil et de refuge</u>, enshrining the ideals of freedom, equality and fraternity, and the harshness and racism of its immigration controls. In the light of the general approach taken in recent years by EC partners to migrant workers, the famous rallying cry of the French Revolution serves only to highlight the hypocrisy of the West in its attitudes towards its former colonies.

Another important development over the last decade, and one which further impedes the fair treatment of non-Europeans in EC countries, is the way in which terrorism and immigration have become dangerously associated. Nowhere is this more apparent than in France where measures to safeguard the country from terrorist incursion have become, for some, inseparable from the fight against illegal immigration. In the name of law and order, a policy has been designed which, in effect, categorises all foreigners as potential criminals. Since terrorism in France has been, in recent years, predominantly associated with the Arab struggle in the Middle East and immigration is seen by many as an invasion of Arabs, it is easy to see how the equation immigrant = Arab = terrorist can come about. This depressing trend, whereby an international phenomenon has become inextricably intertwined with perceptions of Arabs living in France, has had more serious effects on policy since the change of government in March 1986.

NATIONALITY, EXPULSION AND THE NEW RIGHT

On one level, the accession to power in March 1986 of the RPR-UDF coalition led by Jacques Chirac continued the broad lines of the immigration policy of the previous administration. Both Left and Right are vigorously opposed to any new immigration and are committed to the fight against illegal entry and ever-tighter checks and controls of non-EC nationals wishing to enter the country. Both sides are also in favour of the type of voluntary repatriation scheme introduced by the Socialists in 1984, and both, in theory at least, wish to pursue the policy of integration into French society of immigrants legally established in the country. The similarity in approach to the question of immigration led one commentator to suggest, at the time of a major debate on immigration in the National Assembly on 6 June 1985, that 'on fundamental issues, the positions of the major political parties are far closer than one would think'.[30]

A number of measures and proclamations after March 1986 brought a sharper focus to the whole debate, none more so than the proposed change in the Nationality Act (the Code de la Nationalité). First presented at the Conseil des Ministres of 11 October 1986, declared unacceptable and rejected by the Conseil d'Etat on 30 October, the bill was then put in limbo whilst a select committee (the so-called comité de sages) looked into the whole area of nationality. The proposal was finally postponed indefinitely in September 1987 when Jacques Chirac announced that the issue was too sensitive and controversial to be dealt with during the run-up to a presidential election. Although the government was then forced to back down, the proposal itself was nevertheless indicative of the government's approach to the thorny subject of nationality. The article to which the Conseil d'Etat took particular exception and which roused the wrath of opposition parties, immigrant associations, trade unions and churches concerned the proposed suppression of the long-established principle of the loi du sol by which a child of foreign parents, born in France and having resided in the country for more than five years, is automatically accorded French nationality. The government wanted to change this automatic right into a voluntary request for French nationality at the age of eighteen, thereby making each adolescent in such circumstances actively manifest a desire for French nationality at the age of majority rather than passively accept its acquisition. The request for nationality could be made until the age of twenty-two but would be refused to those who had served a prison sentence of more than six months.

The proposed measure had the potential for creating citizens of no state and for denying nationality to someone who had lived all his or her life in France and had known no other country of residence. At the heart of it was the real fear of debasing and diluting the concept of nationality and national identity. It is here that the Chirac government brought a sharper focus to a major issue underlying French policy on immigration in recent times and signalled a sharp turn towards the ex-

treme Right. National identity had clearly been
crucial to the debate for some time but, officially, ideas of what it was, who was entitled to
it and how it was to be safeguarded tended to remain implicit.[31] However, the success of the Front
National in pushing it to the forefront of the political agenda was largely responsible for the decision of the Chirac government to make it a major
policy issue in the RPR-UDF programme.

The nationality issue was merely one episode in
a long list of measures, incidents and proclamations after March 1986 which demonstrated the
growing atmosphere of repression. The increased
police powers of on-the-spot identity checks, used
predominantly to discriminate against North
Africans, were an early indication of how the Socialists' policy of controls and the fight against
illegal immigration had taken on a more sinister
air. Stricter conditions governing the right of
entry and stay and the recognition of political
refugee status were introduced in early August.
These measures were followed by the law of 9
September, by which the decision to expel unwanted
persons from the country was taken out of the
hands of the judiciary and made a purely administrative act, thus speeding up the process and giving any aggrieved party little recourse to a fair
hearing. The reintroduction of visas (14 September) for all non-EC nationals wishing to enter
France was a further move to tighten control over
entry and stay. It should be remembered that these
last measures were introduced at a time when terrorist bombs had killed and maimed in Paris and
the country was in the grip of an intense fear of
and hostility towards Arab terrorism. Viewed in
this context, the introduction of visas might have
seemed a logical attempt to prevent potential terrorists from entering France. Yet, in the introduction of such measures, a dangerous xenophobia
mingled ominously with a genuine fear, with often
appalling consequences for the immigrant population as a whole. Not only were racist attacks in
France a clear example of this,[32] but so were the
injustices in the vetting procedure for North
Africans who had requested visas to enter the
country.

The expulsion of 101 illegal immigrants from
Mali on 18 October 1986 highlights the attitudes
and atmosphere outlined above. The extreme rapidity of the operation and its semi-clandestine and
illegal nature bore witness to the anxiety, hos-

tility and scant regard for human rights shown by the administration when faced with a simple case of illegal entry. In May 1987, whilst expulsions continued at an alarming rate, the insensitivity of the government was revealed once again when the Minister of the Interior, Charles Pasqua, promised to deport illegal immigrants in trainloads. This caused an outcry from opposition parties and immigrant associations who were quick to point out the callous nature and particularly inopportune timing of this remark, delivered at the start of the trial of Klaus Barbie for crimes against humanity, amongst which was the despatch of sealed trainloads of Jews from Lyon to the extermination camps. Not all members of the ruling coalition, however, wished to associate themselves with such statements. Both Michel Noir, the Minister of Foreign Trade, and François Léotard, the Minister of Culture, spoke out strongly against any moves by the government to pander to the racism of the Front National. However, Chirac himself was far less willing to condemn Le Pen's party (having no apparent objection to the numerous alliances between the Front National and the RPR on municipal councils) and showed considerable annoyance at the outspokenness of his two ministers. It would seem that the heavy-handed and ruthless tactics of Pasqua were more indicative of the government's approach to the issue of immigration than the views represented by Noir and Léotard.

The tough line shown by Chirac's government led critics to suggest that the Prime Minister was determined to take away the ground from under the feet of the Front National in the run-up to the 1988 presidential elections. The dominant associations of immigration, delinquency and law and order, which underpin the fundamental message of the Front National, have been consistently echoed (albeit in slightly less extreme form) in the statements of leading members of the government. In the light of this emphasis, statements by ministers condemning racism and arguing for a proper integration of immigrants into French society[33] have a particularly hollow ring to opposition parties, immigrant associations and the immigrant communities who feel that the Chirac government has accentuated the divide between the indigenous and immigrant populations at a time when tensions already run high.

Immigration in France is no longer a question of an influx of foreign workers seeking temporary em-

Travailleurs immigrés

ployment before returning to their country of origin. It now concerns the lives of permanent communities settled in France. Nor can it be compared
to the waves of immigrants before the war who were
assimilated into French society over a period of
time. It is now a question of whether France can
make the transition from the centralising ethos of
the colonial period to the multi-racial ethos of
the post-colonial era. The way seems fraught with
difficulties. Algerian independence in 1962 might
have marked the end of colonial rule in North
Africa but not the end of colonial attitudes towards North Africans. Second generation immigrants
from the Maghreb are resentful of a country which
is their birthplace but whose people often treat
them as undesirable aliens. The former colonies,
with which France wishes to maintain close contacts for reasons of trade and influence, can be
forgiven a certain degree of scepticism about
French overtures when they look at the treatment
of their citizens within and on the frontiers of
metropolitan France. Yet France also has a tradition of welcome and hospitality to foreigners and
commitment to human rights and equality. The future harmony of French society now depends on a
genuine espousal of these ideals.

NOTES AND REFERENCES

1. Quoted in A. Perotti, 'L'Immigration en France
depuis 1900', Projet, numéro spécial: 'Ces Immigrés qui sont
aussi la France', No. 171-72 (1983), p. 17.
2. Quoted in A. Cordeiro, L'Immigration (Editions la
Découverte, Paris, 1983), p. 41.
3. In 1963 the creation of the Bureau pour le
Développement des Migrations intéressant les Départements
d'Outre-Mer (BUMIDOM) also stimulated migration from the
French overseas departments and territories. Although French
citizens, residents from these departments arriving in
France have often found themselves facing the same problems
as immigrants (racism, poor housing, prospects of only un-
skilled work). In one sense they have been even less fortu-
nate than other migrants in that, being French citizens,
they were not eligible for the limited help given to immigrants by the Fonds d'Action Sociale (FAS, established in
1958 to offer aid and support to Algerians in France, but
whose responsibilities were extended in April 1964 to cover
all immigrants). In February 1982 the BUMIDOM was replaced
by the Agence Nationale pour l'Insertion et la Promotion des
Travailleurs d'Outre-Mer (ANT).

4. See, for example, Cordeiro's argument in L'Immigration, pp. 32-3.

5. According to the 1982 census, there had been only a slight increase in the size of the foreign population since 1975 from 3,442,415 to 3,680,100.

6. This aim formed part of the government programme defined by the Conseil des Ministres of 9 October 1974.

7. Travailleurs immigrés: le bilan (Editions C.I.E.M., Paris, 1982), p. 50.

8. For example, at the time of the 1975 census - which put the number of foreigners at 3,442,415 - the Ministry, in its evaluation of 31 December 1974, gave a figure of 4,128,312. Similarly, the 1982 census figure of 3,680,100 was over 500,000 less than the Ministry's estimate of 21 December 1981. The main reason for this discrepancy is explained by the fact that, between censuses, the Ministry of the Interior evaluates the number of foreigners residing in France by the number of residence permits granted. As foreigners who leave France are not obliged to hand in their permits to the authorities, the Ministry's estimate inevitably includes a sizeable number of foreigners who are no longer in the country. (See G. Le Moigne, L'Immigration en France, Presses Universitaires de France, Paris, 1986, p. 12.)

9. This figure includes about 125,000 foreign refugees, the majority of whom are from Southeast Asia (followed by Eastern Europe). Refugee status is accorded by the Office Français de Protection des Réfugiés et Apatrides (OFPRA). For a detailed discussion of Southeast Asian refugees see, for example, P. White, H. Winchester, M. Guillon, 'South-East Asian Refugees in Paris: the Evolution of a Minority Community', Ethnic and Racial Studies, Vol. 10, (January 1987), pp. 48-61.

10. For a detailed discussion of the geographical concentration of the foreign population in France, see P. George, L'Immigration en France (Armand Colin, Paris, 1986).

11. It is interesting to note the correspondence between the main areas of support for the Front National in municipal, parliamentary and EC elections during the 1980s and the areas of largest concentration of foreigners. For a detailed discussion of this phenomenon, see P. Ogden, 'Immigration, Cities and the Geography of the National Front in France', in G. Glebe and J. O'Loughlin (eds), Foreign Minorities in Continental European Cities (Franz Steiner, Wiesbaden, 1986), pp. 163-83, and H. Le Bras, 'Où naissent les lepénistes', Le Nouvel Observateur (4-10 April 1986), pp. 28-9.

12. See C. de Wenden, 'La "Seconde" Génération', Projet, No. 171-72, pp. 100-11; F. Gaspard and C. Servan-Schreiber, La Fin des immigrés (Seuil, Paris, 1985), pp. 180-213; and A. Battegay, 'Les "Beurs" dans l'espace pub-

lic', Esprit, numéro spécial: 'Français/Immigrés', No. 102
(June 1985), pp. 113-9. For a comprehensive guide to recent
Beur writing, see 'La Librairie de l'immigration a changé de
vitrine', Hommes et Migrations, No. 1100 (February 1987),
pp. 10-14.
13. 'For many, and notably the children of immigrants,
10 May was celebrated with a joy never before seen on the
occasion of a domestic political event in France.' Gaspard
and Servan-Schreiber, La Fin des immigrés, p. 89.
14. For a more comprehensive guide to the rights of immigrants in France, see C. Bruschi, 'Le Droit et l'insertion
des immigrés', Esprit, No. 102, pp. 49-63, or L. Richer, Le
Droit de l'immigration (Presses Universitaires de France,
Paris, 1986).
15. However, even with this measure - generally considered to be a good law - problems have arisen, principally
over the interpretation and application of the law. See, for
example, La Croix, 28 February 1986, p. 21.
16. See, for example, W. Safran, 'The Mitterrand Regime
and its Policies of Ethnocultural Accommodation',
Comparative Politics, Vol. 18, (October 1985), pp. 41-63.
17. For an interesting account of the ideological and
institutional representations of immigrants in contemporary
France, see R.D. Grillo, Ideologies and Institutions in
Urban France (Cambridge University Press, Cambridge, 1985).
There is a growing literature concerned with Western representations of the 'other', amongst which it is worth men-
tioning (especially in the French context) the continuing
importance of the work of Frantz Fanon.
18. In fact, the issue soon became an embarrassment for
the government when, in August 1981, the Minister for External Relations, Claude Cheysson, spoke openly to the Algerian
President of the imminent introduction of the measure only
to find, on his return to France, that other members of the
government were being far less positive about its prospects.
19. Cordeiro, L'Immigration, p. 105.
20. 'Illegal immigration itself is not without a certain value, for were we to pursue a policy of strict
enforcement of the rules and international agreements governing this area, we would perhaps find ourselves with an
insufficient pool of labour.' Quoted in Ministére des
Affaires Sociales et de la Solidarité Nationale, 1981-1986:
Une nouvelle politique de l'immigration (Documentation
Française, Paris, 1986), p. 10.
21. Cordeiro, L'Immigration, p. 40.
22. See, for example, M. Ragot, Le Travail clandestin,
Conseil economique et social (Journal Officiel, Paris,
1983); Mission de Liaison Inter-Ministérielle pour la Lutte
contre les Trafics de Main-d'Oeuvre, Bilan de la lutte
contre les traffics de main-d'oeuvre. Rapport au Ministère
des Affaires Sociales et de la Solidarité Nationale

(Documentation Française, Paris, 1983); R. Céalis, F. Delalande, X. Jansolin, C.V. Marie et A. Lebon, 'Immigration clandestine: la régularisation des travailleurs "sans papiers" (1981-1982)', Bulletin mensuel des statistiques du travail, supplément no. 106 (1983); C.V. Marie, 'De la Clandestinité à l'insertion professionnelle régulière, le devenir des travailleurs régularisés', Travail et Emploi, No. 22 (1984).

23. See J.M. Dinand, 'Les Travailleurs immigrés clandestins en France', Regards sur l'actualité, No. 119 (1986), p. 20.

24. See Le Monde, 12 March 1983.

25. 'Unable to secure stable employment in sectors of the economy in difficulty, a certain number of immigrants wish to have the possibility to return to their countries of origin.'

26. See Ministère des Affaires Sociales, 1981-1986: Une nouvelle politique, p. 87.

27. The polarisation of views in the 1980s is evident not only in political manifestations but also in recent literature on the question of immigration. Amongst 'pro-immigrant' texts see Cordeiro, Gaspard and Servan-Schreiber (already cited), T. Ben Jelloun, Hospitalité française (Seuil, Paris, 1984) and B. Stasi, L'Immigration, une chance pour la France (Robert Laffont, Paris, 1984). Amongst 'anti-immigrant' texts see A. Griotteray, Immigration: le choc (Plon, Paris, 1984), J.Y. Le Gallou, La Préférence nationale, réponse à l'immigration (Albin Michel, Paris, 1985) and J. Raspail, 'Serons-nous encore français dans 30 ans?', Dossier Immigration, Le Figaro Magazine, No. 312 (26 October 1985), pp. 123-33.

28. 'The new relations which the Socialist government intends to establish with the Third World, and notably with the countries of emigration, imply a new conception of the relations with the immigrant communities in our country'. F. Gaspard, Le Rapport Gaspard, quoted in A. Perotti, 'La Politique à partir de juin 1981', Problèmes politiques et sociaux, No. 530 (1986), p. 13.

29. J. Costa-Lascoux, 'Droits des immigrés, droits de l'Homme et politique de l'immigration', Regards sur l'actualité, No. 113 (1985), p. 20.

30. R. Solé, Le Monde, 8 June 1985, p. 8.

31. For an excellent discussion of the whole area of nationality, see S. Laacher (ed.), Questions de nationalité: histoire et enjeux d'un code (L'Harmattan, Paris, 1987).

32. See, for example, the motives given by six white youths for killing a Tunisian in Nice on 13 June 1987. 'We're racists.... We killed him because he was an Arab.' Quoted in Libération, 1 August 1987, p. 16.

33. See, for example, Chirac's speech of 8 January 1987 on the occasion of the inauguration of the Commission

Travailleurs immigrés

Consultative des Droits de l'Homme:

> 'Everything must be done to ensure that the dignity of the foreign members of the national community is not compromised. This necessitates a serious consideration of the ways in which relations between immigrants and the administration can be improved. In a more general and profound sense, it means that the struggle to combat racist attitudes and behaviour must be conducted in a more positive and determined manner than ever before'.

Quoted in Hommes et Migrations, No. 1100 (1987), p. 17.

Chapter Five

FRANCE AND AFRICA

Guy Martin

Relations between France and Africa have held a
specific place in French foreign policy since the
1960s. Indeed, almost thirty years after independence, France continues to wield considerable and
exclusive political, diplomatic and economic power
in large sections of Africa. In fact, this continent remains the only area of the world where
France retains enough influence to support its
claims to medium power status in the international
system. The perpetuation of French influence in
the Francophone African states is directly related
to France's continuing quest for prestige and
glory (rayonnement) and to its desire to play a
moderating and independent role between the two
superpowers: 'It is in the Third World that France
finds the political and economic space within
which to disengage from super-power hegemony'.[1] In
that sense, and to the extent that it pretends to
be a third force in world politics, France claims
to be truly non-aligned and, consequently, presents itself as the 'natural ally' of the Third
World.
    France's African policy exhibits specific char-
acteristics such as racism, neo-colonialism, exclusivity, stability and continuity; it is also
based on a variety of economic and politico-
strategic interests. A careful analysis of the
main characteristics and essential mechanisms of
this policy reveals its fundamentally neo-colonial
nature in the sense that it is designed to preserve a status quo that is clearly favourable to
the conservative interests of the Western world in
general, and of France in particular.

THE BASIC FEATURES OF FRANCO-AFRICAN RELATIONS

Racism

Racism has pervaded Franco-African relations ever
since the first encounter between the two civili-

sations. While the French have always portrayed themselves as staunch and dedicated defenders of such lofty ideals and values of the 1789 Revolution as freedom, justice and racial equality, they have consistently considered Africans in a negative light, as being inherently inferior to other human races, totally passive and submissive. First, the Atlantic slave trade and then colonisation contributed to crystallise this negative image in the French collective psyche. Racism became one of the main elements of colonialism. In Memmi's now classic statement:

> Racism summarises and symbolises the fundamental relationship between the coloniser and the colonised.... Racism thus appears as a constituent element of colonialism. It is the clearest expression of the colonial situation, and one of the colonialist's most characteristic features.[2]

According to B.H. Lévy, racism has become one of the constituent elements of the 'French ideology', which is nothing but 'a Fascism with French colours' transcending the traditional political cleavages, and fundamentally anti-democratic, xenophobic and racist.[3]

The consistently negative image of Africans retained by the French collective psyche has survived under the guise of paternalism in the postcolonial era. According to Memmi, 'The paternalist is one who sees himself as generous, once racism and inequality have been established'.[4] This policy has carefully cultivated the image of the African as a perpetual minor, inherently incapable and dependent, permanently in need of a foreign master. In addition, latent prejudices - based on the underlying theme, 'since we left, the Africans are incapable of ruling themselves' - are carefully nurtured by the French media.[5]

Neo-colonialism

In essence, neo-colonialism is 'the survival of the colonial system in spite of formal recognition of political independence in emerging countries which became the victims of an indirect and subtle form of domination by political, economic, social, military or technical means'.[6] This strategy has

been practised by European imperialist powers in
order to enable them to carry on the economic exploitation of their former colonies, while relin-
quishing political power to the comprador national
bourgeoisie.

According to former Ghanaian President, Kwame
Nkrumah, the age-old strategy of 'divide and rule'
is based on 'the principle of breaking up former
large united colonial territories into a number of
small non-viable states, which are incapable of
independent development'.[7] It is such a policy of
'balkanisation' that France has successfully carried out in Africa. Although the locally-elected
nationalist leaders of most of the fourteen states
of the Fédération de l'Afrique Occidentale
Française and the Fédération de l'Afrique Equato-
riale Française expressed their desire to obtain
independence within these larger administrative
frameworks, key French officials manoeuvred in
such a way that this status was finally granted to
each state separately.[8] In fact, the transition
from colonisation to 'co-operation' was smoothed
before the formal grant of independence by the negotiation of agreements between France and the
African states that 'tended to perpetuate a colonial type of domination under a rejuvenated legal
cover'. Co-operation appeared as 'the pursuit of
colonisation by other means'.[9] In effect, the two
notions of independence and co-operation are intimately associated. Through the linkages established between the accession to international
sovereignty and the signing of model co-operation
agreements, France managed to institutionalise its
political, economic, monetary and cultural pre-eminence over a number of African states, which
thereby remained almost totally dependent on
France. In this regard, the new co-operation
agreements concluded between France and its former
African colonies between 1973 and 1977 constitute,
with the exception of Mauritania and Madagascar,
mere adjustments to previous agreements that in no
way affected French hegemony.[10] Behind France's
constant and determined efforts at entertaining
divisions among African states lurks one overrid-
ing concern, namely to prevent at all cost the realisation of African unity.[11]

Exclusivity

Since the early days of imperial expansion,

France's economic dynamism and level of industrial development have been relatively less than those of its major actual or potential rivals. This explains why, as Bustin cogently remarks, protectionism and autarky were systematically applied to France's African empire and continued to shape its colonial and post-colonial policies.[12] France's heavy reliance on explicit legal instruments is codified in the form of a highly normalised set of binding documents (the co-operation agreements) supported by a number of multilateral agencies (franc zone, Franco-African summits, etc.). In Bustin's words, 'This preference for structural linkages may... betray a sense of insecurity and an uncomfortable lack of confidence in one's ability to maintain influence in the absence of formal contractual obligations'.[13]

Ever since their political independence, the Francophone African states have always been considered as belonging to the French traditional sphere of influence by virtue of historical links and geographical proximity. According to this Franco-African version of the Monroe doctrine, it is generally understood that 'France is operating in Africa for itself and within the framework of its responsibilities',[14] and that Africa 'constitutes a territory matching our resources and which we have a duty to develop'.[15] Thus Francophone Africa is seen as constituting a natural French preserve (domaine réservé or pré carré), of limits to other foreign powers, whether perceived as friends (the USA, Canada, the UK, West Germany) or foes (the Soviet Union and other Eastern-bloc countries). Indeed France has, on several occasions, shown a deep suspicion of the motives and actions of these powers in Africa.[16] Although disguised under the label of co-operation, France's African policy is, in fact, primarily motivated by its own conception of national interests and blatantly disregards African concerns and interests. As former President Giscard d'Estaing once bluntly declared, 'I am dealing with African affairs, namely with France's interests in Africa'.[17]

Stability and Continuity

Because they are said to be based on historical links, geographical proximity and linguistic and cultural affinity, relations between France and

Francophone Africa are invested with a special quality in the sense that they are particularly close and intimate, almost familial. According to former Minister of Co-operation Jean-Pierre Cot, 'The relationship between France and its Francophone African partners is based on traditional complicity, on a background of common friendship and references which facilitate contact and dialogue'.[18] Thus, while family feuds may occasionally erupt, differences are never such that they cannot be quickly reconciled within the informal, warm and friendly atmosphere of Franco-African institutions. This explains the extraordinary resilience and stability which characterise Franco-African relations.

One of the most striking characteristics of France's African policy is its continuity throughout the various political regimes of the Fifth French Republic, from 1958 to 1988. There is no doubt that an autonomous and permanent policy exists, transcending the traditional political cleavages, the various regimes and individual political leaders. The successive governments of Charles de Gaulle, Georges Pompidou, and Valéry Giscard d'Estaing have inaugurated and strengthened this African policy. Although François Mitterrand had proclaimed his desire and willingness to somewhat 'liberalise' this policy, his Socialist regime (inaugurated in May 1981) found its room for manoeuvre strictly limited by 'historical' constraints and by the weight of economic, political, and strategic interests. Mitterrand was thus led to manage, rather than to radically transform, this inheritance.[19] In the final analysis, it seems that it is indeed the permanence of these economic, political, and strategic interests which accounts for such remarkable continuity.

THE ECONOMIC, POLITICAL AND STRATEGIC BASES OF FRANCO-AFRICAN RELATIONS

The Economic Basis

The decision-makers responsible for France's African policy usually tend to minimise the role of economic factors in its formulation and implementation. According to them, 'Black Africa is not an indispensable source of raw materials for France. Our investments there are minimal and our trading relations remain fairly limited'.[20] Similarly, Giscard d'Estaing asserted that 'there is no relationship whatsoever between the government's policy and economic interests'.[21] The truth of the matter is that Africa plays a vital economic role for France as a source of raw materials, as a market for its manufactured goods and technology, and as an outlet for its capital investment. Thus it is no exaggeration to say that 'in the short-term, France's economic and social equilibrium depends on its control over Africa'.[22]

Europe in general, and France in particular, are highly dependent on the import of strategic raw materials from Africa. Such minerals are called 'strategic' because they are vital to the functioning of the European high-technology industries, notably in aeronautics, nuclear energy and weaponry. France's current rate of dependency on these minerals from Africa is 100 per cent for cobalt, 87 to 100 per cent for uranium, 83 per cent for phosphate, 68 per cent for bauxite, 35 per cent for manganese and 32 per cent for copper. France's rate of dependency from Francophone Africa is 35 per cent for manganese (Gabon), 32 per cent for chromium and 22 per cent for phosphate (Senegal and Togo).[23]

Uranium is an interesting case in point. France's ambitious nuclear-power expansion programme makes it greatly dependent on long-term African sources of supply. Thus, uranium plays a prominent role in France's African policy. In 1982 Africa accounted for 35 per cent of the Western world's uranium production, the major producers being South Africa (15 per cent), Namibia and Niger (about 10 per cent each), the latter providing 4,646 tons, or nearly 60 per cent of France's requirements. As regards reasonably assured uranium resources, that is known deposits which can be recovered within the given production range, those of South Africa actually represent 14 per cent of the world's total, Niger 9 per cent, Namibia 6.8 per cent, France 3.4 per cent and Gabon 1.1 per cent. Furthermore, France is at present actively prospecting for uranium in Senegal, Mali, Guinea, Mauritania and Zaïre, as well as in South Africa.[24] Two major French parastatals, the Bureau de Recherches Géologiques et Minières (BRGM) and the Compagnie Générale de Matières Nucléaires (Cogema) control most uranium exploitation and prospecting activities in the producing Francophone African countries.[25]

Through custom-made co-operation agreements concluded with those countries at independence,
France managed to secure its supply of all strategic raw materials from them. The co-operation and
defence agreements concluded between France and
most Francophone African countries in the 1960s
and 1970s contain special provisions concerning
French privileged and exclusive access to oil and
gas, uranium, thorium, lithium, beryllium and he-
lium. These are classified as 'strategic raw materials' which, according to the defence agreements
signed between France and these countries, must be
sold to France on a priority basis - and restricted to third countries - as required by 'the
interests of common defence'.[26]

Trade Relations

Franco-African trade relations remain fundamentally asymmetrical. Up to three-quarters of
Africa's trade is realised with industrialised
countries, including 50 per cent with the European
Economic Community (EC), and only 5 per cent represents intra-African trade. Conversely, the EC's
trade is intra-European to the extent of 50 per
cent of all trade and only 5 per cent of its trade
is with Africa. In addition, France's share in
Francophone Africa's total imports and exports remains as high as 40 per cent, while Africa represents only 8 per cent of France's total trade.
Such asymmetrical relations are a reflection of
the great inequalities in economic development and
potential existing between these two partners.
Furthermore, most trade and marketing activities
in the former French African countries are monopo-
lised by the old colonial trading companies - the
Compagnie Française de l'Afrique Occidentale and
the Société Commerciale de l'Ouest Africain -
which have conveniently branched out into import-
export activities, and which operate within the
vast protected market circumscribed by the franc
zone. Similarly, French companies control most of
the activities associated with the shipping of
goods to and from these countries. More than a
quarter of a century after independence, the foreign trade of African countries is still largely
functioning through the 'rules' of the trade economy, according to which the African territories
are restricted to the function of suppliers of raw
materials and agricultural products, while the

European metropoles reserve for themselves the exclusivity of industrial production and the export of manufactured goods. According to a recent study, 48 per cent of France's imports from Francophone Africa in 1986 were made up of agricultural and food products, and 29 per cent of energy and fuel products. During that same year, 63 per cent of France's exports to Francophone Africa were of manufactured goods.[27]

France's main trading partners remain the 'privileged friends' which still constitute the hard core of the 'Franco-African community', namely Cameroon, Congo, Ivory Coast, Gabon, Niger, Senegal and Togo. In 1986, these seven countries together accounted for 89 per cent of France's imports from Francophone Africa, and for 76 per cent of its exports to this region.[28] It is noteworthy that France's balance of trade, which is in chronic deficit compared with other industrialised countries, was almost always positive with Africa between 1975 and 1986. This trade surplus amounted to a staggering 20,337 million French francs in 1986 (5,073 million francs with Francophone Africa), while France's global trade deficit reached a low of 65,748 million francs during that year.[29]

Aid and Investments

Globally, French official development assistance (ODA) to Africa has stagnated (if not diminished) in absolute terms over the last five years. This represented 0.47 per cent of France's GNP in 1981-82, 0.48 per cent in 1983, and 0.53 per cent in 1984-85, still well below the official objective of 0.70 per cent to be attained 'as soon as possible after 1988'.[30] About 50 per cent of these funds for Francophone Africa were allocated for technical assistance, with the remainder available for economic, budgetary and financial help. Until recently, French aid to Africa consisted primarily of public grants, but during the last few years, loans from private sources have contributed an even greater proportion of this 'aid'. Thus, the proportion of loans to total ODA has increased from 16 per cent in 1979 to 30 per cent in 1982, and 34.5 per cent in 1985.[31]

The two main French aid agencies, the Fonds d'Aide et de Coopération (FAC) and the Caisse Centrale de Coopération Economique (CCCE) are, in fact, acting as conduits for the transfer of French public capital to the beneficiary African state agencies, and from the latter to the French firms operating in those countries.[32] Indeed, the 'rate of return' of FAC and CCCE aid is generally estimated at between 67 and 80 per cent.[33] Similarly, about 54 per cent of total French ODA in 1982-83, and 47 per cent in 1985, were partially or totally tied.[34] It is noteworthy that Sub-Saharan Africa received approximately 16 per cent of total French bilateral assistance in 1982-83, and 17 per cent of such assistance in 1983-84.[35] The main beneficiaries of this assistance are France's traditional economic partners, namely the Ivory Coast, Gabon, Mali, Senegal and the Central African Republic. The total French financial flows to these five countries in 1985 amounted to US $184.7, $140.7, $124.8, $82.4 and $50.9 million respectively.[36]

These same countries were in 1974-75 the recipients of 60 per cent of French direct investment in Africa, primarily directed towards oil in Cameroon, Congo and Gabon; phosphate in Senegal and Togo; iron in Mauritania; manganese in Gabon; copper in Zaire; chromite in Madagascar; bauxite and aluminium in Cameroon and Guinea; and uranium in Gabon, Niger and the Central African Republic.[37] Furthermore, the French share of import-substitution and other processing industries usually ranges - depending on the type - anywhere between 60 and 100 per cent.[38] Quite clearly, France's commercial interests in Francophone Africa are considerable, and the franc zone further contributes to its overwhelming economic presence in these states.

The Franc Zone[39]

Almost thirty years after independence, France continues to play a dominant role in the formulation and implementation of monetary policies in Francophone Africa. Through the franc zone, a monetary co-operation arrangement set up between France and its former colonies in West and Central Africa (other than Guinea and Mauritania) following their independence in the early 1960s, France controls the money supply, that is the issue and circulation of their currencies, their monetary and financial regulations, their banking activities, their credit allocation and, ultimately,

their budgetary and economic policies. Through
their acceptance of the strict membership rules of
the franc zone, these African governments have en-
trusted all their monetary and financial responsibilities to France in what amounts to a voluntary
surrender of sovereignty. For instance, the structure of decision-making in the African central
banks is such that the French administrators in
these institutions still retain a quasi-veto
right. Member countries hold their reserves mainly
in the form of French francs and effect their exchange on the Paris market. Similarly, because of
the links established between the two currencies,
any modification in the value of the French franc
against other foreign currencies automatically and
fully affects the CFA franc, the legal tender in
the African member states of the franc zone, without their governments even being consulted prior
to any French devaluation decision.[40] Ultimately,
the CFA franc appears to be a mere appendage of
the French franc, with no real autonomy of its
own. This does however stabilise currencies despite their automatic devaluation when the French
franc is devalued. It also greatly facilitates exports and imports with France (and other Francophone African states), so contributing to France
remaining the major trading partner of its foreign
colonies. French investment in the Francophone
African states is substantially greater than that
of any other state.

Political and Cultural Domination

French political and cultural domination over
Francophone Africa is realised through an elaborate institutional network which enables it to exercise an indirect, but efficient, control over
African political elites and bureaucracies. On
close examination, it appears that the decision-
making structures in the area of French African
policy are characterised by three main features,
namely centralisation, secrecy and specialisation.
    The formulation and implementation of major
African policy decisions has always been, and continues to be, the quasi-exclusive preserve of the
President of the Republic, acting through a small
advisory unit on African affairs.[41] Practically no
exceptions to this principle of 'reserved competence' are allowed. The competence of other Ministries - Foreign Affairs, Co-operation, and

Defence - in African affairs is strictly and
exclusively by delegation of presidential authority.[42] As regards secrecy, as Péan has abundantly
demonstrated, decision-making in African affairs
is based on a complex and elaborate information
network, initiated by Jacques Foccart, de Gaulle's
adviser on African affairs, in which personal relations and the intervention of official or unofficial 'special action' agencies play a prominent
role.[43] As for specialisation, relations with
Francophone African states since independence have
always been the responsibility of a special ministry, the Ministry of Cooperation. It is interesting to note in this respect that Jean-Pierre
Cot's attempt to modify the functional and geographical competence of the Ministry as Mitterrand's first Minister of Cooperation met with resounding failure. There is no doubt that his
forced 'resignation' in December 1982 was brought
about by a coalition made up of rival bureaucracies, the 'neo-colonial lobby' and certain African
heads of state, all of whom had particular reasons
for feeling threatened by Cot's proposed reforms.[44] Undoubtedly, 'the Ministry of Cooperation
will remain the Ministry of the African Neo-
Colonies' for many years to come.[45]

At another level, one of the constant preoccupa-
tions of French decision-makers in Africa has always been to inspire and encourage formal or informal institutional groupings bringing together
all the Francophone African states under the aegis
of France. It is such concerns which have led to
the creation of the Conseil de l'Entente by the
Ivory Coast, Dahomey (now Benin), Niger, and Upper
Volta (Burkina Faso) in May 1959, followed by the
Organisation Commune Africaine et Malgache (OCAM)
which brought together all the moderate Francophone African states in February 1965. It was
partly to make up for the deficiencies of the
rather ineffectual and dormant OCAM that President
Pompidou initiated the Franco-African summit conferences in November 1973. Since then, fourteen
such conferences have been held annually, alternately in France and in Africa.[46] These meetings
constitute in a way the institutionalisation of
the permanent tête-à-tête maintained between the
French president and each of the Francophone
African heads of state. Such intimate contacts are
also preserved through the frequent 'official',
'working' or 'private' visits of the Francophone
African heads of state to France, as well as the

numerous reciprocal visits undertaken by the
French president.[47] At a lower level, a number of
ad hoc conferences periodically bring together the
French and African ministers who deal with similar
areas of competence in their respective countries
-- finance, justice, education and culture,
health, sports, etc. Finally, a wide network of
organisations and conferences - whose hub is the
'Agence de Coopération Culturelle et Technique -
tries, under the heading of Francophonie, to institutionalise the linguistic and cultural links
existing between France and its Francophone satellites.[48]

This complex and elaborate network constitutes a
means whereby France perpetuates its multi-dimen-
sional domination over former colonies, thereby
retarding the process of decolonisation and also
directly or indirectly affecting the state machinery and ruling elites in Francophone Africa. Of
fundamental importance is the fact that the whole-
sale importation of the French administrative,
fiscal, judicial and educational systems by these
states necessarily leads to a situation of acute
cultural dependency. Education and culture constitute a priority area of co-operation and technical
assistance, thereby helping to reinforce the cultural, technical, and political influence of the
former colonial power through the diffusion of its
language, thought processes and behavioural patterns. It is striking to note the priority given
to the language and culture of France throughout
Francophone Africa.[49] This situation obviously results in a significant restriction of the indigenous elite's decision-making autonomy with respect
to Paris, a dependency further reinforced by the
fact that many French technical assistants still
occupy important administrative and management positions, and thus retain significant bureaucratic
responsibilities and power. In the Ivory Coast,
the same two Frenchmen have held the positions of
Chief of the Office of the President and Secretary-General to the Government ever since independence.[50] In Senegal, the Secretary-General to the
Presidency and de facto Minister of Home Affairs
is a French national turned Senegalese, Jean
Collin.[51] In the Central African Republic, a
French military adviser initially assigned to
President Kolingba's personal security, Colonel
Jean-Claude Mansion, has become so powerful that
he has been nicknamed 'Kolingba's President' by
the Centrafrican people.[52]

The neo-colonial system thus set up actually results in a <u>de facto</u> alliance between the French
and the African ruling elites, each defending the
interests of the other to the detriment of those
of the indigenous peoples. Such a situation accounts for the dependent and expectant attitude of
several African leaders towards France, from which
the solution to all of their national problems,
whether political, military, economic, social or
financial, is expected to come.[53] This neo-colonial class alliance also accounts for certain aspects of France's African policy, and particularly
for military interventions in certain states designed to protect, maintain and, if necessary, reinstate some leader or ruling group with which it
entertains privileged relations.[54]

Military Presence and Intervention in Africa

Since independence, France has concluded a number
of defence and military technical assistance
agreements with each of its former African
colonies. These have been renegotiated in the mid-
1970s without significant changes, and they have
even been extended to African countries situated
outside the traditional French zone of influence,
notably to Burundi, Rwanda and Zaïre.[55] Furthermore, France maintains a significant permanent
military presence in Africa, with at least 7,800
troops distributed as follows: Central African Republic (1,650), Ivory Coast (500), Djibouti
(3,800), Gabon (600) and Senegal (1,250).[56] A further 1,278 French military advisers are currently
distributed in 26 African countries.[57] In addition
to its military bases on the continent, which have
been gradually phased out since independence,
France has, since August 1983, set up a 'rapid deployment' airborne force (Force d'Action Rapide)
of 47,000 men that is capable of intervening at
short notice almost anywhere in Africa from its
bases in France.[58] This elaborate network of defence and military assistance agreements and logistical support structures enabled the French
army to intervene twenty times in Africa during
the period from 1963 to 1988.[59] According to the
official French doctrine, military interventions
in Africa are <u>ad hoc</u>, always conducted at the concerned government's specific request, within the
framework of an existing defence agreement, and
designed to counter actual or potential external

aggression.

French leaders also usually link the notion of security and development by arguing that their help in creating strong national armies has contributed to the stability, and hence to the economic benefit, of all concerned. Giscard d'Estaing even went so far as to argue that because the African states have limited resources, they should let France take care of their defence while they grapple with development problems: 'Why do certain states ask us to take care of their security? It is because they just do not have the resources to do it, and it would not be wise for them to use their limited resources to build up modern armed forces. Africa must allocate its resources to development projects'.[60] In fact, the French government's objective in creating African national armies at the time of independence was to build up units which could work closely with French units and effectively serve as branches of the French army overseas. Indeed, 'the French originally saw the role of national armies and French security interests as co-extensive'. The French Ministry of Co-operation continues to subordinate particular African requests in this sector to France's general strategy for Africa.[61]

In this area, as in others, continuity has prevailed over change. Although Mitterrand stated, prior to his coming to power, that 'the resort to the military option in its various forms does not seem to me to be a viable solution',[62] he has declared more recently: 'We shall intervene, if necessary, provided it is within the framework of the agreements signed between France and the African states'.[63] As a matter of fact, the French government decided to intervene directly and heavily in the Chadian conflict by supporting President Hissen Habré against the rebel forces of ex-President Goukoumi Weddeye, who was backed by Libyan troops, from August 1983 to September 1984. In addition to the 3,300 men who made up the 'Manta' intervention force, France provided considerable quantities of arms, equipment and ammunition, as well as logistical support.

The size, location, and mobility of these external armed forces make it very easy for the French to interfere in the African continent. Such a presence, which in effect results in France's strict control over the defence of the Francophone states - one of the foremost attributes of their sovereignty - contributes to further exacerbate their already acute dependency on Paris. First of all, by a policy of co-operation, France is able to control the size and capabilities of most Francophone African armies. Furthermore, as Luckham cogently remarks, 'The presence of French troops and military advisers, the consolidation and reproduction of national military structures through external support and the transmission through military training of metropolitan skills, tastes and ideologies constitute a permanent intervention'.[64] Ultimately, there is no doubt that 'French military co-operation with Francophone African countries has created a dependency which is in the service of French political interests but not always to the long-term benefit of African countries'.[65]

In the final analysis, France's military presence in Africa is determined by three main factors: the size and degree of its economic interests and involvement, the number of French residents and the nature of the links existing between France and the national ruling elites. In this respect, it is interesting to note that the 'core' countries of this defence system are precisely those which are central to France's economic interests, namely Cameroon, the Central African Republic, the Ivory Coast, Gabon and Senegal.[66] Ultimately, one suspects that the main objective is to help pro-French regimes stay in power, as the remarkable political stability and exceptional elite longevity of several Francophone states seem to indicate.

France and the Defence of the West

On the eve of the 1990s, Africa remains the only area of the world where France retains enough power and influence to support its claims to medium power status in the international system. In a way, this position has, historically, always been a matter of political and economic survival for France. As one ideologue of French colonialism saw it at the turn of the century, 'If France were to remain what it is at present, it would cease to exist'.[67] More precisely, 'France will become a great African power or in a century or two it will be a secondary power in Europe'.[68] France, whose economy is shaky and whose international prestige has been seriously affected by unsuccessful colonial adventures, notably in Vietnam and Algeria, is still attempting to raise its global status thanks to the lebensraum offered by the African geo-political space. Such a policy, initiated by de Gaulle and carried on by his successors, is designed to build France into a respectable middle power, free from the hegemony of the USA and the Soviet Union, and truly 'non-aligned'. France thus presents itself as a third force in world politics, the 'natural ally' of the Third World. In this perspective, Francophone Africa constitutes a base from which France can develop relations with countries located outside its traditional sphere of influence. Thus, France has recently developed political and economic relations with a number of non-Francophone eastern and southern African states, notably Angola, Kenya, Mozambique and Zimbabwe. Similarly, Nigeria has become France's main trading partner in Africa, and there is evidence that, overcoming a traditional regional rivalry, Nigeria now seems prepared to share with France the exercise of political and economic influence in west-central Africa.[69] The recent broadening of the participation in Franco-African summits to include non-Francophone African countries derives from the same policy.[70] In this context, there is no doubt that 'France's neo-colonial position in the Francophone countries in some respects has facilitated the extension of her global influence'.[71]

France is acting in Africa not merely on its own account, and in the defence of its own national interests, but also as a proxy gendarme of the Western world. Indeed, 'French actions, whatever their guiding principles, are in the general Western interest'.[72] From this perspective, France appears as a secondary imperial power, included in the Western economy and defence system, with a specific function assigned to it within the NATO alliance, and operating within limits clearly defined by American imperialism.[73] From this point of view, the French military presence and interventions in Africa take on a new dimension and seem to be essentially motivated by three main factors. First of all, they are designed to progressively and permanently integrate the Francophone states into the Atlantic alliance system.[74] Secondly, they are intended to contribute to the protection of the sea lanes through which the Western world's supplies of oil and other strategic raw materials usually travel. Finally, they aim at countering and limiting the expansion of

Soviet military presence and influence in Africa
wherever these might manifest themselves.[75] France
thus appears as a mere instrument - albeit vitally
important - of Western imperialism in Africa,
whose main objective is to ensure the survival of
the states and leaders who act as faithful and
vigilant guardians of Western interests (the <u>in-
terlocuteurs valables</u>, or accommodating African
partners), often against those of their own peoples.

CONCLUSION

This article has attempted to identify the main
characteristics and specific economic, political
and strategic interests which underlie France's
post-colonial policy in Africa. On the basis of
this analysis, the inevitable conclusion has to be
reached that this policy is essentially neo-colonial because it is designed to perpetuate the dom-
inance/dependency pattern prevailing in Franco-
African relations, and because it is clearly
favourable to the conservative interests of the
Western world in general, and of France in particular. Although a process of regionalisation of security structures is currently under way,[76] and in
spite of the traditional dilemma of France's foreign policy (high objectives versus limited
means), the Franco-African economic, political and
security system which now exists is likely to remain in place, with possible minor modifications,
until at least the end of the century. Thus, stability and continuity will probably remain a major
characteristic of France's African policy for the
foreseeable future. It is 'constant, Gaullist and
committed'.[77]
  At the end of the day one puzzling question remains unanswered: 'How can France do everything
that it does in Africa and get away with it?'[78]
Part of the answer to this question lies in the
underdevelopment and dependency, and thus the limited economic and political power, of the African
states within the contemporary international system. While we cannot possibly condone many of
France's activities in Africa, the blame for the
situation now prevailing on the continent cannot
be laid exclusively at its doorstep. France is, in
fact, merely conducting, with all the means at its
disposal, a policy which promotes and defends what
it considers to be legitimate national interests.

France and Africa

It is, therefore, the responsibility of African
leaders to counter such manifestations of neo-
colonialism with innovative and bold policies of
consultation, co-operation, and unity, aiming at
the total political and economic integration of
the continent in the interest of the African peoples. Only thus could French neo-colonialism in
Africa be relegated to where it really belongs,
'the museum of antiquities, by the side of the
spinning wheel and the bronze axe'.[79]

NOTES AND REFERENCES

1. Robin Luckham, 'French Militarism in Africa',
Review of African Political Economy, No. 24 (May 1982), p.
4.
2. Albert Memmi, Portrait du colonisé, précédé du
portrait du colonisateur (Jean-Jacques Pauvert, Paris,
1966), pp. 107-11, translated by the author, as elsewhere in
this article.
3. Bernard-Henry Lévy, L'Idéologie française (Grasset,
Paris, 1981).
4. Memmi, Portrait du colonisé, p. 112.
5. Much the same point is made by Edouard Bustin, The
Limits of French Intervention in Africa: A Study in Applied
Neo-Colonialism (Working Paper No. 54, African Studies Cen-
ter, Boston, 1982), p. 11. For a fairly typical illustration
of French public opinion's and the media's idea of Africa,
see Favilla in Les Echos, 21 January 1983: 'Africa is quite
different from France.... Democracy does not, and cannot,
have the same persuasion there as in the European countries
with an ancient humanist tradition.... Under these inhos-
pitable climes where civilisation has hardly penetrated the
daily exercise of power does not allow for any weakness'.
6. All-African People's Conference, Cairo, March 23-
31, 1961: Resolution on Neo-Colonialism, in Colin Legum,
Pan-Africanism: A Short Political Guide (Pall Mall Press,
London, 1962), p. 254.
7. Kwame Nkrumah, Neo-Colonialism: The Last Stage of
Imperialism (Heinemann, London, 1965), p. xiii.
8. On this process, see W.J. Foltz, From French West
Africa to the Mali Federation (Yale University Press, New
Haven, 1964); J.R. de Benoist, La Balkanisation de l'Afrique
Occidentale Française (Nouvelles Editions Africaines, Dakar,
1979); and G. N'Diaye, L'Echec de la Fédération du Mali
(Nouvelles Editions Africaines, Dakar, 1980).
9. Albert Bourgi, La Politique française de
coopération en Afrique: le cas du Sénégal (Librairie
Générale de Droit et de Jurisprudence, Paris, 1979), pp. 3,
7.

10. A. Bourgi, 'Les Relations avec l'ex-état colonial', in Encyclopédie juridique de l'Afrique (Nouvelles Editions Africaines, Dakar, 1982), Vol. 11, pp. 207-14.

11. This point is further developed in Guy Martin, 'The Historical, Economic, and Political Bases of France's African Policy', Journal of Modern African Studies, Vol. 23 (June 1985), p. 192.

12. Bustin, The Limits of French Intervention in Africa, pp. 3-4.

13. Ibid., p. 10.

14. Televised interview of V. Giscard d'Estaing, quoted in T. Jallaud, 'La Coopération militaire', in La France contre l'Afrique/Tricontinental 1, nouvelle série (Maspéro, Paris, 1981), p. 105.

15. J.P. Cot, A l'Epreuve du pouvoir (Seuil, Paris, 1984), p. 38.

16. Thus there is some evidence that France's interventions in the coups d'état which led to the murder of Sylvanus Olympio in Togo (1963) and to the attempted overthrow of Léon M'Ba in Gabon (1964) were primarily motivated by French fears of the possible prevailing influences of the West Germans (Togo) and Americans (Togo and Gabon). See Yves Bénot, 'Vingt ans de "politique africaine"', in La France contre l'Afrique, pp. 58-60. Similarly, former President Hamani Diori of Niger faced the open hostility of the French 'neo-colonial lobby' when he attempted to develop political and economic relations with Canada. See J. Baulin, Conseiller du Président Diori (Eurafor Press, Paris, 1986), pp. 53-66.

17. Televised interview of V. Giscard d'Estaing, as reported in Le Monde, 29 January 1981.

18. Cot, A L'Epreuve du Pouvoir, p. 63.

19. Much the same argument is made by J.F. Bayart, who goes so far as to assert that it was, in fact, Mitterrand himself who initiated a new deal for Africa when he became Minister for French overseas territories in 1954. 'The real continuity actually starts with Mr Mitterrand and was passed on to General de Gaulle and to his successor' (J.F. Bayart, La Politique africaine de François Mitterrand, Karthala, Paris, 1984), p. 52.

20. Louis de Guiringaud, 'La Politique africaine de la France', Politique étrangère, No. 2 (June 1982), p. 443.

21. Le Monde, 29 January 1981.

22. Pathé Diagne, 'Mitterrand, la Gauche, l'Afrique et le Tiers-Monde', Peuples noirs/Peuples africains, No. 27 (May 1982), p. 6.

23. 'L'Afrique, un partenaire indispensable', Actuel développement, No. 38 (May 1980), pp. 39-40.

24. Figures taken from A.D. Owen, 'The World Uranium Industry', Raw Materials Report, Vol. 2, No. 4 (1984), pp. 6-23. Libération Afrique, 'Les Particules de Giscard:

l'Uranium africain' in La France contre l'Afrique, pp. 144-61 and 'La France et l'Afrique', Marchés tropicaux et méditerranéens, No. 2041 (December 1984), p. 3169.

25. For a more detailed analysis of this issue, see Guy Martin, 'The Political Economy of Africa's Strategic Minerals: Uranium as a Factor in Franco-African Relations', paper for the 14th World Congress of the International Political Science Association, Washington D.C., 28 August-1 September, 1988.

26. P. Lellouche and D. Moisi, 'French Policy in Africa: A Lonely Battle Against Destabilization', International Security, Vol. 3 (1979), footnote 15, p. 116.

27. La Zone Franc: Rapport 1986 (Secrétariat du Comité Monétaire de la Zone Franc, Paris, 1987), pp. 122-5.

28. Ibid., p. 123.

29. Ibid., p. 123; R. Arnaud, 'Commerce: Echanges franco-africains en chute libre', Jeune Afrique Economie, No. 95 (March 1987), p. 34.

30. Development Co-Operation: 1985 Report (OECD, Paris, 1985), p. 295; Development Co-Operation: 1986 Report (OECD, Paris, 1986), pp. 70, 224. According to the newly-adopted computation system, these figures exclude overseas departments and territories.

31. P. Messine, 'Nord-Sud: la Gauche an 1', in Coopération et dépendances/Critiques de l'Economie politique, No. 28 (July 1982), p. 25; Development Co-Operation 1986 Report, p. 276.

32. Richard Joseph, 'The Gaullist Legacy: Patterns of French Neo-colonialism', Review of African Political Economy, No. 6 (May 1976), p. 9.

33. Y. Berthelot and J. de Bandt, Impact des relations avec le Tiers-Monde sur l'Economie française (La Documentation Française, Paris, 1982), p. 43. The rate of return is a measure of the percentage of aid which actually returns to France in the form of purchases of goods and services from that country.

34. Development Co-Operation: 1985 Report, p. 299; 1986 Report, pp. 240-1.

35. Development Co-Operation: 1985 Report, p. 309; 1986 Report, p. 249.

36. Geographical Distribution of Financial Flows to Developing Countries, 1982/1985 (OECD, Paris, 1987), various tables.

37. P. Hugon, 'L'Afrique noire francophone: l'Enjeu économique pour la France', Politique africaine, No. 5 (February 1982), p. 86.

38. E. Jouve, 'L'Afrique, enjeu mondial: le Rôle de la France', in La France contre l'Afrique, p. 82.

39. On this issue, see P. and S. Buillaumont, Zone franc et développement africain (Economica, Paris, 1984); Guy Martin, 'The Franc Zone: Underdevelopment and Dependency in

Francophone Africa', <u>Third World Quarterly</u>, Vol. 8 (January 1986), pp. 205-35; and A.Y. Yarsae, 'Some Problems of Monetary Dependency in French-Speaking West African States', <u>Journal of African Studies</u>, Vol. 5 (Winter 1978), pp. 444-70.

40. These and other problems raised by the functioning of the franc zone system for the African member states are examined in some detail in Martin, 'The Franc Zone, Underdevelopment and Dependency in Francophone Africa', pp. 218-31.

41. Since the March 1986 legislative elections, Right-wing Prime Minister Jacques Chirac has created his own advisory unit on African affairs, headed by an influential and well-connected old 'Africa hand', Jacques Foccart. The creation of this unit, however, does not seem to have affected the presidential African unit's pre-eminence in African affairs. The latter is currently headed by Jean Audibert, assisted by no other than the President's own son, Jean-Christophe Mitterrand; as is often said in France, African affairs are truly 'family affairs'! See in particular 'France: Return of the Old-Guard', <u>Africa Confidential</u>, Vol. 37 (April 1986), pp. 6-7; 'France's Disappointments of Office', <u>Africa Confidential</u>, Vol. 27 (June 1986), pp. 6-7; and P. Michaud, 'French Africa Policy: Continuity with Change', <u>New African</u> (August 1986), pp. 18-19.

42. Cf. Bayart, <u>La Politique africaine de François Mitterrand</u>, p. 48, for an unequivocal statement by Mitterrand during his state visit to Gabon in January 1983: 'It is I who determines France's foreign policy, not my Ministers.... The Ministers are allowed to think or to have an opinion.... It is unthinkable that a policy could be implemented without my agreement, let alone my initiative'. On the principle of the 'reserved competence' of the Presidency in African affairs, see B. Nouaille-Degorce, <u>La Politique française de coopération avec les Etats africains et malgache au sud du Sahara, 1958-1978</u> (CEAN/IEP, Bordeaux, 1982), pp. 104-55.

43. Pierre Péan, <u>Affaires africaines</u> (Fayard, Paris, 1983). Secret societies based on common ideological affinity and close personal relations and loyalty, such as Freemasonry, also constitute an important element in France's relations with Africa; see 'Freemasonry: The French Connection', <u>Africa Confidential</u>, Vol. 28 (May 1987), pp. 1-2.

44. On this episode, see Bayart, <u>La Politique africaine de François Mitterrand</u>, pp. 37-48; also, Cot, <u>A L'Epreuve du pouvoir</u>.

45. Messine, 'Nord-Sud: la Gauche an I', p. 15. On this point, see also K. Whiteman, 'President Mitterrand and Africa', <u>African Affairs</u>, Vol. 82 (July 1983), pp. 335-6.

46. The 13th Conference of the French and African heads of state and government was held in Lomé, Togo, 13-15 November 1986, with 39 participants (25 full members, and 14

observers). The 14th summit, held in Antibes, France, 10-12 December 1987, brought together 37 participants. See <u>Afrique contemporaine</u>, Vol. 26, No. 141 (January 1987), pp. 54-6; <u>Afrique contemporaine</u>, Vol. 27, No. 145 (1988), pp. 55-6; and C. Wauthier, 'Les Sommets franco-africains, symboles de continuité', <u>Le Monde diplomatique</u>, No. 392 (November 1986), p. 30.

47. Thus there have been 32 state visits to Africa by French heads of state between 1960 and 1978 (13 by President Mitterrand since May 1981), and 280 meetings between the latter and their African counterparts during the same period. In addition, during the period 1959 to 1978, the number of visits of all kinds (official or private) by certain African heads of state is impressive: 47 for F. Houphouët-Boigny (Ivory Coast), and 32 for L.S. Senghor (Senegal), to mention just these two; see Nouaille-Degorce, <u>La Politique française de coopération</u>, pp. 463-5. Similarly, former French presidential adviser for African affairs Guy Penne recently revealed that during his five-year tenure, he conducted 81 missions in Africa on behalf of the President and met privately with Francophone heads of state on 205 occasions; G. Penne, quoted in J. Derogy and J.M. Pontaut, <u>Enquête sur un Carrefour dangereux</u> (Fayard, Paris, 1987), p. 254

48. See Chapter 8 on Francophonie by Robert Aldrich and John Connell in the present volume.

49. On this point, see Victor T. Levine, 'Political-Cultural Schizophrenia in Francophone Africa', in I.J. Mowae and R. Bjornson (eds), <u>Africa and the West: The Legacies of Empire</u> (Greenwood Press, New York, 1986), pp. 159-73; and Abdou Touré, <u>La Civilisation quotidienne en Côte d'Ivoire: Procès d'Occidentalisation</u> (Karthala, Paris, 1981).

50. These are Guy Nairy and Alain Belkiri, respectively; see M. Amondji, <u>Félix Houphouët et la Côte d'Ivoire: L'Envers d'une légende</u> (Karthala, Paris, 1984), pp. 219-22.

51. S. Andriamirado, 'L'Homme fort du Sénégal', <u>Jeune Afrique</u>, 6 May 1987, pp. 4-12.

52. According to Roger Delpey, 'For the Centrafrican and the French alike, ... the actual head of the Central African Republic is Mansion...; in Bangui... everyone knows that "Kolingba's President" writes up decrees and speeches, sets the agenda of the Council of Ministers, suggests appointments and demotions, intervenes in economic and budgetary matters, heads the key ministries of the Interior and of Information, chases political opponents, participates in the questioning of political detainees and even helps to fill the prisons'. R. Delpey, <u>Affaires centrafricaines</u> (Jacques Grancher, Paris, 1985), p. 111.

53. Thus the Malagasy journalist Sennen Andriamirado once declared with conviction: 'The futility of debating African affairs among Africans has now become clear. In

order to prevent inter-African conflicts, the Africans must necessarily call on France', 'Comment éviter les guerres', Jeune Afrique, 12 October 1983, p. 49.

54. On this issue, one should consult P. Chaigneau, La Politique militaire de la France en Afrique (CHEAM, Paris, 1984); John Chipman, French Military Policy and African Security (Adelphi Papers No. 201, IISS, London, 1985); John Chipman, Ve République et Défense de l'Afrique (Editions Bosquet, Paris, 1986); J. Guillemin, 'L'Intervention extérieure dans la politique militaire de la France en Afrique noire francophone', Le Mois en Afrique, Vol. 16, No. 186-7 (June 1981), pp. 43-58; Guillemin, 'L'Importance des bases dans la politique militaire de la France en Afrique noire francophone', Le Mois en Afrique, Vol. 16, No. 188-9 (August 1981), pp. 31-44; P. Lellouche and D. Moisi, 'French Policy in Africa: A Lonely Battle Against Destabilization', International Security, Vol. 3 (Spring 1979), pp. 108-33; and Robin Luckham, 'French Militarism in Africa', Review of African Political Economy, No. 24 (May 1982), pp. 55-84.

55. As of January 1988, France had concluded defence agreements with eight countries (Cameroon, Central African Republic, Comoros, Ivory Coast, Djibouti, Gabon, Senegal and Togo), and military technical assistance agreements with 25 others (including the above, the three Maghreb countries, plus Benin, Burkina Faso, Burundi, Chad, Congo, Libya, Madagascar, Mali, Mauritius, Mauritania, Niger, Rwanda, Seychelles and Zaïre); see Chipman, French Military Policy and African Security, Table 4, p. 25.

56. Chipman, Ve République et Défense de l'Afrique, p. 147.

57. Chipman, French Military Policy, Table 3, p. 24.

58. Ibid., pp. 15-26. It should, however, be noted that as early as 1962 a 23,000-men strong Force interarmées d'intervention was set up for a similar purpose; Ibid., pp. 7-8.

59. The list of these interventions is as follows: Gabon (1964); Chad (1968, 1975, 1978, 1980 and 1983); Djibouti (1967, 1974, 1976 and 1977); Mayotte (1977, 1978); Mauritania (1956-63, 1977, 1978, 1980); Central African Republic (1979); Zaïre (1977, 1978); and Togo (1986). (Chaigneau, La Politique militaire de la France en Afrique, pp. 93-100).

60. Televised interview with V. Giscard d'Estaing, reported in Le Monde, 29 January 1981.

61. Chipman, French Military Policy, pp. 21-2.

62. Letter from F. Mitterrand to Libération-Afrique, dated April 1981, quoted in Libération Afrique-Caraïbe-Pacifique, No.14 (September 1982), p. 28.

63. F. Mitterrand, quoted in Messine, 'Nord-Sud: la Gauche an I', p. 24.

64. Luckham, 'French Militarism in Africa', p. 56.

65. Chipman, French Military Policy, p. 24.

66. Luckham, 'French Militarism in Africa', pp. 68-71.

67. Prévost-Paradol, quoted in M. Aurillac, L'Afrique à coeur (Berger-Levrault, Paris, 1987), p. 37.

68. P. Leroy-Beaulieu, quoted in R. Joseph, Gaullist Africa: Cameroon under Ahidjo (Fourth Dimension, Enugu, 1978), p. 6.

69. B. Eyo Ate, 'The Presence of France in West-Central Africa as a Fundamental Problem to Nigeria', Millennium, Vol. 12, No. 2 (Summer 1983), pp. 110-27; O. Anyadike, 'Touching Spheres of Influence', West Africa, No. 3675 (February 1988), pp. 160-1.

70. The following 14 non-Francophone African states took part in the 13th Franco-African summit meeting (Lomé, November 1986) as observers: Angola, Botswana, Egypt, Liberia, Mozambique, Nigeria, Sao Tomé and Principe, Sierra Leone, Somalia, Sudan, Tanzania, Tunisia, Zambia and Zimbabwe; Afrique contemporaine, Vol. 26, No. 141 (January 1987), p. 56.

71. Luckham, 'French Militarism in Africa', p. 78.

72. Chipman, French Military Policy, p. 44.

73. The USA provided logistic support (transport planes) during the French interventions in Zaïre of 1977 and 1978. Similarly, American foreign policy agencies have worked in close co-operation with the French authorities in Chad to provide massive political, military and financial support to the Habré regime in its struggle against the Goukouni-Gaddafi coalition. See Bob Woodward, Veil: The Secret Wars of the CIA, 1981-1987 (Simon and Schuster, New York, 1987).

74. According to a noted French strategist, 'the whole of the African continent... should be considered as an indispensable rear base for NATO'. C.P. Dabezies, 'La Politique militaire de la France en Afrique noire', in D.G. Lavroffe (ed.), La Politique africaine du Général de Gaulle, 1958-69 (Pédone, Paris, 1980), p. 2331; another frankly advocates 'the integration of Black Africa and South Africa within the same geo-political security alliance': J. Leguèbe, L'Afrique du Sud contemporaine (PUF, Paris, 1978), p. 205.

75. It is such motivations which explain the French secret destabilisation actions against the MPLA in Angola during 1975-6, as well as successive interventions in Zaïre in 1977 and 1978; Luckham, 'French Militarism in Africa', Table II, p. 61.

76. Thus, in June 1977, seven Francophone West African states signed the Accord de Non-Agression et d'Assistance en Matiére de Défense (Non-Aggression and Mutual Defence Assistance Pact), with active French encouragement and support. Similarly, support of the OAU as the natural framework for the settlement of inter-African disputes has been a major

principle of France's African policy since May 1981; see
Cot, A L'Epreuve du pouvoir, pp. 136-7.
    77. A. Andereggen, 'Francophone Africa Today', Journal
of Social, Political and Economic Studies, Vol. 12 (1987),
p. 47.In this regard, one can safely predict that France's
African policy is unlikely to be significantly altered after
the 1988 presidential election.
    78. Tamar Golan, 'A Certain Mystery: How can France do
Everything that it does in Africa and Get Away with it'?,
African Affairs, Vol. 80 (January 1981), pp. 3-11.
    79. Friedrich Engels, 'The Origin of the Family,
Private Property and the State', in L.S. Feuer (ed.), Marx
and Engels: Basic Writings on Politics and Philosophy
(Doubleday, Garden City, New York, 1959), p. 394.

Chapter Six

**FRANCE AND THE THIRD WORLD: CO-OPERATION OR
DEPENDENCE?**

Howard Evans

It is now generally recognised that in foreign affairs the arrival of the Socialist government of
President Mitterrand in May 1981 did not herald a
period of major change, and this is certainly true
of France's relations with the Third World. It is
for this reason, notwithstanding the dramatic economic, social and political changes that have
taken place in the Third World since the 1960s,
that it is necessary here to adopt a historical
approach. Not only do many of François Mitterrand's stances appear distinctly Gaullist, but
both the present machinery for the provision of
French development aid to the Third World and the
distribution of this aid were established in the
immediate post-colonial period. It was then that
attitudes were fashioned and a vocabulary forged;
many of the official pronouncements of that time
might be generally endorsed, even by French Socialists, in the 1980s.
  Political debate subsumes ideological debate
and nowhere more perhaps than in the emotive area
of Third World development; the current debate between 'third worldists' and 'cartierists',[1] and by
extension the resonance of Jean-Marie Le Pen's
ideas, can best be understood in the light of the
historical development of the former. Third World
problems, of course, rarely have pride of place in
party political manifestos and usually elicit only
pious platitudes. In both these respects François
Mitterrand's '110 proposals' of 1981 (but not
Jacques Chirac's 1981 programme or the joint
RPR/UDF manifesto of 1986) were an exception. Yet,
through media, especially television, coverage of
conditions in refugee and resettlement camps and
of areas stricken by drought and famine, these
problems probably impinge more directly on the national consciousness than any other aspect of foreign affairs.

126

THIRD WORLD AND THIRD WORLDISM

It is widely considered that the French expression <u>Tiers Monde</u> (Third World) was first used - almost incidentally - by the demographer and economist Alfred Sauvy in <u>L'Observateur</u> on 14 August 1952 to designate those countries then known generally as 'under-developed countries' (<u>pays sous-développés</u>). At the end of an article devoted to the struggle between the Eastern and Western blocs for global hegemony - it was the time of the Korean War, but the East-West rivalry remains a significant factor in France's Third World policy - he stated that, as a result of demographic growth

> pressure is constantly increasing in the global furnace, ...there is a slow yet irresistible, humble yet fierce, push towards life. And the reason is that this <u>tiers monde</u>, ignored, exploited, despised, like the <u>tiers état</u> [Third Estate], also wants to exist in its own right and be recognised.[2]

What is important in this conclusion is not so much the historical allusion to the Third Estate of 1789, the group of representatives of the French bourgeoisie and peasantry which was to bring about the abolition of privilege and set in train the events of the French Revolution (although the analogy is still sometimes to be found in French Third World rhetoric), but the recognition that the under-developed countries, like the Soviet and capitalist blocs, possess a degree if not of unity at least of solidarity of common interests.

This perception was to be reinforced by the meetings of the 'non-aligned' nations at Bandung (April 1955) and Belgrade (September 1961) and the Solidarity Conference of the Peoples of Asia, Africa and Latin America at Havana (January 1966), and by their taking up a central position on the world stage in the early 1960s with the admission to the United Nations of a large number of newly independent states. In France, the Third World debate was to be more highly politicised than in some other countries, partly because of the presence in France of a large number of immigrant workers from the developing countries and, in French universities, of groups of politically

aware students from the French colonies (many of
whom were to become the leaders of the newly independent states in France's immediate post-colonial
period). This debate also coincided with the
colonial wars in which France was engaged at the
time, Indochina until 1954 and then the Algerian
War. Les Damnés de la terre, by Frantz Fanon, a
doctor of West Indian origin and an anti-colonial-
ist activist, published in 1961 with a preface by
Jean-Paul Sartre,[3] was to have a considerable impact on French intellectuals. As an ideology, le
tiers-mondisme ('third worldism') was to give
Left-wing intellectuals an alternative to the Soviet model of society, while allowing them to
maintain their critique of capitalism as an economic system exploiting not only the proletariat
of the industrialised countries but also the im-
poverished underdeveloped countries. These elements were to provide the seed-bed for the emergence in the 1970s of the Socialist Party's Third
World doctrine. A major role was also played both
by French Protestants, and (in the wake of the en-
cyclicals Mater et Magistra and Populorum Progres-
sio) by French Catholics in the development of
third worldism in the immediate post-colonial period. Public attention was also drawn to Third
World problems by the publication of a large number of best-selling books on the subject, among
which mention might be made of the agronomist René
Dumont's L'Afrique noire est mal partie (1962)
(Black Africa has Got off to a Bad Start), the
sale of which was banned in some newly independent
former French colonies.[4]

Since the mid-seventies there has been a growing
reaction in French public opinion against third
worldist ideas. Many reasons may be adduced for
this. Not the least of these was the oil crisis of
1973-74, associated in the eyes of the general
public with the end of a sustained and unprecedented period of economic growth in France. Increasing unemployment, linked by some with the
large immigrant workforce in France and the competition to traditional French industries of cheap
Third World imports,[5] as well as the alleged mis-
use and waste of Western aid to the Third World,
constituted themes exploited by proponents of what
is known in French as le cartiérisme,[6] French
withdrawal from involvement with under-developed
countries, and not least in more recent years by
Jean-Marie Le Pen's extreme right-wing Front National. The recent controversy over the Carrefour

du Développement[7] has provided further ammunition to the anti-third worldists. Pascal Bruckner's <u>Le Sanglot de l'homme blanc</u> epitomises their arguments: third worldism is based on bad faith and hypocrisy and beneath the virtuous pronouncements lie egoism and pride:

> Solidarity with the oppressed peoples was from the beginning a vast war machine directed against the West. Its logic is a logic of war and its action a continuation of the Cold War by other means, the underdeveloped countries having replaced 'reformist' Soviet Russia in its role as world wide adversary of imperialism.[8]

At the same time there have also been in <u>Le Figaro magazine</u> and other Right-wing publications attacks on religious and charitable organisations concerned with Third World aid, such as the Comité Catholique contre la Faim et pour le Développement (CCFD), accused of propagating Marxist ideas.[9]

Third worldism has also come under scrutiny from the Socialist Left. In 1978, <u>Le Nouvel Observateur</u> published a series of articles, subsequently issued in book form,[10] criticising the Socialist Party's earlier lack of realism, and in 1984, following his resignation as Ministre délégué de la Coopération et du Développement in December 1982, Jean-Pierre Cot published a critique of the Mauroy government's Third World policies.[11]

After the earlier optimism and idealism, despite the Brandt reports and the pronouncements of the Club of Rome, but in face of the magnitude and complexity of the problems to be solved, the widespread famines, growing inequalities, the debt problem and the lack of success of initiatives such as the North/South dialogue and the New International Economic Order, disillusionment has entered French public opinion, exacerbated by the growth of nationalism and the outbreak of frontier wars in the Third World, by tribal rivalries and the violation of human rights in many African and other developing countries. Perhaps, it has been suggested, not all the ills of the Third World can be imputed to the earlier colonial powers, to capitalist exploitation and the 'unequal exchange'. Although this has not diminished the impact of the fund-raising campaigns by French non-governmental organisations (NGOs), especially at times of famine and drought, such aid represents only a small fraction of total French aid to the Third World and statistics indicate that in France wallets and cheque-books are taken out less readily than in some other countries.[12] It is against this background that French co-operation policy must be studied.

CONTINUITY AND CHANGE

It might be useful to recall here that the term 'Third World' itself, although widely used and convenient, defies easy definition. Various alternative expressions have been suggested: 'developing countries' (pays en voie de développement, or PVD), for example, but this term is in many cases contradicted by economic realities. The radical 'centre/periphery' dichotomy is open to intellectual and practical objections, and Mao Tse-tung's 'Three World' model (the two superpowers constituting the First, dominating, World; the other industrialised countries, both dominating and dominated, the Second; all the others - under Chinese leadership - making up the Third World) has also been contested. Subdivisions have emerged within the Third World, including on the one hand, the Newly Industrialising Countries (nouveaux pays industrialisés, NPI), and on the other, the Less Developed Countries (pays moins avancés, PMA), sometimes known as the Fourth World (Quart Monde). The purely statistical criterion (based on GNP per capita) having proved to be misleading, firstly because it fails to subsume areas such as health and education and secondly because in many cases the quasi-totality of a country's wealth is in the hands of a minute minority of a country's population, more specific criteria have been suggested. These have not been without their drawbacks, and in a United Nations context, a country is usually considered to be under-developed if it states that it is so.

For the purpose of this chapter, the term 'Third World' will be used, not in the broad sense of all those countries that do not belong either to the Western/capitalist or to the Eastern/Communist bloc, the original 'non-aligned' countries now representing three-quarters of the world's population, but in the narrower sense of those countries that are in receipt of French development aid in

one form or another; China is thus excluded
(although in some senses it may be considered as a
Third World country), as are most Middle East
countries (several of which are very poor). This
is not, however, as we shall see, to suggest that
the granting of Official Development Assistance
(ODA), to use the OECD terminology, is exempt from
geopolitical considerations (as in the French policy of interventionism in Sub-Saharan Africa) or
that it can be dissociated from the French vision
of its place in the world. Furthermore, it is not
always easy to separate economic, technical and
cultural aid, aimed at promoting development, from
military aid (the case of Sub-Saharan Africa again
being particularly relevant here). The French
Overseas Departments and Territories (the DOM-
TOMs) have been excluded here since they are not
sovereign states (and it is to the credit of the
post-1981 Socialist governments that in official
statistics DOM-TOM aid, variously calculated as
being between a third and a half of French bilateral public aid, has been clearly and separately
identified). Development aid can take many forms
(gifts and grants, loans, export credit guaran-
tees, technical and cultural assistance, preferen-
tial tariff arrangements, scholarships, etc.), may
be public (provided from state funds) or private,
bilateral or multilateral, and the latter is administered both by the various international institutions, including the United Nations' agencies, and by the EC.

In what must perforce be a 'broad brush' approach, this chapter examines a series of questions that throw light on France's place in the
world today. To what extent does the French colonial experience still colour current attitudes? To
what extent has there been continuity (or change)
from de Gaulle to Mitterrand, and then to the Mit-
terrand/Chirac 'cohabitation'? What exactly is
coopération, a term that has been used in French
since the immediate post-colonial period, in preference to aide/assistance au développement? To
what extent do the rhetoric of official discourse
and reality coincide?

France has significant potential for (and interest in) influencing EC policies and it is surely
not an accident that the post of Commissioner for
Development has largely been a French preserve. It
has indeed been argued that one of the purposes of
the Yaoundé Agreement, the predecessor of the Lomé
Agreements, the main instrument of EC-Third World

relations, was to permit France to share with its Community partners the burden of aid to its former colonies. With the accession of the UK, this aid was extended to the developing countries of the Commonwealth, and the EC now has partnership agreements with some sixty African, Caribbean and Pacific countries (the ACP countries) and other agreements with another sixty or so developing countries. However, Latin American and Southeast Asian programmes are limited, and most EC aid - which takes the form essentially of food aid, tariff preferences and guaranteed prices and quotas for some primary agricultural products - is channelled to former colonies of Community members.[13] As far as the international organisations are concerned, one can say in general terms that France has adopted, at least since the early seventies, a relatively high profile in the meetings of the United Nations' agencies (UNCTAD etc.), of the IMF and the World Bank,[14] that in these circles it enjoys a certain prestige in the eyes of Third World countries, in particular in its opposition to the USA' policies, but that its influence is limited by its position as only a medium-sized economic power. In GATT negotiations France has tended to adopt a more guarded position.

However, a constant feature of French development aid policy, not significantly reversed during the Socialist administration (1981-86), has been the preference shown for bilateral, at the expense of multilateral, aid. In 1964, Georges Pompidou, then Prime Minister, put forward the following arguments against multilateral aid: it is more bureaucratic, expensive and inefficient than bilateral aid; its priorities are established by majorities in the organisations concerned and are thus just as politically oriented as bilateral aid (with the unspoken assumption that the decisions might not be to France's liking); thirdly, international organisations foster the domination of the English language: 'But for us French there is a sort of need to maintain the influence of the French language, and therefore a fundamental reason for maintaining bilateral aid'.[15] There is little doubt but that these sentiments would be generally endorsed by official sources in France in the 1980s, whether the Left or the Right is in power.[16]

In addition to the importance attached to bilateral rather than multilateral aid, one can also detect, again in general terms, other aspects of

132

France's relations with the Third World where there has been, between de Gaulle, Pompidou, Giscard d'Estaing and Mitterrand, more continuity than change, and it has been suggested that, at least as far as the last three are concerned, the element of change has been rather between a certain renewal of policy at the beginning of each septennat and a subsequent return to a previously established pattern.[17] In the case of François Mitterrand, this seems to have been the case, for different reasons, both in respect to Algeria and to Latin America.

Although it would be wrong to suggest that the Fourth Republic was not concerned with development aid, the essential features of this pattern were established by de Gaulle during the early years of his Presidency, following the peaceful accession to independence of a large number of French colonies (and the effective demise of the French Community established by the Constitution of 1958) and the more dramatic solution to the Algerian problem. Although a late convert to the principle and process of decolonisation, de Gaulle came to accept its inevitability; indeed, in his frequent visits abroad, he wished to be seen as the champion of the newly liberated nations of the Third World in their struggle against imperialism. Independence was not to be seen as the breaking of French economic, military and cultural ties, the first two being marked by the franc zone and continued security involvement. He paid particular attention to Third World problems and during his Presidency French aid (expressed as a percentage of GNP) was the highest in the world, and at a level which it has not since reached (but a long way below the 3 per cent of GNP set as a target by the UN in the heady immediate post-war years). It cannot be denied, however, that the unpublicised activities of Jacques Foccart, a counter-espionage expert and de Gaulle's specialist in African affairs responsible for relations with the newly independent African states, present a more ambiguous side to France's relations with these states during de Gaulle's Presidency, involving direct intervention in the internal affairs of sovereign states. De Gaulle's Third World policy must clearly be seen as part of his overall objectives of restoring France to what he considered to be its rightful place in the world, of breaking down the division of the world into two opposing blocs and of countering the global influence of the USA.[18] It might be argued that certainly the first of these objectives, and, to a lesser and varying extent, perhaps the other two have remained a constant of France's Third World policy to this day.

John Frears is no doubt right to emphasise the continuity between de Gaulle and Giscard d'Estaing in Third World and particularly African affairs:[19] Giscard's mondialisme was little different from de Gaulle's grandeur; Giscard's rhetorical allusions to France's 'civilising mission' often echoed those of de Gaulle; foreign policy was still conducted from the Elysée Palace, and if Giscard dispensed with what John Frears has called the 'cloak and dagger' services of Jacques Foccart,[20] his successors were close associates of Foccart. If there was some decline in development aid to the Maghreb, especially Algeria, special importance was still attached to Sub-Saharan Africa. However, one also notes changes in emphasis in Giscard's policies, some initiatives (which often did not achieve anything like the desired results) and a deterioration in France's relations with many - if not all - developing countries. De Gaulle had enjoyed a certain prestige in the eyes of many Third World heads of state which Giscard did not share, partly because of a certain number of, to say the least, clumsy decisions.

The Paris Conference on International Economic Cooperation, CIEC (1975-77) (often called the North/South Dialogue) can hardly be said to have been in practical terms a resounding success, although it probably strengthened the unity and resolve of the Third World to bring about a new monetary order. Giscard's plan for an Arab-African-European trilogue was still-born. On the other hand, to the obvious displeasure of some African Francophone leaders, he opened up the annual Franco-African summits, established by his predecessor, Georges Pompidou, not only to former Belgian colonies but also to non-French speaking nations (former British and Portuguese colonies). Although it is difficult to discover any tangible results from what has been irreverently called the annual 'Franco-African High Mass', it still constitutes, with an increasing number of participants, and in spite of the different types of regime represented and the tensions between some of its members, a useful diplomatic forum.[21]

It is, however, in the strictly economic field that with Giscard d'Estaing one notes the most significant changes. These can perhaps be linked, to a large extent, to the oil crisis and the growth of competition in French and world markets from the Newly Industrialising Countries. It was recognised officially that there were limits to France's aid programme; Giscard d'Estaing's Prime Minister Raymond Barre stated in 1979: 'The industrialised countries' efforts in favour of the developing countries cannot be greater than in the past'.[22] Furthermore, less emphasis was laid on developmental aid in the strict sense of the term (for basic infrastructure, agricultural development, etc.) and more on commercial investment, large contracts (such as the Cairo underground railway) and credits for French exports. Such a policy, which has not been confined to France, has, it might justifiably be argued, exacerbated the Third World debt problem in the 1980s and favours countries expected to 'take off' economically, at the expense of the Less Developed Countries. Of course, de Gaulle had never concealed the economic advantages he expected France to reap from coopération, both in terms of French exports and of guaranteeing for French industry supplies of raw materials.[23] Nevertheless, in the 1970s, a clear change of emphasis may be noted.

A comparison between three official reports, the Jeanneney report (1963), the Gorse report (1970) and the Abelin report (1975), shows the evolution of policy towards the Third World. The first, entitled A Policy for Co-operation with the Developing Countries, stressed that co-operation must be disinterested and not based on the expectation of any political, economic or military advantage in return. Global solidarity should be the sole motive. Although never fully implemented, the Jeanneney report is indicative of the climate of the 1960s and remains the benchmark for more progressive French Third World policies. The Gorse report, commissioned by Georges Pompidou's first Prime Minister and advocate of the 'new society', Jacques Chaban-Delmas, was highly critical of French aid policy: it was too self-interested, too 'Africa-oriented' and transformed the countries in receipt of aid into clients; too great a place was taken by the teaching of the French language and by arms sales. The Gorse report was never published and President Pompidou expressed deep reservations about its contents.[24] The Abelin report, on the other hand, is marked by unashamed 'realism':

Our aim is one of mutual benefit; we must affirm in frankness and without any sense of guilt that France intends to develop its commercial and cultural relations with those regions of the world whose human development it wishes to foster, not only by reason of their raw materials but also of their human resources, their geographical importance and their historical echoes.[25]

A year after the publication of the Abelin report, the Minister for Co-operation, Robert Galley, stated:

The exploitation of these [African mineral] resources requires advanced technology and should be the occasion for greater industrial investment by [French] nationalised and private firms.... The French government's co-operation policy is not disinterested: in the long term, what is at stake is France's future, and not only her cultural influence [rayonnement] but also her political and economic security.[26]

A greater degree of regional specialisation, emphasis on 'mutual' benefit and reliance on private investment (with the expectation of tangible returns) characterised the Giscard era, together with a concern to avoid 'destabilisation' in sensitive areas and continued military presence in particular in Africa.[27]

Third World problems had never enjoyed a prominent place in French (or indeed any other) election manifestos. This was, however, not to be the case in 1981 with François Mitterrand's '110 Proposals for France'. Among the first of these were:

condemnation of US aid to Latin American dictatorships, call for an independent Chad, respect for Cambodian sovereignty, support for self-determination in Eritrea and the Western Sahara, priority to the North/South dialogue for the establishment of a new World Economic Order, the increase in public aid to the Third World to 0.7 per cent of the GNP in each developed country, definition of a new world monetary system through

reform of the IMF and the World Bank and
of the 'basket of currencies', a debt
moratorium and fresh liquidities for the
poorest countries of the Third World.[28]

Mitterrand's programme was both ambitious and
generous. For him widespread famine is nothing
short of genocide, and France's food aid programme
and financial transfers to Third World countries
should be increased as a matter of priority; emphasis should be placed on training in agricultural techniques and in computing. If demand were
stimulated, world economic recovery would be fostered, and this would benefit French industry and
agriculture. He called for new types of co-operation that would decrease the dependency of Third
World countries and denounced a situation whereby
the prosperity of the developed world was founded
on the poverty of the Third World. Human rights
also played an important part in Mitterrand's new
French policy for the Third World. Finally, he
promised to bring greater clarity into the real
magnitude of French co-operation with the Third
World by ensuring that DOM-TOM transfers would be
excluded from the official statistics of French
development aid.[29] Furthermore, in a policy statement by the newly-elected President of the Republic, published in July-August 1981 in Actuel-
Développement, he added the intention to restruc-
ture France's official aid and development machinery, to concentrate less on Sub-Saharan Africa and
other Francophone countries, to reduce assistance
to reactionary regimes, to favour aid that would
foster self-reliance and economic independence
(développement auto-centré) rather than aid based
on essentially French commercial or other considerations, actively to promote initiatives in international organisations and in the EC, and to
provide greater support to the activities of Non-
Governmental Organisations.[30] (Subsequently the
Socialist governments of 1981-86 were to lay great
stress on the value of associations, the voluntary
organisations.)

Election promises, of course, are exactly that.
And it is understandable that in the first flush
of victory the Socialist President should put forward aims that proved to be beyond his grasp. In a
very lucid and cogently argued article, particularly concerned with Africa,[31] Tony Chafer has
analysed the internal and external reasons why
Mitterrand's innovatory 'new deal' has not materi-

alised: his margin for manoeuvre was limited,
there was disagreement even within the government
in respect to the implementation of the aid programme, and, in order to preserve jobs in France,
he was unable to resist pressure from the industrial lobby in favour of major projects not
specifically designed to increase the self-sufficiency of Third World countries. For example, the
Burundi colour television project, personally approved by François Mitterrand, against the advice
of his Minister for Co-operation and Development,
Jean-Pierre Cot, was arguably not the first priority for that country, though its government, no
doubt for reasons of prestige, presumably at least
agreed to its installation.

On the other hand, bilateral state aid (aide
publique au développement, APD), which had declined during the Giscard era, began to move
steadily towards the target of 0.7 per cent of
GNP, as can be seen from the following figures
(with the DOM-TOMs excluded): 1979 - 0.34 per
cent; 1980 - 0.36 per cent; 1981 - 0.45 per cent;
1982 - 0.49 per cent; 1983 - 0.48 per cent; 1984 -
0.52 per cent; 1985 - 0.54 per cent; an average
annual increase of 10.1 per cent between 1979-80
and 1984-85.[32] Although in questions of aid and
development, where the quality of the assistance
is usually of greater importance than the volume
and statistics need to be treated with more than
usual caution, it might be noted that in 1985 this
placed France in joint fifth position (with Belgium) among the eighteen member states of the
OECD Development Assistance Committee (DAC), below Norway, the Netherlands, Denmark and Sweden,
but above, for example, the Federal Republic of
Germany (0.47 per cent), Japan (0.29 per cent),
the UK (0.34 per cent) and the USA (0.24 per
cent).[33]

The dominant position still held by Sub-Saharan
Africa among the recipients of French bilateral
aid may be seen from the following percentages
(1984, DOM-TOMs excluded): Southern Europe, 1 per
cent; North Africa, 12.4 per cent; Sub-Saharan
Africa, 55.4 per cent; Latin America, 5.1 per
cent; Near East, 2.3 per cent; Southern Asia, 3.8
per cent; Far East and Oceania, 5.6 per cent (no
breakdown by region is possible for the remaining
14.4 per cent).[34] Thus, in spite of Mitterrand's
much publicised visit to Central America for the
Cancun Conference of October 1981, development aid
to Latin America is still a relatively small

proportion of total French aid, given the needs of that continent. With respect to the Near East where, in particular in Lebanon and to a lesser extent in Syria and in Egypt, France had for many years enjoyed a privileged educational and cultural presence, there are clear indications that this influence has declined and is continuing to decline rapidly.[35]

Total French aid in 1984 (DOM-TOMs excluded) was 65.3 billion francs (1.53 per cent of GNP), broken down as follows:

(a) Bilateral aid - 16.9 billion francs
(b) Multilateral aid - 5.4 billion francs
(c) Other contributions from the public sector - 9.3 billion francs
(d) Contributions by the private sector - 33.8 billion francs (of which 18.5 billion are guaranteed export credits, 15 billion loans and investments and 0.2 billion gifts by charitable organisations).

Perhaps the main feature that distinguishes French bilateral aid from that of other OECD DAC countries is the predominance of cultural and technical assistance, more than half of the total, in the form of specialists on short-term secondment to Third World countries, known in French as coopérants. The majority of these, 8,022 out of 10,811 in 1982, are teachers,[36] and many are graduate volunteers who, instead of doing their national service in the French armed forces, opt to spend a longer period in a Third World country. Although the number of coopérants has fallen significantly since the end of the Gaullist era, France provides more assistance in this form than any other country of the North. As may be expected, for linguistic if for no other reasons, most are appointed to French-speaking countries.

In spite of Mitterrand's programme (with which the first Socialist Minister for Co-operation and Development, Jean-Pierre Cot's, statements were not entirely consistent), and in spite of a not insignificant increase in multilateral aid, bilateral rather than multilateral aid is still the principal channel for French public aid.   Furthermore, it can safely be assumed that, with the exception of the charitable gifts, the contributions of the private sector are made as much in the expectation of an early profit as in the interests of the recipients.

Mitterrand achieved, in spite of an inauspicious domestic economic climate, a significant increase in French state aid. However, as has been shown conclusively by Adrian Hewitt,[37] although the Elysée continued to show a close interest in Third World problems, Mitterrand failed to modify substantially other established patterns of French relations with the Third World. No significant change was noted in the 'tied' aid policy, Africa still received the lion's share of French aid and the decision-making process in Paris was still marked by inter-ministerial rivalry.[38] Of course, it can be argued that changes such as those put forward by Mitterrand in 1981 can only be achieved gradually, prior commitments have to be honoured and structural and administrative inertia surmounted.

Even within the government, voices were heard extolling the virtues of combining 'continuity' with 'change' in co-operation policy. In September 1982, Cot wrote:

> I have never claimed to have broken with everything that has been done in the past.... The main difference [from my predecessors] is perhaps that we have not only made speeches, but we have put into concrete application the conclusions of certain analyses made in the past but which have never been translated into political action.[39]

Cot's forced 'resignation' in December 1982 highlights not only the difficulties encountered by the Socialists in implementing their Third World policies but also some of the ambiguities of France's activities in this field and the gulf that often seems to exist between discourse and effective action. It seems clear that, in addition to clashes of personality and the traditional rivalry between the Ministry for Co-operation, the Foreign Ministry and the Presidential advisor for African and Madagascan affairs (a post maintained by Mitterrand and first held by Guy Penne with, as his assistant, the President's son, Jean-Christophe Mitterrand), Cot, an enthusiastic and generous third worldist and adversary of 'prestige' aid projects (such as the Burundi television), had alienated certain heads of state of African countries whose friendship the Elysée valued (including, it has been suggested, those where respect for human rights is not the first priority). It has been claimed that Cot had wished to achieve greater diversification of French aid to continents other than Africa, to provide greater support for the voluntary aid and relief organisations, to decrease drastically the amount of French aid devoted to maintaining costly bureaucracies in the recipient countries and to reduce French links with South Africa to a strict minimum. While the President maintained that it was possible to reconcile the constraints of reality and of existing commitments with the ultimate goals to be achieved, Michel Rocard, in an article in Le Monde defending Cot and claiming that Cot had while in office pursued the policies advocated by the Socialists when in opposition, wrote: 'It is thanks to him that a new wind is blowing through France's co-operation policy, which still bore the marks of the colonial inheritance'.[40]

Thus, in recent years continuity has been the dominant feature of French relations with the Third World, and things could hardly have been different for the period since March 1986, with a Socialist President and professed third worldist (who, however, had failed from 1981 to 1986 to achieve more than a few of his ambitious and generous aims and for whom Realpolitik was to become the basis of his action), 'cohabiting' with a Right-wing Prime Minister, a proponent of 'neo-liberalism' who yet remains, as far as France's place in the world and the pre-eminent place of French-speaking Africa in France's aid programme are concerned, in the Gaullist tradition. For Jacques Chirac (not unlike Mitterrand) it is the private banks, the USA and Japan, which are responsible for the dramatic debt situation of some Third World countries.[41] Unlike Chirac's New Caledonia policy, which François Mitterrand has not hesitated to criticise publicly, France's co-operation policy does not seem to have created any major problems between the President and his 'cohabiting' Prime Minister. In the 1988 budget, prepared by the Minister for Co-operation and close associate of Jacques Chirac, Michel Aurillac, provision has been made to increase ODA to 0.54 per cent of GNP in 1988 and to increase the number of coopérants.[42] Chirac is formally committed to achieving the 0.70 per cent target 'as soon as possible', with a high priority attached to sub-Saharan Africa.[43]

CONCLUSION

Although co-operation policy should not only be considered as a branch of foreign policy, they are of course very closely linked. The influence of the advisor on African and Madagascan problems, from Jacques Foccart to Guy Penne, appointed by successive Presidents (who under the Fifth Republic have a special responsibility for foreign affairs), and the fact that a significant proportion of development aid is channelled through the Ministry of Foreign Affairs, provide evidence of this. Co-operation policy thus tends to follow the dictates of foreign policy, not only in its broad geopolitical, strategic or economic orientations, in its adherence to the doctrine of national independence,[44] in its ambitions for maintaining and strengthening France's place in the world, in its concern to prevent destabilisation in particular regions of interest and - one must add - in maintaining French-speaking Sub-Saharan Africa as a privileged zone of influence, but also in France's relations with particular Third World countries, be they 'friendly', hostile or just important suppliers of much needed raw materials. Recently, for example, it was decided to reduce French aid to Vanuatu in view of the latter's hostility to French policy in New Caledonia.[45] Frequently security involvement and French military presence, not to speak of arms sales, all of which which lie beyond the scope of this chapter, go hand-in-hand with co-operation.

French co-operation policy exhibits a degree of duality[46] and even of ambiguity.[47] The term 'co-operation' itself is ambitious, implying as it does an equality in partnership, active participation of the recipient countries, freeing them from the frustration they feel at their inequality and relieving them of their burden of being assistés. Yet there has been in France itself, as well as abroad, no shortage of critics accusing successive French governments of paternalism, neo-colonialism and imperialism. Official discourse is based on the notions of solidarity and interdependence, but also on France's 'civilising mission', an idea going back to the nineteenth century, and the importance of French culture and the French language (the famous rayonnement). The emphasis on aid to former colonies, characteristic not only of France but also of the UK, Belgium, Australia and elsewhere, may be seen as a continuation, in other forms, of a colonial past or, on the other hand, as a normal tendency, given the common links of language, tradition and habit. The franc zone probably has disadvantages as well as benefits for those Third World countries it embraces. Although it is possible to criticise the types of aid provided by France (and, in particular, the 'tied' nature of much of this aid), nevertheless, as far as volume is concerned, France's position among the industrialised countries of the North is a respectable one. Given the present climate of protectionism and the concern to improve the balance of payments and save French jobs, the evolution of French co-operation with developing countries may depend on the ability of governments to convince public opinion that Third World development aid is at least as important as assistance to the relatively poor regions of metropolitan France, in other words to go beyond what is seen by many Frenchmen as a stark alternative: le Zambèze ou la Corrèze?[48]

NOTES AND REFERENCES

1. After the journalist Raymond Cartier, see note 6 below.
2. Sauvy's paternity has been contested by Peter Worsley ('How Many Worlds?', Third World Quarterly, Vol. 1 (1979), p. 101). Citing Claude Bourdet, Worsley argues that the term tiers monde was in general use as early as 1949, but primarily in connection with internal national politics in European countries, rather than with governments or states. The extract from Sauvy's Observateur article is quoted in Yves Lacoste, Contre les anti-tiers-mondistes et contre certains tiers-mondistes (Editions La Découverte, Paris 1986), p. 68. Yves Lacoste is one of the major French writers on Third World problems, and in this, his latest work, he attempts 'to demystify third worldism in order to make it more effective'. See also by Lacoste: Géographie du sous-développement (PUF, Paris, 5th ed., 1982); Unité et diversité du Tiers-Monde (Maspéro, Paris, 1980); Les Pays sous-développés (PUF, Paris, 7th ed., 1984).
3. Frantz Fanon, Les Damnés de la terre, preface by Jean-Paul Sartre (Maspéro, Paris, 1961).
4. René Dumont, L'Afrique noire est mal partie (Seuil, Paris, 1966). In his latest work, Pour l'Afrique, j'accuse. Le Journal d'un agronome au Sahel en voie de destruction (Plon, Paris, 1986), Dumont's prognosis remains equally sombre.
5. When the Socialists, committed third worldists,

came to power in 1981, they immediately commissioned a study
of the impact of the evolution of the Third World on the
French economic and employment situation; it has been published as Yves Berthelot and Jacques de Bandt, Impact des
relations avec le Tiers-Monde sur l'économie française, 2
vols. (Documentation française, Paris, 1982).

6.   After the journalist Raymond Cartier, whose articles in Paris Match in the 1960s advocated French withdrawal
into the Hexagon. See, in particular, 'Attention, la France
dilapide son argent' ('Watch out! France is throwing its
money down the drain'), Paris Match, 29 February, 7 and 14
March 1964.

7.   The director of an organisation for developing
greater public awareness of Third World problems, established by the Minister for Co-operation and Development under the Socialist government, had been accused of gross mis-
appropriation of public funds. At the end of 1987 he had not
been brought to trial, and although the facts are far from
clear, as is the degree of involvement of the Minister himself, Christian Nucci, who is to be arraigned before a Parliamentary High Court, the 'scandal' has received widespread publicity.

8.   Pascal Bruckner, Le Sanglot de l'homme blanc. Tiers
Monde, culpabilité, haine de soi (Seuil, Paris, 1983), p.
36. See also 'Les Impostures du Tiers-Mondisme', Paris
Match, 22 February 1985.

9.   See 'Ces Archanges qui pourfendent l'hérésie', Le
Monde diplomatique, June 1986, p. 6.

10.   André Burguière (ed.), Le Tiers Monde et la Gauche,
Preface by Jean Daniel (Seuil, Paris, 1979).

11.   Jean-Pierre Cot, A l'Epreuve du pouvoir. Le Tiers-
mondisme, pour quoi faire? (Seuil, Paris, 1984). For details
of Cot's critique, see below.

12.   For an analysis of French Third World NGOs, see
Charles Condamines, 'Le Grand Bazar de la Charité', Le Monde
diplomatique, September 1986, pp. 20-21. In 1983, $45 mil-
lion was received by these organisations from private
sources (i.e., excluding government grants); the correspond-
ing figures for some other developed countries were: West
Germany $398 million, the Netherlands $120 million, UK $116
million, Sweden $83 million. Among the more important French
Third World NGOs may be noted: the Comité catholique contre
la Faim et pour le Développement, the non-confessional
Fréres des Hommes, Secours Populaire Français, the French
section of UNICEF (to which the French are the largest contributors after Canada and the USA), and, in the field of
health care and training, Médecins sans Frontiéres and
Médecins du Monde, which in late 1987 took over SOS Sahel.

13.   See Carol Cosgrave Twitchett, 'The European Community and Regional Co-operation in the Third World', in
Kenneth J. Twitchett (ed.), European Co-operation Today

(Europa Publications Ltd., London, 1980), pp. 71-86.

14. However, for a recent French critical analysis of these organisations, see Gilles Nicolas, 'Faut-il brûler les banques d'aide au développement?', Le Monde, 29 September 1987, p. 31.

15. Quoted in Patrick Cadenat, La France et le Tiers-Monde, vingt ans de coopération bilatérale (Documentation française, Paris, 1983), p. 6.

16. In Le Monde of 30 September 1982, Jean-Pierre Cot wrote: 'France will have a preference for bilateral aid which is more efficient and effective both for the donor and for the recipients'. The contradiction between this and Mitterrand's pronouncements on the same subject in 1981-82 is apparent.

17. Hervé Cassan, 'France and the Third World' in Peter Morris and Stuart Williams (eds), France in the World (Association for the Study of Modern and Contemporary France, Nottingham, 1985), p. 87. For other studies of France's Third World policies see: Yves Berthelot, 'France's Third World Policy: Problems of Change', in Christopher Stevens (ed.), EEC and the Third World (Hodder and Stoughton, London, 1983), pp. 28-41; J. Barron Boyd, 'France and the Third World: the African Connection', in Phillip Taylor and Gregory A. Raymond (eds), Third World Policies of Industrialised Nations (Greenwood Press, Westport, 1982), pp. 45-65; Miles Kahler, 'International Response to the Economic Crisis: France and the Third World in the 1970s', in Stephen S. Cohen and Peter A. Gourevitch (eds), France in the Troubled World Economy (Butterworth, London, 1982), pp. 76-96; W. H. Morris-Jones and Georges Fischer (eds), Decolonisation and After: The British and French Experience (Frank Cass, London, 1980); Hassan M. Selim, Development Assistance Policies and the Performances of Aid Agencies (Macmillan, London, 1983), especially pp. 80-96.

18. For a detailed analysis of de Gaulle's Third World policies, see Charles de Gaulle and Institut du Droit de la Paix et du Développement, De Gaulle et le Tiers-Monde (Pédone, Paris, 1984).

19. John Frears, France in the Giscard Presidency (Allen and Unwin, London, 1981), pp. 96-7 and 109-20.

20. Ibid., p. 109.

21. For the development of these summits, see Claude Wauthier, 'Les Sommets franco-africains, symboles de continuité', Le Monde diplomatique, November 1986, p. 30.

22. Quoted in J.-Y. Carfantan and C. Condamines, Qui a peur du Tiers-monde? (Seuil, Paris, 1980), p.109.

23. In, for example, his press conference of 31 January 1964.

24. Cadenat, La France et le Tiers Monde, p. 20.

25. Quoted in Carfantan and Condamines, Qui a peur du Tiers-Monde?, p. 106.

26. Ibid., p. 106.
27. For an analysis of French military involvement in Africa, see John Chipman, French Military Policy and African Security (International Institute for Strategic Studies, London, 1985).
28. Quoted in C. Manceron and B. Pingaud, François Mitterrand - L'Homme, les Idées, le Programme (Flammarion, Paris, 1981), pp. 170-1.
29. Ibid., pp. 146-7.
30. Summarised in Adrian P. Hewitt, 'France, the Third World and the North/South Dialogue in the 1980's: Old Habits Die Hard', in Morris and Williams (eds), France in the World, pp. 91-92.
31. Tony Chafer, 'Mitterrand and Africa: 1981-1984. Policy and Practice', in Modern and Contemporary France, Vol. 23 (October 1985), pp. 3-12.
32. OECD figures, quoted in Quid 1987 (RTL-Robert Laffont, Paris, 1986), p. 1461, and OECD, Development Co-operation: 1986 Review (OECD, Paris, 1987), p. 52.
33. OECD, Development Co-operation: 1986 Review, p.72. These figures do not, of course, indicate the variations in the type of aid provided: Denmark and the Netherlands, for example, have a preference for multilateral aid; French, Swedish and Norwegian aid is made up essentially of grants, whereas the Federal Republic of Germany prefers loans. France, Belgium and the UK concentrate their aid effort on their former colonies. France was not one of the ten OECD Development Assistance Committee members who, in 1975, signed a Memorandum of Agreement 'untying' aid grants.
34. The source of these figures, and of those that follow, is Quid 1987, p. 1461.
35. See J.-P. Péroncel-Hugoz, 'La Coopération franco-libanaise en question: réaménagements ou restrictions?', Le Monde, 25-26 August 1985, p. 10, and 'La Politique française au Proche-Orient. Hier et aujourd'hui', a debate published in Esprit, N.S. 11, June 1987, pp. 54-80.
36. Patrick Cadenat, La France et le Tiers-Monde, p. 162.
37. Adrian P. Hewitt, 'France, the Third World and the North-South Dialogue in the 1980's: Old Habits Die Hard', in Morris and Williams (eds), France in the World, pp. 91-97.
38. Since 1962, when the first Ministère de la Coopéra-tion was established, it has traditionally been responsible for France's ex-colonies, thus, at least initially, provid-ing a degree of continuity with the colonial administration, while other Third World countries have been the responsibil-ity of the Foreign Ministry. However, the latter has a close and direct interest in all Third World countries, and this has periodically led to difficulties within the administra-tion. The post of Minister for Co-operation was abolished in 1966 only to be re-established by Giscard d'Estaing in 1974.

Under the Socialists, both Jean-Pierre Cot and his successor, Christian Nucci, held the title of Ministre délégué,
responsible to the Foreign Minister. In Chirac's 1986 administration, the Ministry for Co-operation has again become an
autonomous Ministry. Other government departments, for example the Ministries of Education, Agriculture, Telecommunications and, of course, Finance, together with certain
specialised agencies (especially the Caisse Centrale de
Coopération Economique, CCCE, and the Fonds d'Aide et de
Coopération, FAC) have overseas development responsibilities
which they jealously guard. And, of course, each of the
Fifth Republic Presidents has taken a close interest in
Third World problems and has appointed to his staff a specialist solely responsible for this area of national policy.
For a detailed analysis of the administration of French co-
operation, see Cadenat, La France et le Tiers-Monde.

39. Quoted by Cadenat, La France et le Tiers-Monde, p.
20.

40. Quoted in L'Année politique - 1982 (Editions du
Moniteur, Paris, 1983), p. 103. See René Backmann, 'La
Dernière colère de Jean-Pierre Cot', Le Nouvel Observateur,
11-17 December 1982, p. 28, and Georges Mamy, 'Affaire Cot:
Mitterrand s'explique', Le Nouvel Observateur, 18-24
December 1982, p. 25. Also Le Monde, 9, 10 and 15 December
1982.

41. Le Monde, 2 September 1987, p. 3.

42. Le Monde, 18 September 1987, p. 31.

43. OECD, Development Co-operation - 1986 Report, p.
70.

44. In this respect, the granting of French aid to
Nicaragua in 1981 is symptomatic: Mitterrand was committed
to providing more aid to Latin America, but in doing so provoked the hostility of the United States; he based his decision on the need to prevent the Sandinistas from falling
into the Soviet orbit.

45. Le Monde, 3 October 1987, p. 6.

46. Hervé Cassan, 'France and the Third World', in
Morris and Williams (eds), France in the World, p. 87.

47. Cadenat, La France et le Tiers-Monde, p. 21.

48. Carfantan and Condamines, Qui a peur du tiers
monde?, p. 110.

Chapter Seven

REMNANTS OF EMPIRE: FRANCE'S OVERSEAS DEPARTMENTS
AND TERRITORIES

John Connell and Robert Aldrich

The base for France's role in world politics is
not limited to the Hexagon. Indeed, the territory
of the Republic extends beyond Europe to the Atlantic and Caribbean, the Pacific and the Indian
Ocean. In its ten départements et territoires
d'outre-mer (DOM-TOMs), the remains of its colonial empire, Paris enjoys a right of sovereignty
in all the world's oceans and can legitimately
claim to be neighbour to all the globe's continents. The DOM-TOMs provide prestige, natural resources, access to vast maritime zones, strategic
possibilities, voters, migrants and tropical cli-
mates. Constitutionally, Fort-de-France, Martinique, and Saint-Dénis, Réunion, are as much a
part of France as Dijon or Aix-en-Provence. Some
of the islands have been attached to France longer
than Franche-Comté, Nice or Corsica, yet activists
within and critics outside have demanded that
France 'decolonise' its possessions. The space
launches from French Guiana (Guyane), the nuclear
experiments in French Polynesia and the violent
confrontation in New Caledonia testify to the
value, and the controversy, of the French outre-
mer. Often overlooked in studies of France, in reality, these far-flung outposts occupy a central
position in France's global strategy. Jacques
Chirac is quoted as saying 'Without the DOM and
TOMs, France would only be a little country'.[1]
    The remnants of France's massive colonial empire
are mostly quite large islands, some larger than
Corsica. They have a combined population of more
than 1.6 million people and jointly command an 11
million square kilometre Exclusive Economic Zone
(EEZ), giving France the third largest maritime
zone in the world. The departments are closely
tied to France, with Paris represented by prefects
(Préfets-Commissaires de la République) like those
of French metropolitan departments, and though
they have conseils généraux and conseils ré-
gionaux, these have limited powers. The territo-

148

ries are generally administered by High Commis-
sioners alongside an assembly that has more substantial powers than that of a department. Collec-
tively the departments and territories are the
brief of the French Ministry of Overseas Departments and Territories. Together they constitute a
significant proportion of the 'confetti of empire'
that remain in the world.[2]

Table 1   French Overseas Departments and
           Territories

	Population 1983	Area (Sq.kms)
Departments		
French Guiana (Guyane)	73.012	91.000
Guadeloupe and Dependencies	328.400 *	1.780
Martinique	326.428 *	1.100
Réunion	515.814 *	2.510
Territories		
French Polynesia	166.753	4.000
New Caledonia and Dependencies	145.368	19.000
Wallis and Futuna	12.391	.274
TAAF	-	
Territorial Collectives		
Saint-Pierre and Miquelon	6.041 *	.242
Mayotte	55.000 approx.	.275

* 1982 population figure.

THE HISTORICAL ROLE OF THE DOM-TOMS

Of all France's DOM-TOMs Guadeloupe, Martinique
and Réunion are the oldest, the three island anciennes colonies through which France established
its imperial power. Acquired in the 1630s, all

three regions in two oceans, have had similar patterns of development, as the sugar-fields of
France, and all have similar ethnically mixed populations and high population densities. Saint-
Pierre and Miquelon, two tiny islands with a fishing base off the south coast of Newfoundland, are
all that remains of France's formidable North
American empire, and Guyane, which only formally
became a French possession in 1816, is France's
only South American territory. The Pacific territories were more recent acquisitions; in Oceania,
there was less of a contest for colonies, other
than with the British, whom France narrowly beat
for both New Caledonia and French Polynesia.
France established a protectorate over Tahiti and
the Marquesas in 1842 and took formal possession
of New Caledonia in 1853. In the 1880s, France annexed Tahiti and neighbouring islands (now called
French Polynesia) and took over the small islands
of Wallis and Futuna, which lie midway between New
Caledonia and Tahiti.

France also over the years acquired rights to
various uninhabited islands in the Antarctic
ocean, as well as rights to Terre Adélie on the
Antarctic continent; these, administered from
Paris and without a permanent population, are
grouped as the Terres Australes et Antarctiques
(TAAF). Finally, there is, in a sense, the last
DOM-TOM to be acquired. When the Indian Ocean Comoros islands moved to independence in the 1970s
the residents of Mayotte voted almost unanimously
against inclusion in the new republic and France
retained control of the island.

The three anciennes colonies were run by semi-
private companies for most of the first century of
their existence and, through sugar and slavery,
became prosperous. However, since the the nineteenth century, their history has been difficult.
The abolition of slavery did not lead to any economic diversification and a serious shortage of
labour resulted. Through migration, especially
from India, in conditions little different from
slavery, sugar cane briefly revived until beet
production in Europe caused a disastrous slump.
This migration precipitated an even greater mixture of ethnic groups in the populations. Guyane
experienced a gold rush in the late 1800s but was
better known as a penal colony; it remained thinly
populated and unproductive. In each of the anciennes colonies, though direct exploitation inevitably waned, the colonial era was far from

over, and sugar continued to dominate the economy through the first half of the twentieth century.[3]

French interests in the Pacific were initially strategic (and missionary) rather than economic. However France was the largest European importer of copra in the nineteenth century, and the Pacific was the major supplier. By the end of the 1800s, New Caledonia was the world's largest exporter of nickel, essential as an alloy in steel and in increasing demand for armaments. Phosphate was later mined in French Polynesia. The islands also provided a source of various tropical products, including coffee, vanilla, pearls and, for a time, cotton, but none ever flourished over long periods. France also used New Caledonia as a penitentiary, in preference to Guyane, and transported some 10,000 convicts and political prisoners to Oceania. Lack of labour, capital, markets and greater shipping connections with France, however, limited economic development. Settlers were slow in migrating to the French Pacific, although New Caledonia eventually became France's only real settler colony other than Algeria. Colonists then imported Asian workers for their plantations and mines and marginalised native Melanesian and Polynesian islanders. The indigenous population diminished considerably after the European arrival, not to begin a recovery until the 1920s. Polynesians retained much of their land, but colonists in New Caledonia confined Melanesians to reservations. These structures were consolidated in the first half of the twentieth century with programmes for economic development, most of which were abject failures, and continued Asian immigration.[4]

Elsewhere, fish made up Saint-Pierre and Miquelon's only export. Wallis and Futuna, in the Pacific, and Mayotte, in the Indian Ocean, had subsistence economies and almost no exports. By the mid-twentieth century, the future DOM-TOMs were primarily producers of raw materials and importers of French manufactured goods and capital. Multicultural populations existed in most of the territories, and included white settlers, Africans, Indians, Asians and, in the regions which had been inhabited when the French arrived, indigenous residents; in the Antilles and Tahiti, frequent intermarriage had also produced a mixed-blood population. At this time, when the French empire included much of Africa, Madagascar and Indochina, these small islands were minor members of the imperial family.

THE CONTEMPORARY DOM-TOMS

The period after 1945 brought substantial economic
change to this group of colonies, which the con-
stitutions of the Fourth and Fifth Republics
transformed into <u>départements et territoires
d'outre-mer</u>. Already they seemed less than healthy
economies.[5] Only emigration seemed to offer real
prospects for any kind of development. In the
decades to come dependence worsened and from each
of the <u>anciennes colonies</u> in the Caribbean and Indian Ocean, now French departments, migration to
France boomed. In the TOMs, France reasserted its
authority, funding steadily increased and these
territories entered into a new phase of change
that virtually took them, in little more than a
century, from subsistence to subsidy.

Martinique, Réunion and Guadeloupe have now
reached a situation of economic crisis, with the
collapse of the sugar industry and minimal diversification, exacerbated by high population densities, excessive rural-urban migration, high unemployment, a chronic balance of payments deficit
and urbanised societies that have come to rely exceptionally on French transfer payments. Agriculture has declined, the terms of trade have worsened, imports are many times the value of exports
(in Réunion eight times), and in the French
Caribbean there is now an 'economic fiasco, a society which consumes but which produces practically nothing',[6] simply a 'consumer colony'.[7] More
than two-thirds of all employment in each of the
DOMs is in the tertiary sector; salaries account
for more than half of all government expenditure
in Réunion. Once the backbone of so much of the
West Indies and the Indian Ocean, the sugar industry has largely given way to tourism and bananas,
another commodity that has an uncertain future and
is particularly hazard-prone, though it remains
the dominant export in Réunion. Although constant
reference to high standards of living, amongst the
highest in the Caribbean and the Indian Ocean, is
used to justify the French presence, to the extent
that there is a 'fetishism of money',[8] huge income
disparities between French bureaucrats, the white
land-owning bourgeoisie and unemployed farm
labourers are difficult to disguise. Caribbean activists argue that only independence can destroy
the feudal powers of the colonial oligarchies,
propped up by the French state, though <u>indépendan-
tistes</u> remain a tiny minority and are virtually

non-existent in Réunion.

Lack of employment opportunities in the DOMs has
emphasised the standard West Indian response to
limited development: emigration. Migration to
France increased steadily in the 1960s, and by the
1970s the annual emigration had created a static
population in the islands. For two decades migration was sponsored by the Bureau pour le
Développement des Migrations intéressant les Départements d'Outre-Mer (BUMIDOM), founded in 1963
to reduce island unemployment and introduce cheap
labour into France.[9] So rapid has emigration from
the anciennes colonies become that at the time of
the 1982 census 282,300 migrants from the DOM-TOMs
lived in France, the vast majority from Martinique
(95,700), Guadeloupe (87,000) and Réunion
(75,700); this total was 64 per cent greater than
during the 1975 census, so that more than one person in five born in the Caribbean now lives in
metropolitan France.[10] The remittances from these
migrants contribute a key element in the economic
organisation of the overseas departments. Emigration has encouraged assimilation, decreased unemployment and reduced discontent; for Michel Debré,
RPR deputy for Réunion, and former French Prime
Minister, not only does migration assist in incor-
porating the DOM-TOMs more firmly into France but
'the direct consequence of ending migration would
be a revolutionary situation'.[11]

The DOMs, French Polynesia and especially New
Caledonia have also seen a steady migration of European French, so much so that in the Caribbean
'the recent influx of métropolitains looking for a
place in the sun has only made a racially dis-
turbed and unequal situation worse.[12] Large numbers of white immigrants to the islands have entered the civil service, professions and busi-
nesses, even taking up menial jobs. This migration
has reduced the proportion of the black population
so severely in the Antilles that some West Indians
have spoken, somewhat unrealistically, of genocide
by substitution, whilst in New Caledonia, Melanesians have been reduced to a minority of the total
population.

The situation of Guyane is almost as unbalanced
as in the Caribbean islands. The major activity is
the French space station at Kourou, which largely
employs metropolitan engineers and technicians.
Some 65 per cent of the formal workforce are in
the tertiary sector (almost all in the bureaucracy) and no more than 15 per cent work in the

agricultural sector. Agriculture has steadily declined, little land is cultivated and the young
are increasingly uninterested in an agricultural
career. With an area a sixth that of metropolitan
France, Guyane is by far the largest and most
thinly-populated DOM-TOM, with a wholly undevel-
oped interior still dominated by forests and Indian subsistence economies. Massive financial assistance has contributed to high wages and living
standards. Though official attempts to encourage
the growth of a settler colony failed, with the
exception of a settlement of Laotian refugees, a
substantial influx of illegal migrants has come
mainly from Surinam, Haiti and Brazil. The population doubled in two decades and, in 1982, only 57
per cent of the population had been born there,
and a further 11 per cent in metropolitan France.

The only other French possession in America and
the smallest of France's territories, Saint-Pierre
and Miquelon, has a slowly growing population of
6,000 since its decline to 3918 in 1921. Before
colonial days the islands had no indigenous population, and most of its present residents were
born there. Previously a department, in 1985 it
became a 'territorial collectivity' giving it
marginally increased autonomy and better trade relations with North America. With an economy solely
dependent on fishing, and a trivial amount of
tourism, and imports twice the value of exports it
is propped up by French finance and most employment comes from the bureaucracy. Emigration to
Canada rivals migration to France.

The productive economy of the 'territorial collectivity' of Mayotte remains wholly agricultural. Exports have declined since 1981; imports
have increased to the extent that their value is
more than thirty times that of exports, creating a
massive trade imbalance that must be supported by
French assistance. France directly provides almost
40 per cent of the budget, much of which is directed towards creating an economic infrastructure
and of building up the bureaucracy. Even in the
brief period since secession from the Comoros in
1975 every form of agriculture has slumped as
agriculturalists have preferred wage labour. In
less than a decade the island that was once the
poorest in the Comoros has become the richest and
most dependent.

In some respects Mayotte is similar to the least
known French territory, Wallis and Futuna. Both
Polynesian islands have highly stratified soci-

eties where the kings retain considerable authority, now alongside the Catholic church. The combination of one church, three monarchies, cultural
homogeneity on each island, small size and unusual
isolation have given the territory an exceptionally conservative social and economic system. The
description of the territory as being in a situation of 'total dependency'[13] is most apt. The only
exports in the 1980s have been trochus shells (1.5
tonnes in 1983); imports total more than a thousand times the value of exports. Though the subsistence economy remains viable (despite high population densities), cash crops have been wholly
unsuccessful, tourism is insignificant, the first
bank only opened in mid-1977 and the territory is
reliant on remittances from over 10,000 migrants
in New Caledonia and French financial assistance.
Virtually no employment exists outside the tiny
public sector, and a rapidly growing population
(one of the fastest in the world) means migration
has been crucial to development.

French Polynesia by contrast is one of the
largest territories in the world, although very
little is land. Composed of five major archipela-
goes, the territory is absolutely dominated by the
central island of Tahiti, the first to be
colonised and now home to two-thirds of the territory's population. As in the Caribbean DOM-TOMs
and New Caledonia, the capital city and its bureaucracy are pre-eminent, though here there is
one exception: nuclear testing on Mururoa atoll. A
substantial tourist economy has developed around
Tahiti and, as in other DOM-TOMs, the traditional
agricultural economy (based in copra production)
has declined and given way to employment in the
bureaucracy, in nuclear testing and in the service
industries that have grown up around these core
activities. Nuclear testing led to substantial migration from France, improvements in infrastructure, a dramatic increase in employment, primarily
in the service sector, and much higher wage levels. Two-thirds of the labour force work in the
service sector; 3,000 people hold jobs associated
with the nuclear experiments. French Polynesia had
become, to some, the world's first 'nuclear
colony'.[14] Nowhere in the South Pacific has witnessed such a drastic and rapid economic transformation 'from copra to the atom'[15] as French Polynesia. The rapidity of change, however, has created problems of inadequate housing, income inequalities, pollution and high prices; the slow-

down of nuclear testing has also increased unemployment.

In New Caledonia a much less dramatic transformation occurred. The Second World War ensured rising demand for nickel and chrome and a mining boom
was matched by a commercial boom, high levels of
consumption and unprecedented prosperity. In the
post-war years, as the mining industry grew, the
agricultural sector declined to only one-fifth of
the workforce and the tertiary sector (both public
and private) absorbed the bulk of the wage labour
force. After a 'nickel boom' in the early 1970s,
linked to high prices for nickel during the Vietnam War, and massive migration to New Caledonia
from the other French Pacific territories, the
mining industry declined dramatically, expensive
plant fell idle and during the 1980s depressed
nickel prices resulted in the need for heavy subsidies. Tourism developed rapidly in the 1970s as
mining waned, but was highly concentrated in
Nouméa, the capital. The city increasingly dominates the economy, as employment shifts out of
agriculture and mining. Regional and ethnic economic inequalities have consequently worsened in
the past decade. Melanesians, who make up 43 per
cent of the population, are incorporated into the
periphery of the New Caledonia economy through
wages, taxes, pensions, medical assistance and a
variety of legal and institutional means. There is
no longer a 'traditional' self-reliant Melanesian
economy, just as there is no self-reliant Polynesian economy in French Polynesia.

As other DOM-TOMs, New Caledonia has also become
a transfer economy. By far the most important elements of New Caledonia's budget are direct contributions and grants from the metropole. In 1984 of
total territorial revenue thirty per cent was a
direct payment from France. Budget demands have
contributed to the massive growth of the exter-
nally subsidised public service, which has doubled
in size since 1970; in each of the Pacific territories it employs almost a quarter of the wage
labour force and contributes virtually half the
wages and salaries in New Caledonia. Thus the DOM-
TOMs, through transfer payments, migration and remittances, consumerism and culture have become
firmly tied to France, even if by doing so, they
have become isolated from surrounding local regions.

Certain structural similarities exist throughout
the DOM-TOMs. Political status has resulted in the

growth of a large well-paid bureaucracy that dominates the employment sector; many bureaucrats are
metropolitan French, repatriate significant proportions of their incomes and return to France
after brief service. The dominance of the public
sector, and the commerce that derives from it, has
led to the widespread decline of the commercial
and subsistence agricultural sector, the absence
of fisheries (except in Saint-Pierre and Miquelon)
and, with complex official procedures and high
wage levels that deter French or foreign investment in the economy (despite recent changes), productive economies have become 'consumer colonies'
heavily dependent on substantial French financial
assistance. Uneven economic development between
regions and ethnic groups has emphasised inequalities. Welfare provisions, however, have contributed to standards of living and life expectan-
cies that are invariably better than in nearby
countries.

THE CHALLENGE TO FRANCE

The winds of change that blew through Africa and
Asia, sweeping a variety of colonies to independence, did not avoid the French empire, even if
decolonisation was not a process that France embraced enthusiastically. In protectorates such as
Syria and Lebanon France had little choice but departure and France reluctantly also left Morocco
and Tunisia. In Indochina and Algeria only sustained warfare forced France to relinquish its
colonies. In sub-Saharan Africa, France's departure was much more like that of the UK; nonethe-
less the newly independent African states remained
closely tied to France. For France decolonisation
was virtually over, yet already demands for independence in the DOM-TOMs sounded.
    In the immediate post-war years, for example,
demands for greater autonomy in French Polynesia
were led by a prominent Polynesian politician who
ultimately won 70 per cent of the votes in elections in 1951 and advocated transforming the territory into a Tahitian Republic.[16] However, a
decade later at the 1958 constitutional referendum, 64.4 per cent of the electorate voted in
favour of remaining with France. The expansion of
employment, and the improvement of services, in
the wake of the nuclear testing programme in the
1960s dampened the demand for independence. Never-

157

theless a substantial autonomist movement achieved
internal self-government in 1977. A multitude of
parties battled for control of the territorial assembly, including several pro-independence groups
- which increased in strength - but a Conservative
party retained control and gained a statute of autonomy in 1986 which gave French Polynesia a ministerial executive and such symbols of identity as
a flag and anthem. This did not, however, silence
those calling for independence, nor did it prevent
internecine strife within the dominant party.

In New Caledonia the genesis of nationalism was
contemporaneous with that in French Polynesia. The
first significant multiracial party was founded in
1951 and its mild reformist policies attracted
considerable Melanesian support. However, Melanesian frustrations with the slow pace of reform,
racial discrimination, continued opposition to
their aspirations, and particularly denial of land
rights, produced a radicalisation of politics in
the 1970s. A number of purely Melanesian parties
emerged, and consensus evaporated. In opposition
to the Melanesian parties fragmented conservative
parties consolidated into the Rassemblement pour
la Calédonie dans la République (RPCR), a primarily European and Polynesian party.

Land issues dominated politics and emphasised
divisions between the European New Caledonians
(Caldoches) and Melanesians, who had only been
legally allowed to move from reservations after
the war. Melanesians still owned little property,
the economy was totally controlled by European interests, and Melanesians were absent from the economic, political and cultural elite. In many
Melanesian reservations land pressures were emphasised by natural increase and return migration
which limited the potential of cash-cropping and
cattle-ranching and stimulated demands for land
reform. Though the speed of restoring land to
Melanesians increased in the 1960s and 1970s it
was still far short of Melanesian expectations and
needs.[17] By 1980 demands for greater autonomy
and land rights had given way to the first calls
for independence. The formation of the pro-independence coalition of Melanesian parties dates
from the early 1980s. This metamorphosed into the
Front de Libération Nationale Kanak et Socialiste
(FLNKS) in 1984; the name of the group indicates
its political orientation.

Election of a Socialist government in metropolitan France in 1981 had frightened Caldoches who

thought the Parti Socialiste willing to 'abandon'
New Caledonia, while Melanesian activists hoped
for redress of their grievances. A solution proved
impossible to find, and High Commissioner Edgard
Pisani's proposal for 'independence-association'
in which New Caledonia would accede to independence but cede certain areas of government
(notably external relations and defence) to Paris
incurred strident criticism from both sides. A
subsequent Socialist plan, implemented in 1985,
divided the territory into four regions, three
coming under FLNKS control. Meanwhile, violence
erupted and more than twenty people have since
been killed. The Chirac government has resolutely
refused to accept talk of independence, has ha-
rassed the FLNKS and sent several thousand police
and soldiers to the islands. Chirac, despite President Mitterrand's reservations, held a referendum
on independence in September 1987. The FLNKS boycotted the vote, but the remaining voters (just
over fifty per cent of the electorate) chose almost unanimously to remain part of the French
Republic. Most observers felt that this exercise
would not bring peace to the troubled territory.
  Outside the two largest Pacific territories demands for independence have been less strident -
and totally absent in Saint-Pierre and Miquelon
and Wallis and Futuna - and opposition to France
has take quite different forms. In the Antilles,
only a tiny minority have ever voted for independence, in part because of 'an attitudinal framework emphasizing security-mindedness and material-
ism, and the lack of a visible and charismatic
pro-independence leader'[18]. Though the French Socialist government decentralised some power to the
islands, this did not stifle growing opposition
and the celebrated poet, Aimé Césaire, a French
deputé for Martinique, has demanded progress
towards greater autonomy. Césaire's concept of
négritude had been vital in the development of a
Creole identity, and the ideas of such Antillais
intellectuals as Frantz Fanon and Edouard Glissant
inspired cultural and political movements of various persuasions inside the Caribbean and elsewhere. Radical (often Marxist-inspired groups) demanded independence and, in Guadeloupe, terrorists
mounted bombing campaigns. Neither in Guadeloupe
nor in Martinique did pro-independence groups at-
tract more than 5 per cent of votes, however, and
mainstream parties (including the local affiliates
of the PCF) accept departmental status, although

arguing for more self-control and even greater subsidies.

Guyane has seen some support for independence during the 1980s. However, many Guyanese are recent migrants from a variety of places, and others are indigenous Indians, hence a collective Guianese identity is not apparent. Rapid migration, a fragile economy, and the absence of stable and coherent political parties discourage indépendantiste attitudes and it is widely believed that France would step up its settlement programme if independence sentiments increased; geopolitics and the French investment in space technology at Kourou mean Paris would react strongly against any attempts to gain independence.

Réunion in the Indian Ocean, the largest in population of the DOM-TOMs, has been one of the least troubled by pressure for independence. Though occasional demands for greater autonomy have been voiced, an independence movement is conspicuous by its absence, a function certainly of a situation where Réunion has received massive financial assistance from France - more per capita than any state in Africa - and welfare services are superior to those in some French metropolitan departments. More than elsewhere, in Réunion the theme of decolonisation has been argued to be not independence but integration; a Réunion Senator, Albert Ramassamy, has argued that 'for the old colonies that have become departments, integration is a means of decolonisation, just as much as independence for those who have chosen that'.[19] Hence pressure from Réunion is for greater assistance from France. It is precisely this perspective that informs contemporary French policy towards the DOM-TOMs. As Bernard Pons, the Minister for DOM-TOMs under Chirac, has stated: 'There are two ways of ending decolonisation: secession or the achievement of full French citizenship'.[20] Implicitly, 'secession', rather than 'independence', would be an illogical and foolish choice. In Réunion, and in the other anciennes colonies, widespread support exists for this view.

Mayotte, having voted against independence with some 99.4 per cent of the electorate choosing France, now seems destined to remain French for the foreseeable future. Since the Comoros, with a population more than six times that of Mayotte, is one of the poorest states in the world, the prospect of renewed integration seems unlikely. In fact, the strongest political movement in Mayotte favours closer integration with France through Mayotte becoming a département. Paris has hesitated, arguing that greater development of the island is necessary before such an institutional change can be adopted or even seriously explored.

With the exception of New Caledonia, independence movements seem to be losing ground in the DOM-TOMs. The encouragement of migration from and also to the DOM-TOMs, lavish financial support, including unemployment benefits and the construction of a massive centralised bureaucracy have ensured incorporation and maintained dependency. Such material advantages of DOM-TOM status have discouraged contestatory movements, which have thus tended to focus on cultural aspirations, relative deprivation, unemployment, inequality, self-reliance and self-determination, rather than on economic gains from local control of the economy. This is most apparent in French Polynesia, where the independence movement was strongest before the start of the nuclear testing that transformed the economy, and in the Caribbean, where independence is primarily a cultural rather than a political or economic issue. The structural problems of the economies of most DOM-TOMs have resulted in high levels of unemployment. This, rather than stimulating demands for an independent economy, have often emphasised the strengthening of ties with France to ensure the maintenance of unemployment benefits and the large but artificial public sector. This is well exemplified in Martinique where

a growing economic dependence on the metropole, stemming from a plunge in the productive capacity of the island, a shift from the primary to the services sector (with no intervening expansion of industry), the growth in transfer funds (particularly family allocations), the ballooning of the local bureaucracy, and the growing exodus of what is considered the more dynamic, enterprising, and often skilled part of the island's youth - nevertheless combined with a visible heightening in the population's standard of living, health, education, services and level of infrastructure - could only intensify Martinicans' perceived political dependence on, and the fierceness of, their loyalty to France.[21]

Demands for independence arise primarily from
small urban protest movements, and more out of
protest over inequality than over support for a
coherent political programme, again with the exception of the broadly-based claims of indépendan-
tistes in New Caledonia.[22] France has stressed the
development problems of nearby independent mini-
states, and argued that independence does not constitute the only form of decolonisation, that
colonialism may merely be replaced by a more rapa-
cious, less controllable, neo-colonialism or even,
in some circumstances (such as Guyane) that independent states might simply be annexed by larger
neighbouring states. This view has been widely accepted in the DOM-TOMs and the probability of
greater movement towards independence is very
slight; in most DOM-TOMs this would only follow
unlikely unilateral metropolitan French action.

Continued French control of the DOM-TOMs, however, has caused diplomatic headaches for Paris.
The Conference of Non-Aligned States regularly
condemns French 'colonialism', as do such meetings
as a 'Conference of the Last French Colonies' held
in Guadeloupe in 1985 and a meeting hosted by
Libya in 1986. The Organisation for African Unity
has called for the return of Mayotte to the Comoros. The South Pacific Forum - a group of mainly
independent states from which French Polynesia and
New Caledonia are excluded and even denied observer status - has condemned French policy in New
Caledonia. In 1986, the Forum states including
Australia and New Zealand - whose relations with
France have been embittered by New Caledonia,
nuclear testing and the Rainbow Warrior incident[23]
- successfully campaigned for the UN to relist New
Caledonia on its roster of territories to be decolonised. France is able to ignore such pronouncements, despite a certain humiliation, and its
clientelistic connections with Third World countries and ties in the EC and Atlantic Alliance
easily overpower and subvert such censure.

THE TIES THAT BIND

France's construction of transfer economies in re-
mote and largely unproductive islands that were
increasingly firmly tied to the Hexagon, at a time
when other colonial powers were withdrawing, appears paradoxical. For a country that has avowedly
championed liberation this is doubly so. Neverthe-

less explanations for France's continued presence
in distant seas suggest themselves. French sensi-
tivities over the loss of territory are unusually
strong, emphasised by the reacquisition of Alsace
and Lorraine at the end of the First World War,
the occupation of France itself in the Second
World War, colonial wars in Indochina and especially Algeria and, finally, France's reluctance
to withdraw from the New Hebrides in 1980. France
has departed only when colonial possessions appeared indefensible. Ethnicity and secession are
widely viewed with suspicion and the DOM-TOMs have
a powerful hold on the sentiments of many
metropolitan French. It was not merely rhetoric
that provoked the present Minister of the Interior, Charles Pasqua, to declaim in New Caledonia
that 'the defence of Bastia begins in Nouméa'. The
belief in the united and indissoluble state remains exceptionally powerful in a country marked
by the centralising tendencies of the ancién
regime and arguments against greater autonomy
within France, especially in Corsica, or for the
DOM-TOMs, have traditionally reinforced each
other.

The simplest argument for a continued French
presence is a legalistic one: residents of the
DOM-TOMs are fully-fledged French citizens. Until
and unless a majority of voters in any particular
DOM or TOM decides to withdraw from the Republic,
Paris cannot grant independence. In fact, the constitution of France does allow for the TOMs to accede to independence and would also permit greater
autonomy, even the sort of 'independence-association' envisaged by Pisani for New Caledonia. However, the constitution also charges the president
with maintaining the integrity of the Republic,
and international law recognises France's
sovereignty in the DOM-TOMs.

Though there are some prospects for economic development in the DOM-TOMs, including cobalt
prospects in New Caledonia and timber in Guyane,
the only real economic prospects lie in the two
hundred mile Exclusive Economic Zones, particularly in the possibility of extracting minerals
from the continental shelf or from polymetallic
nodules on the ocean floor. Currently such benefits are elusive and distant but for French Polynesia they offer some hopes of future economic
growth and, more generally, it is argued that 'the
outre-mer is the key to France's oceanic future'.[24] Around Saint-Pierre and Miquelon the EEZ

has increased fish catches and fisheries conflict with Canada, but outside the Pacific the EEZs are of no real significance. The economic benefits from the DOM-TOMs are, as they have almost always been, a hope for the future rather than an immediate reality. Classic economic arguments for retaining the DOM-TOMs are minimal though economic goals give sustained credibility to the necessity for a French presence; as a French minister explained in 1981:

> Why disguise the fact that our national interest is to stay in the Pacific? Thanks to our territories and their zones of sovereignty, France has the third largest maritime economic zone in the world. The core of humanity's hope lies in the sea and under the sea. What's more, the major powers of the twenty first century are to be found around the Pacific: the United States, the USSR, Japan, China, Indonesia and so on. So it's natural that France should be there.[25]

Strategic reasons have come overwhelmingly to shape the structure of France's presence in distant seas, much more important than just the Centre d'Expérimentation du Pacifique (CEP) at Mururoa in French Polynesia, established after France was forced to transfer its nuclear experiment station from newly-independent Algeria. Guyane is dominated by a sole activity, the European space centre and satellite station at Kourou. In both places strategic issues have led to the 'recycling of a forgotten colony' which, in Guyane at least, has gone 'from Green Hell to Outer Space'.[26] Réunion has some strategic value, along with Mayotte, for the surveillance of the principal crude oil route in the Indian Ocean. Moreover there is an obvious chain from Djibouti (where France retains a substantial military presence), through Mayotte and Réunion, to Kerguelen and the French Antarctic. Unpopulated Kerguelen could even prove to be a future nuclear testing site if France decides to leave Mururoa.

Not only are there specific strategic reasons for France's presence in each of the three oceans, but these regions give France a firm physical stake in global affairs. Moreover, the DOM-TOMs complement each other: nuclear testing in French

Polynesia and the space station in Guyane, which may monitor global military activity, benefit from back-up provided by the Pacific and Caribbean territories, respectively, and Réunion and Mayotte provide facilities in the Indian Ocean for French fleets and shore bases. Unoccupied islands, such as Kerguelen or Clipperton, far from the Mexican coastline, could provide airstrips and bases for French activity should they be needed.[27] It is the Pacific, described by the prestigious Institut du Pacifique as the 'new centre of the world',[28] that is the jewel in the contemporary colonial crown, and where France anticipates playing a substantial future role, holding the balance of power between the USA and the Soviet Union, to create amicable relations and encourage a sense of 'co-responsibility' in the region. With the increasing importance of the Pacific France argues that security and prosperity can be best assured by continued control over the foreign policy and defence of the islands, an independent nuclear deterrent and strong conventional defence forces. Moreover the interests of the superpowers in the region, with the Soviet Union's presence being increasingly apparent (most recently in a fishing treaty with Vanuatu), makes a French presence even more vital.[29] Thus France, in this strategic arena so distant from the Hexagon, and through its global physical presence, is performing as a superpower.

France has not retained the DOM-TOMs for economic reasons. Pierre Messmer claimed with more widespread validity, 'It is not material interests which tie Réunion to the metropole, it is political, human, physical and spiritual unity. Réunion is France in the Indian Ocean'[30]. More accurately, the converse is true: material interests tie the DOM-TOMs to the metropole but political and cultural issues tie France to the DOM-TOMs. The voters of the DOM-TOMs are of a certain importance in vigorously contested and often narrowly won national elections and French representatives from the DOM-TOMs include such notable figures as Michel Debré, Raymond Barre and Aimé Césaire.

Beyond this the French presence is a mixture of intangible influences: ambitions of a global role cherished by the French educational system but especially the vision of at least a thin line of French culture, religion, technology and language encircling and civilising the globe.[31] It is this perspective that has also nurtured Francophonie and suggested that the DOM-TOMs are 'windows on

the world' in both a cultural and an economic
sense. Because of the DOM-TOMs France can claim to
act as a sovereign indigenous power in regional
and international affairs affecting the Atlantic,
the Caribbean, the Pacific and the Indian Ocean -
a feat no one other country can manage. More
recently they have been suggested as not merely
windows for France but as a 'meeting place for
France and the European Community' in the outre-
mer, even a 'tropical Europe'.[32]

The costs of maintaining the DOM-TOMs has been
variously estimated at between 0.2 per cent and
2.3 per cent of the total French budget. Although
a substantial sum, this is minimal for a country
with France's resources. By falling below the
global aid levels of some other comparable world
powers, France can finance the DOM-TOMs and concentrate its overseas assistance on territories
from which the 'leakage' to France in the private
sector is very high. A substantial proportion of
the public money spent in the DOM-TOMs, perhaps as
high as 90 per cent in the smallest states like
Guyane and Wallis and Futuna, returns to France
through the private sector. The real costs of
maintaining the DOM-TOMs are thus very small.

France's ambitions have ensured that the DOM-
TOMs remain firmly in place, an apparent anomaly
that strengthens France's global presence. Yet
their existence may not be so anomalous. Most
small territories, even where politically independent, have invariably been partly integrated into
the economies of metropolitan states through aid,
trade or migration. The smallest colonies and independent states have increased their ties and
moved from productive to rentier status.[33] Despite widespread and continuing external arguments
that the independence of New Caledonia is inevitable and that only doubts over the timing and
structure of that independence remain, currently
it seems much more certain that this will not
occur. It is even more certain that other DOM-TOMs
will not gain independence. A number of other territories in the Pacific and the Caribbean have
reached a satisfactory negotiated dependence based
on high levels of aid and access to migration opportunities. They may be more appropriate prece-
dents than the nearby independent states and, in
this century at least, the era of decolonisation
appears to have drawn to a close. For all that, it
is a paradox that France, widely viewed as a country that not only supports liberation but by los-

ing an empire found a role in a world which saw liberation as a moral right, even a necessity, should retain (Britain's control of Hong Kong temporarily apart) the largest colonial empire. Except in the Pacific it is not a global presence that is widely challenged. The existence of the DOM-TOMs, and the powerful demand for independence in New Caledonia, emphasise the ambiguities of France's domestic and international policies.

NOTES AND REFERENCES

1. Quoted in Le Canard enchaîné, 22 October 1986.
2. There is no recent detailed account of the DOM-TOMs. The main account that covers most of them is a useful but outdated report by Jean-Claude Guillebaud, Les Confettis de l'empire (Seuil, Paris, 1976), which partly omits Réunion. A special issue of the journal Hérodote (Vol. 37-38, 1985) on 'Ces Iles oú l'on parle français' reviews particular issues in each of the DOM-TOMs, except Mayotte, Wallis and Futuna and Guyane, and has a valuable introduction.
3. Serge Mam-Lam-Fouck, Histoire de la societé guyanaise (Editions Caribéennes, Paris, 1987); Alain-Philippe Blérald, Histoire économique de la Guadeloupe et de la Martinique du dix-septième siècle à nos jours (Karthala, Paris, 1986).
4. Robert Aldrich, The French Presence in the South Pacific, 1842-1940 (Macmillan, London, in press).
5. Jean Gottman, 'The Isles of Guadeloupe', Geographical Review, Vol. 35, (1945), pp. 182-203.
6. B. Petitjean-Roget, 'Pour comprendre la situation économique des Antilles', Les Temps modernes, No. 441-2 (1983), p. 1866.
7. Beverley Ormerod, 'Discourse and Dispossession: Edouard Glissant's Image of Contemporary Martinique', Caribbean Quarterly, Vol. 27 (1981), p. 2.
8. Alain-Philippe Blérald, 'Guadeloupe-Martinique: a System of Colonial Domination in Crisis', in F. Ambursley and R. Cohen (eds), Crisis in the Caribbean (Monthly Review Press, Kingston and London, 1983), p. 155.
9. Ivor J. Butcher and Philip E. Ogden, 'West Indians in France: Migration and Demographic Change', in P.E. Ogden (ed.), Migrants in Modern France: Four Studies (Queen Mary College, Department of Geography, Occasional Paper No. 23, London, 1984), pp. 43-66.
10. INSEE, Recensement général de la population de 1982. Les Populations des DOM-TOMs en France métropolitaine (Secrétariat d'Etat chargé des départements et territoires d'outre-mer, Paris, 1985), p. 49.

11. Michel Debré, <u>Une Politique pour la Réunion</u> (Plon, Paris, 1974).

12. P. Marshall, 'Martinique and Guadeloupe', <u>Latin American and Caribbean Review</u> (World of Information, London, 1985), p. 213.

13. Karl Rensch, 'Wallis and Futuna: Total Dependency', in A. Ali and R. Crocombe (eds), <u>Politics in Polynesia</u> (Institute of Pacific Studies, Suva, 1983), pp. 4-17.

14. Bengt and Marie-Thérèse Danielsson, <u>Poisoned Reign: French Nuclear Colonialism in the Pacific</u> (Penguin Books, Melbourne, 1986).

15. Claude Robineau, <u>Du Coprah à l'atome</u> (ORSTOM, Paris, 1984).

16. Virginia Thompson and Richard Adloff, <u>The French Pacific Islands: French Polynesia and New Caledonia</u> (University of California Press, Berkeley, 1971).

17. Alan Ward, <u>Land and Politics in New Caledonia</u> (Australian National University, Department of Political and Social Change, Monograph No. 2, Canberra, 1982).

18. S.B. MacDonald and A.L. Gastmann, 'Mitterrand's Headache: The French Antilles in the 1980s', <u>Caribbean Review</u>, Vol. 16 (1984), p. 20.

19. Albert Ramassamy, <u>La Réunion, décolonisation et intégration</u> (AGM, Saint-Denis, 1987), p. 8.

20. <u>France-Antilles</u>, 26 June 1987.

21. William F. S. Miles, <u>Elections and Ethnicity in French Martinique: A Paradox in Paradise</u> (Praeger, New York, 1986), p. 158. A similar French perspective is that of Claude de Miras, 'L'Economie martiniquaise: développement sans croissance', <u>Iles Tropicales, Insularité, 'Insularisme'</u> (CRET, Talence, 1987), pp. 399-420.

22. Recent publications on New Caledonia are reviewed in John Connell, 'Towards Kanaky? Politics and Land in New Caledonia', <u>Oceania</u>, Vol. 57 (1987), pp. 294-303. Detailed accounts include John Connell, <u>New Caledonia in Crisis</u> (Routledge, London, in press) and Michael Spencer, Alan Ward and John Connell (eds), <u>New Caledonia: Essays in Nationalism and Dependency</u> (University of Queensland Press, Brisbane, 1988).

23. This incident has now been widely documented: R. Shears and I. Gidley, <u>The Rainbow Warrior Affair</u> (Counterpoint, Sydney, 1985); J. Dyson, <u>Sink the Rainbow</u> (Reed Methuen, Auckland, 1986); Insight Team, <u>Rainbow Warrior: The French Attempt to Sink Greenpeace</u> (Century Hutchinson, London, 1986); D. Robie, <u>Eyes of Fire: The Last Voyage of the Rainbow Warrior</u> (London Press, Auckland, 1986).

24. <u>France-Antilles</u>, 26 June 1987.

25. Quoted in <u>Pacific Islands Monthly</u>, Vol. 52, April 1981, p. 15.

26. F. Schwarzbeck, 'Recycling a Forgotten Colony: From

Green Hell to Outer Space in French Guiana', Caribbean Review, Vol. 16 (1984), pp. 22-5, 47-8.

27. Pierre Messmer, the former Prime Minister and architect of the nickel boom migration to New Caledonia, has even stated that 'Wallis and Futuna are in a strategic position in the centre of the South Pacific and this will become increasingly important in the future' (Les Nouvelles Calédoniennes, 14 October 1986).

28. Institut du Pacifique, Le Pacifique, 'nouveau centre du monde' (Berger-Lavrault, Paris, 2nd ed., 1986).

29. Georges Ordonnaud, 'Les Enjeux politiques, économiques et stratégiques', Politique étrangère, Vol. 52 (1987), pp. 35-46; Robert Aldrich, 'France in the South Pacific', in John Ravenhill (ed.), No Longer an American Lake? Alliance Problems in the South Pacific (University of California Press, Berkeley, in press); Alan Ward, John Connell and Michael Spencer, 'Introduction', in Spencer, Ward and Connell (eds).

30. Guillebaud, p. 25.

31. Jean Chesneaux, 'France in the Pacific: Global Approach or Respect for Regional Agendas?', Bulletin of Concerned Asian Scholars, Vol. 18 (1986), pp. 73-80.

32. 'Le Rendez-vous de la France et de L'Europe pour l'outre-mer', Bernard Pons, Press Conference, Paris, 26 May 1987. Cf. 'L' Outre-mer français: une Europe tropicale?', France-Antilles, 13 November 1987.

33. John Connell, Sovereignty and Survival. Island Microstates in the Third World (University of Sydney, Department of Geography, Monograph No. 3, 1988).

Chapter Eight

FRANCOPHONIE: LANGUAGE, CULTURE OR POLITICS?

Robert Aldrich and John Connell

France prides itself on being the home of a particularly rich culture and on having a vocation to
spread this culture overseas. Stimulated by the
universalism of the Enlightenment and the ideals
of the Revolution of 1789, this vocation in the
nineteenth century became a <u>mission civilisatrice</u>,
intimately tied with French expansion and the phenomenon of imperialism. This occurred, ironically,
at a time when the French language was spoken only
in the royal courts of Europe, some diplomatic
circles and the intelligentsia but not by all the
people of France itself. Even after the difficult
era of decolonisation, France retains its claim to
be the centre of an international culture and to
pursue a policy of cultural <u>rayonnement</u>. Underlying this quest is a belief in the innate value of
the French language which dates back to the foundations of the Académie Française in the 1600s and
Rivarol's championing of the philosophical clarity
and unmatched beauty of French in the 1700s. The
great contemporary French historian Fernand
Braudel stressed that 'La France, c'est la langue
française'.[1] But cultural pride has also been
mixed with a desire to preserve that heritage from
outside intrusions, a need to spread the culture
beyond the Hexagon and a claim to associate or as-
similate foreigners to the ideals of French civilisation by imparting to them the essentials of
that language and culture. Cultural diffusion thus
entails elements of an ideology and a political
programme which can be used to reinforce France's
presence outside the country.

The concept used to organise the world's French-
speakers and the countries sharing, at least
partly, in French civilisation is Francophonie.
The term was probably invented in the late nineteenth century, during the period of French colonial expansion, by Onésime Reclus, a geographer
whose specialty was North Africa and who wanted to
group together those people and territories where
French was spoken as a mother tongue or an adopted

language. Reclus, a republican and patriot, also
thought that France could spread its ideas of lib-
erty, equality and fraternity through its language
and culture. The term fell into disuse soon after-
wards, although the idea of an international culture and a 'greater France' was just coming into
its own. Francophonie was revived in 1962, the
year Algeria became independent, in a special issue of the journal Esprit devoted to the French
language; among the contributors were Tunisian
president Habib Bourguiba and Senegalese president
Léopold Sédar Senghor. By the late 1960s the word
was used in official circles and had entered most
French dictionaries; from the 1960s and 1970s on-
wards some 200 private and public international
organisations, mostly headquartered in Paris, were
established to promote and defend the French language and maintain ties between France and other
French-speaking lands.[2]

Exactly what Francophonie represents, however,
is not clear. For some it means only the use of
the French language, or even languages influenced
by French (notably Creole); for others it refers
to countries where French has an official status,
even if other languages are in common usage. Generally, most users of French see Francophonie as
an element of shared identity, in which French-
speakers in multilingual societies (as in Canada)
can associate with each other or by which citizens
of countries with no indigenous national language
(as in the majority of black African states) can
communicate with each other inside the state and
in their regions. Promoters of Francophonie also
see it as demarcating a world separate from that
of the English-speaking one and a way of guarding
against encroachment from 'Anglo-Saxon' civilisation. Some observers, couching their defence of
French in almost mystical or overtly chauvinistic
forms, see the language and culture of France as
possessing unique and priceless characteristics.
These may be connected with supposed special
traits held by those who know French or, in
racialist terms, characteristics of the French
people. In this nationalistic extreme, Francophonie becomes a more abstract concept, francité,
the distinguishing marks of French civilisation.
Acceptance of this view is not limited to white
Frenchmen. Senghor - poet, statesman and apostle
of négritude - says that Francité is a 'mode of
thought and action, a certain way of asking questions and looking for solutions. It is a spiritual

community: a noösphere around the globe. In brief,
Francophonie goes beyond language, it is French
civilisation: more precisely, the spirit of civilisation, that is to say, French culture'. In most
contexts francité and Francophonie have been
merged without distinction. Almost all definitions
of Francophonie have been at best vague, and it
has generally been seen as a sort of umbrella term
to encompass various concepts, organisations or
even links among French-speaking countries.[3] What
is implied is the inclusion of people outside
France in the culture (in a broad sense) of France
itself. In the colonial era, this was first the
policy of 'assimilation', the total political,
economic and cultural absorption of colonies and
colonial peoples into France; when that failed,
the French changed the approach to 'association',
which recognised the autonomous identity of
colonies and cultures. Francophonie can be seen as
a variation on these doctrines, a principle mod-
ernised to fit the post-colonial age.[4]

Relations between non-Frenchmen and French
civilisation, however, are not appreciated in the
same fashion everywhere. French, after all, was
the vehicle for the discourse of independence
movements in the French colonies, and some of
France's old possessions have declined participation in Francophone organisations. In Algeria, for
example, Francophonie has been denounced as merely
a new form of colonialism.[5] Writers such as
Edouard Glissant, who is from Martinique, have
charged that French culture alienated West Indians
both from their African roots and their Caribbean
moorings, and some radicals in the French West
Indies call for a rejection of French in favour of
Creole. For French speakers in multilingual societies, such as Belgium, Switzerland, Canada and
Lebanon, French was what one writer calls an
'identity shield'. In North Africa, where Islam,
Arabic culture and nationalism already created a
powerful sense of identity, French became
'problematic', while in black Africa, without the
heritage of unifying languages and states which
existed previous to the colonial epoch, it was a
'legacy'.[6]

The boundaries between language, philosophy and
political policy are never evident. Xavier Deniau,
president of the Comité de la Francophonie and
author of one of the most widely distributed books
on the topic, insists: 'Francophonie is not political, at least in the muddled sense of the term:

it is so only in the sense that it is preoccupied
with the interests of the "cité francophone".
Francophonie cannot be confused with an ideology:
it refuses all assimilation, close or distant,
with "ism" notions, imperialism, racism, colonialism, which define themselves by the negation of
the other and the arrogant affirmation of some
supremacy'.[7] President Valéry Giscard d'Estaing,
however, implied a different understanding of
Francophonie: 'There is an interdependence between
the economic power of a nation and the radiation
of its culture. I mean, interdependence, advis-
edly. This means not only that the material presence of a nation opens the way to its intellectual
presence, but also that this, in turn, thanks especially to the vehicle of language, contributes
to economic dynamism on world markets. This is why
the spread of French culture in the world must be
ceaselessly reinforced and extended. This is why
this linguistic and intellectual community one
calls Francophonie must be considered an essential
element in our political policy'.[8] The creation of
an Haut Conseil de la Francophonie by François
Mitterrand after his election in 1981 and the subsequent appointment of a Secrétaire d'Etat à la
Francophonie by Jacques Chirac in March 1986 testify to the interest political figures across the
spectrum have taken in the issue and imply that it
is not solely a cultural phenomenon but another
significant element in France's external relations.

THE GEOGRAPHY OF FRANCOPHONIE

The number of people who speak French is difficult
to estimate and depends on whether the statisti-
cian wants to include those who speak French as
their normal language of communication, those who
speak it fluently or those with some training in
it. Certainly more than one hundred million can
speak French usefully, and at least thirty-five
nations accord some official status to French. In
Europe, French is the language of France and
Monaco, one of the national languages of Belgium,
Luxembourg and Switzerland and is spoken by many
of the residents of the Val d'Aosta region of
Italy. More people speak French outside France
that within the Hexagon. French has become, with
English, one of the two genuinely successful
'colonial' languages. In Africa, French is in com-

173

mon use in Algeria, Morocco and Tunisia and in the countries south of the Sahara which were part of the old French and Belgian empires. It is used in the Indian Ocean in Madagascar, Mauritius and the Seychelles and is preserved in the old French outposts on the Indian subcontinent. French is still used in Vietnam, Laos and Cambodia. In Vanuatu, the old Anglo-French condominium of the New Hebrides, it is an official language. French is also an official language of Canada, where the Québécois are one of the largest concentrations of French-speakers in the world. French is spoken by a minority in Louisiana; it is the official language of Haiti and is used in Dominica and St. Lucia. Such nations as Greece, Portugal, the Vatican and the former Portuguese colonies in Africa use French as their diplomatic language. In addition, French is the language of the ten départements et territories d'outre-mer that give France a presence in every ocean. In many other countries, benefitting from its long association with culture and education, French is studied by significant numbers. In the non-Francophone world, French is taught as a foreign language by 250,000 instructors to some twenty-five million students. French-speaking communities are large enough to make possible the publication of French-language newspapers in such nations as Australia, Turkey, Lebanon and Egypt.

In the mid-1960s various attempts were made to define Francophonie in linguistic terms. A fourfold classification identified, firstly, countries which had only French as the national language (Haiti, Monaco and France), secondly, countries using French as one of two or more national languages (Canada, Belgium, Switzerland, Luxembourg), thirdly, countries using French for official purposes (the 'Francophone' states of Sub-Saharan Africa) and fourthly, countries where French is used but not as the national language (Lebanon, Indochina and the Maghreb). At the same time a further classification was used which introduced additional criteria, such as historical ties with France and economic development.[9] As the empire was dismembered, French rarely declined; only exceptionally, in Southeast Asia, has its use diminished though Prince Sihanouk was one of its most ardent supporters. By contrast in many Francophone African states its use has expanded, stimulated by educational systems, radio, newspapers and other communications media, and the return of migrant

workers from France. Elsewhere, in the twentieth
century, French has dominated the foreign language
classes of schools and tertiary education institutions throughout the world and organisations such
as the Alliance Française have found new markets
for language instruction. French is an official
language of most international organisations and,
with English, the working language of the UN and
the EC. French has thus spread beyond the former
empire, but Francophonie remains in many ways a
colonial legacy and a much more concrete and functional entity than the 'spiritual community' that
Senghor suggested for francité.

The level of knowledge of French - and interest
in French civilisation - varies from one country
to another. In the Caribbean and the Indian
Ocean, the daily language is Creole, and some
Francophone states (including Mauritius, St. Lucia
and Dominica, all of which were British colonies)
use English as their official language. French itself also differs from region to region, even
within France, with distinct accents and vocabu-
laries or even recognisable dialects (such as
joual in Quebec). Local writers and politicians in
these outposts of Francophonie must make a decision whether to use one or other language. In
Canada, politicians often switch between English
and French from paragraph to paragraph; the President of Haiti, Leslie Manigat, switches from
French to Creole in his speeches and similar tran-
sitions occur in Mauritius.

The multilingual situation of most former
colonies has ensured not only that French was the
means of national unity but that it was also an
instrument of social stratification. Many countries have one or more native languages (Berber
and Arabic in North Africa, Malgache in Madagascar, dozens of languages in black Africa and
Vanuatu) which are spoken by the ordinary people;
French in such cases is the language of the elite,
for official communication or for exchanges between different ethnic groups. 'There can be no
doubt that the francophone African leaders owe
much of their political and economic power as well
as their social standing to their skill in the
French language'.[10] (By contrast where local political leaders, such as Pouvanaa a Oopa in French
Polynesia, had limited French speaking ability
their power was substantially weakened.) Senghor
in 1983 was elected an immortel, a member of the
prestigious Académie Française. Not surprisingly

the Francophone African elite at least has a vested interest in the retention of French in formal contexts. In sub-Saharan Africa only Djibouti and Mauritania have adopted a second official language (Arabic) alongside French, though Rwanda and Madagascar give equal status to their national languages. In every case French remains the medium of education.

Even in recent years French has thus been seen as a language of colonialism. For instance, in French Polynesia,

> at the present time, with the development of secondary education, it constitutes more than ever the intellectual tool that allows it to colonise a swollen administration (a growing middle class) whilst also allowing it to consolidate its position in other sectors (such as the elite). Moreover it is well integrated into a political, administrative, economic and cultural system, which reproduces with several purely formalistic adaptations, the metropolitan system.[11]

In this way elites were and are firmly linked in many different ways to metropolitan culture and economy across a significant part of the globe.

THE CHALLENGE TO FRENCH

Though French was the language of colonialism, cultural contact and commerce it could not become wholly triumphant in situations of pre-colonial linguistic diversity, nor even in distant lands where lifestyles were so different from those of the Hexagon that new concepts were required. Even in New Caledonia, where French settlers dominated large parts of the island, their close association with Australia ensured that such words as 'station' 'creek' and 'paddock' became part of their own language as a particular Caldoche dialect emerged. Where French was the language of a handful of traders, missionaries and administrators, education systems were not always adequate to diffuse it successfully, other linguistic influences (especially English in the Caribbean) reduced its purity and Creole became the principal medium of communication in some parts of the empire.

French Creole languages are widely spoken in the Caribbean, in many of the islands between Haiti and Trinidad, though predominantly in Guadeloupe (and its dependencies), Martinique, St. Lucia and Dominica. Most of the Indian Ocean islands, notably Mauritius, Réunion and the Seychelles, also have Creole-speakers. (Elsewhere, in other areas of French colonialism such as Africa, Asia and the Pacific, Creole languages were rare; usually indigenous languages remained important with French itself becoming a means of communication between different groups.) Invariably Creole languages were despised by colonial authorities. Attempts to establish orthodox French were least successful in the Caribbean where French colonists identified less with their new homes than did Spanish or English colonists. 'In the French possessions... the presence of a universalistic religion, early frequent manumission and considerable inter-racial mating probably accelerated cultural creolization'.[12] As the Guadeloupe novelist Maryse Condé recently recorded:

> Since Creole has always been considered inferior to, and dependent on, the French language, which is the language used in education and government, it has been confined to a sort of "ghetto" [and] has thus become incapable of dealing with any other situations outside the "ghetto". In 1960 West Indian militants broke down some of these barriers, started using slogans in Creole, writing in Creole on the walls and it started to become a political language. Creole started to leave its "ghetto" behind and to find the vocabulary it needed for the situation.[13]

Creole is accepted as a language of Antillais popular culture: such music groups as the Compagnie Créole, Kassav and Malavoi have scored triumphs with their Creole songs in the West Indies, France itself, Franchopone Africa and areas of the West Indian diaspora.

In many Francophone regions Creole especially, but also indigenous languages, have become symbols and structures of resistance to a perceived French colonial presence. This is most obvious in Guadeloupe, Martinique and Réunion where some autonomist and independentist literature is written or titled in Creole, rather than in the French

that characterises more conservative publications:
slogans on walls announce <u>Kanaky Gwadloup, Mem
Kombat</u> and <u>On Sel Chimen. Lendependans</u>. In New
Caledonia, where Melanesians speak more than
thirty languages, the independence movement uses
French, but the Ecoles Populaires Kanaks (EPK),
which emerged in the wake of the 1984 political
tension, are oriented to strengthening Kanak culture in terms of language, customs, art and agriculture and to improving knowledge of local languages. French therefore became the second
language, rather than the medium of instruction
that it is in other schools. Underlying cultural
aims are political aims; children 'can't express
themselves properly in French because it isn't
their language and they can't speak their language
because it's forbidden. So the emphasis on expression in one's native language is a kind of reaction to white schooling'.[14] Significantly, no
Creole language or culture evolved in New Caledonia - a situation which one scholar sees as a
cause of political and social polarisation.[15] Similarly, but much less dramatically, Left-wing and
independentist groups in French Polynesia demanded
that Tahitian be the medium of school education,[16]
and Tahitian now enjoys an equal status with
French as the two official languages of the territory. There are also parallels in the association
of the nationalist surge in Quebec in the 1960s
with the defence of <u>joual</u> as a national language
and demands for greater use of Creole in pre-inde-
pendence Mauritius. Restoration of lost traditions, linguistic as much as economic, are quite
central to the demand for independence and ethnic
identity.

Though Creole and indigenous languages became a
form of resistance to colonialism, transcending
the role that Creole once played, nowhere could
such forms of resistance ever hope to displace
French. Even in the New Caledonian EPKs, where
language was highly politicised, French was regarded as the crucial second language, since
though

> we're right in an anglophone environ-
> ment... you can't take away a hundred
> and thirty years of French presence....
> And politically speaking, we say when we
> want to fight someone, well, we have to
> use his weapons to fight him with; so in
> order to confront the French, in the

Xârâcúú EPK we are teaching French with
three aims in mind: first, to be able to
speak to the person facing us, that is,
communication. Second, to be on an equal
footing with him, and for that, we have
to master his techniques, everything
that makes up that world we're not
afraid of. Third, you don't only communicate with the colonists. French enables us to communicate with the
world.[17]

Where politicisation has been weaker, the role of
French has been more important; the use of Creole
may be most pervasive in countries like Haiti,[18]
the Seychelles and Mauritius, where direct French
colonialism has long since disappeared.

Throughout most of the Francophone world, including such parts of the Hexagon as Corsica and
Brittany, languages other than French are often
widely spoken amongst the masses, are symbols of
cultural (and ethnic) distinctiveness and are
forms of resistance against French domination in
particular contexts. They are then a challenge to
the imperialism of language. Even in such overseas
departments as Guadeloupe, Réunion and Martinique,
usage of relatively standard French is principally
confined to the mass media, politicians (and then
only part of the time), schools (and tertiary institutions) and the aspiring middle class, for
which French itself is of major symbolic importance. The French language is sometimes merely a
thin veneer over very different languages and cultures.

French has also been under attack from Arabic in
North Africa and the Middle East. After the independence of Algeria, Tunisia and Morocco, their
governments made an effort to 'Arabise' education
and culture. For example, Arabic gradually replaced French as the language of instruction for
tertiary education. More radical Algeria was especially intent on reducing French language influence. The militant nationalism of Nasserite Egypt
reduced the role of French there, and French practically disappeared from Syria, which France had
controlled under a League of Nations mandate before its independence. In Lebanon, French held
ground against Arabic, but the civil war has de-
prived Beirut of its role as the cultural and financial capital of the Middle East.

For all the significance of Creole, Arabic and

other local languages, the principal challenge to
French comes from the increasing global domination
of English, in culture, the media and as the means
of communication in international meetings. If
over one hundred million people speak French, four
times that many speak English. The diplomats and
businessmen of most Asian countries choose English
as their primary Western language, and English
outdistances French as the major European language
in black Africa. This challenge from English is
also powerful in France, where the Académie
Française has waged a zealous and ceaseless struggle against an invasion of alien words and in
defence of a mythical linguistic purity. Beyond
the Hexagon these concerns are transformed into
opposition to any form of institutionalisation of
Creole and other languages. Yet language choice is
not merely cultural; it is also political.

French therefore remains with English a genuinely global language and one capable of express-
ing a variety of sentiments. At the first Francophone summit in 1986 President Didier Ratsiraka of
Madagascar, a country at least nominally Marxist,
rhetorically questioned his own presence: 'I am
French educated and proud to speak French, and my
country uses French to communicate with the outside world and as the teaching language of our
university....In the four corners of the planet
there are people who speak your language, who love
your country and who are your friends'.[19] To the
same summit, the now deposed President of Burkina
Faso, Thomas Sankara, sent a message that in
French he could sing the 'Internationale' and
speak to oppressed people in New Caledonia.[20]
Ultimately the Guadeloupean novelist Maryse
Condé's analysis concerning the Antillais is applicable to many French-speakers; there is a

> 'love-hate relationship that all West
> Indians have towards the French lan-
> guage. Initially the French language
> was, for West Indians, the outward sign
> of defeat by the French. Subsequently
> this became a victory because...we did
> manage to speak French very well, better
> than most French people. Finally this
> victory became a kind of mutilation,
> which prevented us from fully exploiting
> the resources of another language which
> our ancestors created in the slave
> ships, Creole'.[21]

With the increased emphasis on Creole, Arabic and other languages - and the importance of English for international business - many French-speakers are bilingual. France itself, thanks to migration, greater education and the cultural creativity of ethnic minorities, is becoming a culturally pluralist society.

French has served as a conduit to and from France for ideas, and cultural imports have revivified native French language and thought. Early in the twentieth century the Senegalese Senghor and the Martiniquais Aimé Césaire used French to work out a philosophy and literature of blackness, négritude. The black West Indian Frantz Fanon and the Tunisian Jew Albert Memmi used French to castigate French colonialism in classical works of political contestation. Such authors as Hector Bianciotti have moved to Paris from their own countries, from Argentina in Bianciotti's case, and switched to writing in French. Non-French authors writing in French have been awarded literary prizes; the Moroccan Tahar Ben Jelloun won the Goncourt Prize in 1987 for novels that, amongst other things, are models of purity and elegance in the use of French. On a more mundane level, expressions from outside French have enriched the French language - from 'baraka' and 'bled' to 'hamburger' and 'milkshake' - much to the concern of those who would like to maintain the French language free of such foreign imports. 'Native' French does not always dominate the culture of France itself.

INSTITUTIONS OF FRANCOPHONIE

Of the multitude of organisations and conferences through which Francophonie takes on an institutionalised form, four are of particular importance: the Agence de Coopération Culturelle et Technique (ACCT), the annual Franco-African summit conferences, the regular meetings of Francophone countries from around the world and the new French Secretariat of State for Francophonie. The ACCT is one of the oldest and most permanent of the Francophone institutions and the one which has the most concrete programme. The association was set up at a meeting in Niamey, Niger, in 1969 under the aegis of French novelist and former Minister of Culture André Malraux. The ACCT's purpose was to group together those countries where French is

used in a non-political organisation for, as its
name implies, cultural and technical co-operation.
The organisation was seen to be a way of channel-
ing development aid from the wealthier Francophone
countries (particularly France and Canada) to the
lesser developed ones, but also as a means of popularising the cultures of the African, Caribbean
and Asian Francophone societies in Europe and
America. Funding for the organisation came directly from the states which joined. France agreed
to provide 48 per cent of the budget, and Canada
would give 30 per cent; the rest was to be contributed by other states. The headquarters of the
organisation was set up in Paris; the secretary-
general was initially a Québécois Canadian who was
succeeded by a Gabonese.

The ACCT's first activities were to provide educational assistance. It arranged, for instance,
for Canadian French-language school books and
other pedagogical materials to be distributed in
black Africa. The organisation also aimed to promote culture and set up awards for novels and
films and sponsored various festivals. It co-pro-
duced films, set up oral literature study centres
in Africa, provided scholarships to students and
gave subsidies for such projects as translation.
It sponsored an international school in Bordeaux
for training in management. The ACCT also began to
act as the official representative of the Francophone movement in international meetings; in 1978
it gained recognition as a permanent observer at
the United Nations.

The ACCT has not been immune to internal strife
and criticism. Some Africans criticised the organisation for being neo-colonial and doing little to
promote African culture. Use of funds was also
controversial, particularly since half the budget
in some years went to pay the salaries of employ-
ees of the organisation. Critics charged the ACCT
with having an inflated and ossified bureaucracy.
Jockeying for power in the administration has
occasionally surfaced, particularly in manoeuvring
between Canada and France for domination of the
organisation. This was complicated by a situation
where the exact domain of the ACCT's activities
has never been entirely clear. Should it, for example, only fund French-language projects or
should it also encourage foreign-language ones
(where these were African or Creole languages) in
Francophone countries?

Because of heated debate over such issues and

France's frustrations in implementing its preferred policies in the ACCT, the new conservative
Prime Minister, Jacques Chirac, created in 1986
the Secrétariat d'Etat à la Francophonie. The new
secretariat was effectively designed to replace
the ACCT, a body that had become sclerotic over
time and over which France could exercise only
limited control. At the first summit meeting in
Paris in 1986 organised by the new Secrétariat
d'Etat à la Francophonie, a management committee
(Comité de suivi) was appointed to control the
ACCT budget. The Quebec summit a year later allocated no new funds to the ACCT, and France and
Canada directed their funds (46 per cent and 32
per cent respectively) to the management committee
rather than to the ACCT itself.[22] For a time, an
organisation which had sought to challenge French
cultural hegemony appeared near extinction.

There has also been conflict between France and
Canada over the future of the ACCT. As French interest declined both Canada and Quebec emphasised
their support for the organisation and, along with
a large number of other members, sought for the
ACCT to become the permanent secretariat of Francophonie rather than France's own organisation.[23]
A compromise 'provisional consultative committee'
was established at the 1986 Francophone summit
conference. Canada also then promised to double
its contribution which, with that of Quebec, would
have turned Canada into the major financial supporter of the ACCT, had France not responded in a
similar vein. Culture had become more obviously
politicised.

The ACCT, even with these problems, has proved
itself capable of acting as a useful co-ordinator
of activities. Occasionally it has also managed to
act in an unofficial diplomatic role when relations have been strained between Francophone countries or to arrange for substitutes of educational
and technical personnel when they have been withdrawn. After the Comoros broke official diplomatic
relations with France in 1975, the ACCT managed
the replacement of French coopérants - who formed
almost all of the country's corps of teachers -
with Belgian and Canadian substitutes. More recently, as relations between France and Vanuatu
have become strained and France has recalled some
of its coopérants in Vanuatu, the ACCT has arranged for them to be replaced by Tunisian staff.
The organisation can, therefore, 'tide over' relations during a difficult period and set up con-

tacts between countries which would probably not
otherwise exist. Since it is still perceived as a
non-governmental organisation, it has a margin of
manoeuvre denied to other agencies. Given the
large role played by France in the ACCT, however,
Paris is certainly a beneficiary of such activities.

French has remained crucial in education and in
establishing telephone, telex, radio and television links. The role played by French radio,
cinema and television in disseminating French language and culture is considerable, especially in
the smaller African states where the cost of funding domestic content is considerable. French remains central to cultural rayonnement. At a Francophone film festival in Martinique (November
1987) the Secretary of State for Francophonie
derided Creole: 'If a West Indian film is made
solely in Creole it gets put in the ghetto. I
have seen African films, but without subtitles who
can understand them?'.[24] Similarly Tahar ben
Jelloun feared that if he had written in Arabic
his work would remain largely unknown in Europe.[25]
Not only in the Ministry do other languages remain
in the ghetto. Beyond loosely cultural ties, this
cultural hegemony contributes to France's consolidation, for example through commercials, as the
major market for Francophone Africa; as Jacques
Rigaud notes, 'It is not without worth to admit
that there exists a close relationship between
cultural and economic relations'.[26] Yet in a similar vein Canadian challenges to France over the
leadership and direction of the ACCT have been
seen by some in France as attempts 'under the
cover of "Francophone militancy" to seize French
commercial interests in the African and Arab
World'.[27] The African states, in whatever arena,
are central to Francophonie.

Inevitably the role of French as a colonial language has ensured that, in many respects, French
is also an element in more nebulous post-colonial
influence. In all former French colonies French
continues to play an important role and an examination of France's bilateral relations with the
independent African states affords some evaluation
of the extent to which Francophonie is merely a
'spiritual community' occupied by French speakers,
or whether it has more overtly political connotations. After all, as early as 1966, Senghor had
called for the establishment of an 'inter-
parliamentary association of all the nations where

French is spoken' which would lead to a community of nations.[28] Such an analysis also stresses the concepts of association and assimilation, and their relationship to Francophonie.

One of the oldest systematic expressions of official Francophonie is the regular Franco-African summit. The origins of this encounter lie in the decolonisation of French Africa, and Paris' desire to maintain contacts with its former possessions. Such was the aim of General de Gaulle in his proposal for a French Community, a project torpedoed by the unwillingness of the newly-independent African states (notably Guinea) to agree to such an organisation. Many African leaders, however, were willing to maintain regular contacts in the hope of winning financial and technical aid from Paris and also because of their cultural links with the former metropole. In 1959 de Gaulle invited three of the most pro-French African leaders to Paris to discuss future relations; this meeting between de Gaulle, Léopold Senghor of Senegal, Hamani Diori of Niger and Félix Houphouët-Boigny of the Ivory Coast, at least symbolically, was the first Franco-African summit. But the conferences did not become regular meetings until the administration of Georges Pompidou in the 1970s (and after the formation of the ACCT). Subsequently, the meetings became annual, alternately held in France and in Africa. They are not attended by all of France's former African colonies (Algeria and Madagascar, for instance, have refused to take part), but the meetings of some forty heads of state have become a standard institution in French foreign policy (much like the regular consultations between France and West Germany). They again underline the centrality of Africa to the concept of Francophonie.

As with the ACCT, the exact purpose of the summits has not always been clear. Indeed, from initially limited objectives, the Franco-African summits have expanded the range of issues that concerned them and have become a forum for France's wider African interests. Critics charge that they are another opportunity for France to pursue its neo-colonial goals in the Maghreb and black Africa. Some have seen unnecessary overlap (or even intentional upstaging) between the summits and other conferences, such as the Organisation of African Unity (OAU) and the meeting of countries in the franc zone. Leaders like Senghor have emphasised the cultural and political role of the summits, while Houphouët-Boigny sees them as having a more directly economic character. Clashes among members are not uncommon, and the political problems of the African states - the various coups and insurrections - have troubled meetings. Controversial, also, has been the policy of gradually expanding the summits to include non-Francophone states; President Giscard invited the President of Liberia to attend the conferences, and President Mitterrand has opened the meetings to several of the former Portuguese colonies in Africa. With the attendance of these states and the ex-Belgian colonies (and the recent joining of the franc zone by Equatorial Guinea) France has found a way of expanding its presence in Sub-Saharan African outside the bounds of its former empire and also a way to cement ties with its old possessions. The difficulties which beset the OAU also mean that the Franco-African summits have taken on a larger role as a forum for pan-African meetings.

In order to broaden France's connections with Francophone countries outside black Africa, an objective of Socialist policy, the Mitterrand government set up another meeting, held in French-speaking countries. The first Francophone summit meeting, held in February 1986 in the splendour of Versailles, also marked a distinct movement towards the politicisation of Francophonie. With some 40 participating states (out of 42 invited ones) Francophonie formally had as many members as the British Commonwealth (with five states - Canada, Dominica, St. Lucia, Mauritius and the Seychelles - belonging to both) but with greater diversity, since the French group incorporated Arab and socialist states. The conference heard a variety of fairly predictable speeches from heads of delegations, the most welcome being the praise of Francophonie from Madagascan President Ratsiraka, whose country had declined to participate in the Franco-African summits. Political questions appeared when Vanuatu Prime Minister Walter Lini turned his speech into a diatribe against nuclear power, and Vietnam unsuccessfully proposed a motion condemning Zionism. The summit did, however, vote its disapproval of South African apartheid. The meeting agreed to set up a Francophone television agency, undertake agricultural cooperation and design an international baccalauréat. Participants and the media hailed the summit as marking a new stage in the Francophone movement. Le Monde titled its editorial 'The Birth of Francophonie'

Francophonie

and Canadian Prime Minister Brian Mulroney said,
'The Paris summit should mark the birth of a new
international club more or less analogous to the
Commonwealth'.[29]
Soon after the summit concluded, French legislative elections led to the 'cohabitation' arrangement with Jacques Chirac as Prime Minister.
Chirac created a Secrétariat d'Etat à la Francophonie, and appointed as head of the department
Lucette Michaux-Chevry, a politician from Guadeloupe. Known for her energetic temperament and
political volatility - she was once a Socialist -
Madame Michaux-Chevry was a strong supporter of
Chirac's policies, including his opposition to independence movements in France's overseas territories. Soon after taking office, Madame Michaux-
Chevry stressed that 'Francophonie is a fight...
for a new international solidarity, for a new in-
tricate and manifold cultural identity, and for a
common development'. She added: 'The French language is both a language of the people and an
agent of modernity.... It helps us to dialogue
against contemporary violence... it even helps us
to dialogue on subjects which divide us'. As a
native of the Antilles, she saw her nomination as
a gesture of France to its overseas citizens.
Madame Michaux-Chevry stated that in her portfo-
lio, 'The politics of Francophonie implies several
dramatic actions, but above all, it is a patient
and prudent construction'. The Secretary of State
has travelled widely to spread her message of
Francophonie, attending conferences, presiding
over Francophone film festivals and sometimes dis-
pensing money for particular projects. She has
favoured educational and cultural activities, arguing, 'If the French language is to recover and
hold a predominant position in the world, why
should it not be as a language of celebration and
gaiety through the arts?'[30] Critics of Madame
Michaux-Chevry, however, see her gestures as
largely symbolic.
The peculiarity of 'cohabitation' meant that the
second Francophone summit - a meeting initiated by
the Socialists - would have as one of its major
participants the RPR Secretary of State for Francophonie - proof for some that Francophonie tran-
scended political divisions, for others that different political groups had simply tried to tri-
umph over each other in the creation of new
Francophone institutions.
The second Francophone summit was preceded by a

meeting of Francophone African foreign ministers in Bujumbura, Burundi, in July 1987, an indication of both the privileged status of African states within Francophonie and French attempts to ensure African support in the face of possible future challenges from Canada. The summit, co-hosted by Canada and Quebec, and held in Quebec in September 1987, was attended by thirty seven states and delegations from Quebec and Wallonie (Belgium), with 'special guests' from Louisiana, the Val d'Aosta (Italy) and Francophones in the New England states of the USA. Only the former French colonies of Algeria, Cameroon and Vanuatu were unrepresented. The summit approved a series of resolutions on international issues, including the Middle East, South Africa and the Iran-Iraq war; most were predictably innocuous or in support of more genuine development in the South. The conference also resolved to create special funds to support development in Chad and Lebanon and to fund a series of specific development projects, many in the field of communication. Underlying these resolutions and commitments were common hopes that the summits would continue to evolve into something akin to the Commonwealth. Symbolic of these aspirations was the decision to stage a sports meeting in Morocco in 1989, a clear parallel to the Commonwealth Games. The Comité International du Suivi du Sommet Francophone, composed of Canada, Quebec, Senegal and France, meeting in Marrakesh in March 1988, continued to work on these projects and discussed the future of the ACCT, which should become 'the permanent secretariat of Francophonie'. Notable was the fact that Morocco hosted the gathering and will host the 1988 Franco-African summit; Rabat let it be known that it would welcome holding the fourth Francophone summit in 1991 in Morocco and might put forward a candidate for the secretary-generalship of the ACCT.[31]

After the summit President Mitterrand concluded that even 'without cumbersome institutions, the Francophone movement is becoming established; it is progressing and it has decided to live on'.[32] Yet the Canadian Prime Minister noted that it 'remains a young and fragile undertaking',[33] alluding to Franco-Canadian rivalry for leadership of the organisation, its modest finance and the distaste among some members for the human rights record of others. Governments criticised on the eve of the summit included Vietnam, Benin, Zaïre, and Lebanon and political problems were also reflected in the coup that overthrew the President of Burundi while he was attending the summit. Some countries, including Vietnam, even opposed the word Francophonie, though supporting the idea, preferring instead 'countries sharing the use of French', a more complex phrase but one deliberately opposed to the hegemony of France.

FRANCOPHONIE: ESPACE CULTUREL OU POLITIQUE?

Francophonie is not devoid of contradictions. Is it a cultural or a political phenomenon? A meeting of equals or an agent for French co-operation, or tutelage, or neo-colonialism? Are French and other languages complementary or competing? Can national identities in countries outside Europe be adequately expressed in a European language? Anomalies are evident from French policy. In a period when Basques and Bretons, Corsicans and Alsatians affirmed their local identity, was there a 'contradiction of the French government [in] discouraging linguistic regionalism at home, while defending it in the Val d'Aosta, Louisiana and Quebec'?[34] Do the invitations to Portuguese- and Spanish-speaking countries to the Franco-African summits water down the whole concept of Francophonie? Ought France to encourage the use and learning of French, to the exclusion of other languages (notably English) or should it promote multilingualism and recognise the importance of English? These more obviously cultural issues that marked the consolidation of Francophonie are also reflected in political forms.[35] The 1987 Burundi meeting emphasized the conflict and rivalry between Canada, Quebec and France within Francophonie, and the emphasis of both Canada and Quebec that Francophonie should be 'above all multilateral' rather than France-dominated.[36] French politicisation of Francophonie presents new problems for France for which there is no real parallel within the British Commonwealth, where the UK is the unquestioned dominating force.

The evolution of Francophonie from the early 1960s is clear. From being primarily a cultural organisation with the aim of preserving and strengthening the use of French language and culture, it has taken on the aspect of being the conduit for the channelling of aid from developed French-speaking countries to developing ones. More recently, with the pronouncements issued at the Quebec summit, it has shown itself capable of making statements on international political questions. With this development, Francophonie has become a roughly parallel organisation to the UK Commonwealth, complete with its own bureaucracy, international meetings and even sports competitions. The two organisations are not however alike; no member country of the Francophone group except France acknowledges the French President as head of state, unlike the Commonwealth's acknowledgement of the Queen of England. Criticism of France has been more muted inside the Francophone summits than criticism of England at the Commonwealth Heads of Government Meetings; the castigation of British policy towards South Africa that regularly troubles the Commonwealth meetings is absent from French summits.[37]

Growing French interests in Africa, now encompassing non-Francophone states, that have followed President Mitterrand's increased aid levels and even President Giscard's greater concern for multilateralism within Francophonie, have ensured that African states especially were drawn by early loose linguistic and cultural ties into an organisation that increasingly became economic and political. Francophonie therefore could be seen as a form of neo-colonialism, especially amongst the very poor countries of Sub-Saharan Africa, yet, at the same time, as the Haitian President, Leslie Manigat, has suggested, it can also be a means of redistributing global resources through stronger multilateral ties.[38] In an interdependent world both these relationships are not incompatible. Even in its older form, in the mid-1970s, Francophonie was seen as the kind of 'transnational organisation which the modern world produces out of its dominating centres'.[39] One writer hypothesized: 'Were it to become an organised movement with coherent central direction, Francophonie would become an important transnational actor in world politics'.[40] That time appears almost to have arrived. In any case Francophonie is now much more precise and focused than the formless umbrella-like phenomenon that characterised its origins two decades ago.

The wider implications of Francophonie's future evolution are unclear. A statement by Madame Michaux-Chevry is intriguing: 'There is a Francophone region which is cultural, geographic, strategic and commercial. What is Francophonie? It is five continents that share the same language and who communicate with each other in that language'.[41] There has also been some assessment of whether there might be a Francophone economic region.[42] The strategic and commercial potential of Francophonie has not been fully discussed, and some leaders would probably object to Francophonie taking an active role in these domains. For critical observers, such action would simply highlight what they see as the role of Francophonie as an agent of French neo-colonialism.

It would be unfair, however, to judge Francophonie as simply an element of French foreign policy, much less a tool of neo-colonialism. After all, it was three African leaders - Senghor, Bourguiba and Diori - who proposed the idea. The Gaullists in France were late converts; the General was cool to the idea and not all of his followers have been ardent supporters. Even without the concept and the institutions, France would probably have strong relations with the countries which were its former colonies, and the Francophone organisations have not replaced the other institutions of external relations such as the Ministries of Foreign Affairs and Co-operation and the advisers on African and Malgache affairs at the Elysée Palace. Yet Francophonie provides a useful medium for the combination of cultural and political policy through semi-official channels. Undoubtedly what began in black Africa as a primarily cultural and linguistic phenomenon has come to be dominated by France, despite Canadian rivalry, in what is now a political and economic arena. A cultural organisation has become a political institution.

NOTES AND REFERENCES

1.   Quoted by Mort Rosenblum, Mission to Civilize: The French Way (Harcourt Brace Jovanovich, San Diego, 1986), p. 8.

2.   These are listed in Xavier Deniau, La Francophonie (Que Sais-Je?, Presses Universitaires de France, Paris, 1983) and W.W. Bostock, Francophonie: Organisation, Co-ordination and Evaluation (River Seine Publications, Melbourne, 1986); the standard reference work is the Dictionnnaire général de la Francophonie (Letouzey, Paris, 1986) and the Annuaire biographique de la Francophonie (Nathan, Paris). This paper has paid particular attention to the more general aspects of Francophonie and their political

implications. However, many of the most active Francophone organisations have very precise domains of activity. For instance, the Association des Universités partiellement ou entièrement de Langue Française (AUPELF), founded in 1961 in Montreal, groups together 156 universities plus 450 French studies departments from non-Francophone countries. The AUPELF, avowedly apolitical, has organised conferences, arranged visits and exchanges of students and scholars, and worked with other educational organisations, such as UNESCO and the UN University (Compte-Rendu de la Huitième Assemblée Triennale, AUPELF, Montreal, 1984).

3. S.K. Panter-Brick, 'La Francophonie with special reference to educational links and language problems', in W.H. Morris-Jones and G. Fischer (eds), Decolonisation and After (Frank Cass, London, 1980), p. 342.

4. On these concepts, see R.F. Betts, Assimilation and Association in French Colonial Theory (Columbia University Press, New York, 1961) and Michalina Vaughan, 'Assimilation versus Association: Separate Recipes for Failure', Modern and Contemporary France, No. 21 (March 1985), pp. 3-8.

5. Le Monde, 6 May 1980. At the Franco-African summit in Nice, the Algerian president publicly rejected Francophonie 'as an expression of economic and cultural colonialism'.

6. David C. Gordon, The French Language and National Identity (Mouton, The Hague, 1978). On the West Indies, see Edouard Glissant, Le Discours antillais (Seuil, Paris, 1981).

7. Deniau, La Francophonie, p. 6.

8. Quoted in Gordon, The French Language and National Identity, p. 56.

9. Panter-Brick, La Francophonie. p. 338.

10. Anton Andereggen, 'Francophone Africa Today', Journal of Social, Political and Economic Studies, Vol. 12 (1987), p. 42.

11. François Ravault, 'Le Français dans une société pluri-culturelle: l'exemple de la Polynésie', Anthropologie et Sociétés, Vol. 6 (1982), pp. 103-4.

12. Sidney W. Mintz, 'The Socio-Historical Background to Pidginization and Creolization', in D. Hymes (ed.), Pidginization and Creolization of Languages (Cambridge University Press, London, 1971), pp. 487-8.

13. Quoted in 'La Parole en Exil', in P. Morris and S. Williams (eds), France in the World (Association for the Study of Modern and Contemporary France, Nottingham, 1985), p. 104.

14. Marie-Adèle Néchéro-Jorédié, 'A Kanak People's School', in M. Spencer, A. Ward and J. Connell (eds), New Caledonia. Essays in Nationalism and Dependency (University of Queensland Press, Brisbane, 1988), p. 202.

15. Alain Saussol, 'Peut-on parler de créolité en

Nouvelle-Calédonie?', in Iles Tropicales, Insularité, 'Insularisme' (Centre de Recherches sur les Espaces Tropicaux, Talence, 1987), pp. 157-64.

16. Ravault, 'Le Français dans une société pluri-culturelle', p. 99.

17. Néchéro-Jorédié, 'A Kanak People's School', p. 206.

18. Mintz, 'The Socio-Historical Background to Pidginization and Creolization', p. 488.

19. Quoted by Rosenblum, Mission to Civilize, p. 13.

20. Op. cit., p. 14.

21. 'La Parole en Exil', p. 100.

22. J.P. Péroncel-Hugoz, 'Le Sommet de Québec: Francophonie An II', Le Monde hebdomadaire, 3 September 1987, p. 10.

23. Le Monde, 12 July 1987.

24. France-Antilles, 11 November 1987, p. 19.

25. Bostock, Francophonie, p. 104.

26. Jacques Rigaud, Les Relations culturelles extérieures (La Documentation Française, Paris, 1980), p. 77.

27. Le Monde, 12 July 1987.

28. W.W. Bostock, 'From Empire to Voluntary Association: the Commonwealth and Francophonie in Comparative Perspective', World Review, Vol. 24, No. 2 (1985), p. 27.

29. Le Monde, 20 February 1986, p. 15.

30. France-Antilles, 24 October 1986.

31. Le Monde, 15 March 1988.

32. Le Monde, 6 September 1987.

33. Sydney Morning Herald, 7 September 1987.

34. Gordon, The French Language and National Identity, p. 102.

35. Christine Souriau, 'Arabisation and French Culture in the Maghreb', in W.H. Morris-Jones and G. Fischer (eds), Decolonization and After, pp. 310-29.

36. Le Monde, 12 July 1987.

37. Bostock, 'From Empire to Voluntary Association', p. 35.

38. L. Manigat, 'Réflexions sur la fonction politique du Commonwealth et de la Francophonie', in A. Jacomy-Millette (ed.), Francophonie et Commonwealth: Mythe ou Réalité (Choix, Québec, 1978), pp. 241-50.

39. Souriau, 'Arabisation and French Culture in the Maghreb', p. 315.

40. Brian Weinstein, The Civic Tongue. Political Consequences of Language Choices (Longman, London, 1983), p. 167.

41. France-Antilles, 11 November 1987, p. 19.

42. Philippe de Saint Robert, 'D'abord, les moyens d'une vraie solidarité', Le Monde diplomatique, No. 401 (August 1987), p. 18.

Chapter Nine

THE QUAI D'ORSAY AND THE FORMATION
OF FRENCH FOREIGN POLICY IN HISTORICAL CONTEXT

Mark B. Hayne

Since the end of the Second World War, the influence of the Quai d'Orsay, the Ministry of Foreign
Affairs, in the formulation and execution of foreign policy has substantially changed. The inher-
ent ministerial instability of the Third and
Fourth Republics had allowed the Quai a pre-eminent, even excessive role in the decision-making
process. The institutionalisation of the authority
of the presidency of the Republic with the 1958
constitution, and the utilisation of foreign policy as a major weapon in creating a more cohesive
domestic situation, have considerably diminished
the position of the Foreign Ministry in the area
of policy formulation. Moreover, the previous
diplomats' virtual monopoly on foreign affairs has
come under serious challenge. Various groups outside the government, such as big business, the
press, finance and lobby groups, can exert considerable influence on the formulation of foreign
policy. Even within the administration, forces
such as the president's and prime minister's offices, various ministries and secretariats, and
parliament, have augmented their authority.

However, the Quai d'Orsay remains the central
agent for the implementation of policy. The Quai
has not responded belatedly to the complexities of
modern international relations. Through continual
reorganisation of its structures and its recruitment procedures, and re-orientation of its intellectual appreciation of contemporary problems, the
Quai remains the dominant force, if not in the
formulation of policy, then for its administration.

THE MAKING OF FOREIGN POLICY, 1871-1958

The relative influence of the Quai d'Orsay since
1871 has been largely dependent upon the power
that the various presidents and prime ministers

might theoretically and practically wield. The
constitutional laws of 1875 empowered the president to negotiate and even to ratify treaties, and
he was not obliged to inform the legislature if
the interest and safety of the state dictated otherwise.[1] However, the political crisis of 1877 and
fear of a possible anti-republican coup d'état
weakened the presidency to the extent that future
incumbents rarely attempted to rule.[2] There were
some obvious exceptions in the realm of foreign
policy before 1914 - Jules Grévy, who provided
stability after the failed Conservative coup and
who oversaw the purging of monarchists in the
Quai;[3] Félix Faure, who steadied the Republic during the Dreyfus Affair and who proffered sound advice to Foreign Minister Delcassé during the
Fashoda Crisis with England in 1898; and most notably Raymond Poincaré. The last, both as Premier
in 1912 and President from 1913, wielded very
demonstrable power.[4] Through his rigid adherence
to the system of alliances, he hoped to maintain a
balance of power between the Triple Entente and
the Triple Alliance. But such influence owed more
to the person of the president than to his institutionalised authority. Even Poincaré's power was
diminished immediately prior to the First World
War.[5]

In such an atmosphere, the bureaucrats of the
Quai d'Orsay and the ambassadorial elite abroad
were given a relatively free rein in the formulation and administration of foreign policy. Foreign
ministers arrived and departed with startling rapidity.[6] On average, governments lasted seven-and-
a-half months between 1880 and 1914. Given such
instability, the Ministry provided substantial
consensus concerning the continuity of policy-making and execution. In the Moroccan crises of 1905
and 1911 and the July crisis of 1914, the Quai
substantially helped to hold foreign policy together in the midst of considerable internal disarray. Indeed, the most notable ambassadors, such
as Paul and Jules Cambon, who held the London and
Berlin embassies respectively immediately prior to
the First World War, and the rather notorious Maurice Paléologue in St. Petersburg, could act on
their own authority, even against governmental
prerogatives. In particular instances, such as the
July crisis of 1914, when domestic politics preoccupied political leaders and when leadership was
significantly absent, they might establish something akin to an 'ambassadorial dictatorship'.[7]

While such an exceptional authority was lessened slightly in the inter-war period, diplomats and bureaucrats were of paramount importance between 1919 and 1940. In twenty years, fourteen Ministers of Foreign Affairs (in forty-one governments) attempted to guide France but frequently presented confusing and even divergent attitudes. At the same time the role of the presidency gradually weakened to such an extent that it became largely a ceremonial role.[8] The Quai attempted, albeit unsuccessfully, to plug the gap. The creation of a secretary-generalship during the First World War, a position of ultimate authority and still a permanent feature, was one such measure. Only two people held this post between 1920 and 1940. Philippe Berthelot, the favourite of Aristide Briand and the éminence grise of the period, at least held foreign policy together. However, he and his office temporarily fell into disgrace in the 1920s when he and his brother were linked to a financial consortium in China.[9] Alexis Léger, his successor in 1933, was by no means as authoritative. French society was meanwhile polarising. French political leaders had no clear vision of the future, nor a clear response to the menace of Hitler in the 1930s. Finally, the Quai itself was in disarray, a legacy in part of Berthelot's personal rule and patronage.[10] As the Second World War approached, continual ministerial instability and wavering left a large vacuum in the formulation of policy. At times the direction given to the Quai was simply non-existent.

The Fourth Republic (1946-58) was similarly wracked by party politicking and internal upheaval. The lack of unity on the Left, the rising Centrist force, the unsteadiness of the Right, and the emergence of factional groups such as Poujadism and Gaullism, created uncertainty in parliamentary politics. Such a situation reflected deep cultural, social, economic and political rifts and highlighted interests of groups such as the North African colons and French winemakers. The Republic came to be known for its inertia both domestically and in the foreign arena. The failure of the French parliament, after two years of deliberation, to ratify the 1952 Pinay proposal to join a European Defence Community highlighted such paralysis. In the 1950s France was deeply divided over the whole process of decolonisation and over its decline to the rank of a second rate power. French defeat in Vietnam in 1954 and the Suez de-

bacle in 1956 produced a sense of helplessness labelled <u>molletisme</u> (after the French Premier Guy
Mollet). By 1956 the collapse of the parliamentary
system seemed imminent, and the Algerian conflict
had worsened. Votes of no confidence in cabinets,
periods when no government existed and a myriad
succession of premiers created a void. In such an
atmosphere, the Quai d'Orsay remained an agent of
the first magnitude. Diplomats <u>sur place</u> could
present the foreign minister with <u>faits accom-
plis</u>.¹¹ In 1953, for example, the Sultan of Morocco was deposed by French representatives, and
three years later, a Moroccan nationalist leader
was abducted by French secret forces. Premier
Mollet could only approve after the event. Mollet,
under pressure from the Quai, agents in the field
and military officers who acted without orders,
then virtually adopted their more hardline approach to the Algerian rebels.¹²

But the Foreign Ministry itself was hardly functioning in a co-ordinated fashion. Like parliamentary politics, it had fallen into disarray during
the Second World War. Drastic restructuring of its
administration, alterations to personnel and infu-
sion of new blood into Free France after 1944 all
had their effects. Moreover, the complexity of international relations after 1945, with an increase
in the appointment of technocrats, the re-posi-
tioning of agents as France decolonised and the
inflow of recruits from the new Ecole Nationale
d'Administration (ENA) all aided in breaking the
closed club inherited from nineteenth-century tra-
ditions.¹³ As permanent bodies such as NATO and
the EC evolved, the problem of the co-ordination
of such agencies with the Quai d'Orsay was not
properly addressed. Moreover, despite its ineffi-
ciency, the Fourth Republic was marked by a return
to the parliamentary (rather than executive) control inherited from the French Revolution. Ministers also demonstrated a marked tendency as well
to work with their private cabinets to the exclusion of the Ministry.¹⁴

FOREIGN POLICY IN THE FIFTH REPUBLIC

The Fifth Republic somewhat reversed the parliamentary and ministerial role by allowing the president of the Republic executive control, whereby
foreign policy almost became his <u>domaine réservé</u>.
The constitution of 4 October 1958 gave the presi-

dent substantial powers. According to Article 5, he protects the independence of the nation, the continuity of state and the validity of treaties and agreements. Through Articles 14 and 15, the president accredits ambassadors and envoys to foreign powers and has foreign ambassadors and envoys personally accredited to him. He is the head of the armed services and chairs the higher committees on national defence. The constitution, moreover, gives the president three special powers lacking before this period. The first (contained in article 16) was that no counter-signature of the premier is required for the president to decree emergency powers; de Gaulle called on Article 16 between 23 April and 30 September 1961 during the Algerian War. Second, the president has power either to accept or refuse a governmental or parliamentary request for a referendum. Third, the president can refer to the Conseil d'Etat, the government's chief advisory body on legislative matters, any agreement pertaining to foreign relations which might appear unconstitutional.[15] Clearly, de Gaulle's purpose in writing these measures into the constitution was to allow the presidency a much stronger measure of executive control, an authority which was readily employed in the 1960s.[16] However it would be erroneous to view this strengthening of powers as deriving solely from the constitution. Articles 16, 20, 21, 35 and 53 make it clear that the president must share his foreign policy responsibilities and collaborate closely with the parliament and government. The personality of de Gaulle and the Algerian situation in the early 1960s, as well as the new procedures for election to the presidency after 1962, have weighted constitutional convention and practice more favourably towards the presidency.[17]

Through tenure of a seven-year term, the president provides the constitutional and executive continuity which neither the parliament nor the government can match. In practical terms, the president's power of nomination to political and bureaucratic positions strengthens his authority in the foreign policy arena. Moreover, while parliament is empowered to ratify certain agreements, mostly of a fiscal or legislative nature, the essence of political treaties falls largely outside its purview. Parliament also has a limited means of modifying the Foreign Ministry's budget and cannot apply the same pressure on the French government as, for example, the US Congress can apply to the chief executive of the USA.

Because a certain cohesion and unity have gradually built up over foreign policy since 1969, the presidency has been able to exert a dominant influence down to the present day, provided it remains within a certain framework.[18] The framework is determined by such factors as long-term security needs, including the nuclear force, France's desire to remain a powerful influence in the world, restraints imposed by public opinion, economic capacity and the constitution. Another determinant is the restriction imposed by conflicting interests within French society.[19] President Mitterrand's opposition to the German Socialists in the February 1983 European parliamentary elections reflected the manner in which a certain cohesion in presidential decision-making, combined with practical restraints, has developed in the 1980s.

Indeed, Mitterrand, despite the rhetoric of the French Socialist and Communist movements, has positively enhanced the Gaullist instruments of the 1960s: the strengthening of the Fifth Republic's institutions, especially the role of the presidency; the maintenance of a nuclear capacity, which is no longer a focus for bitter Left-right factionalism; and the maintenance of an armaments and a technology policy which is not necessarily narrowly linked to perceived friends and allies. Equally as striking has been Mitterrand's personal involvement in foreign affairs, as much a legacy of de Gaulle's presidency as a reflection of Mitterrand's resolve to be a great actor in foreign affairs. Such personal involvement has been witnessed in the meeting of Colonel Ghaddafi and Mitterrand in November 1984 in Crete, a failed attempt to solve the problem of troop withdrawal in Chad. In December 1985, Mitterrand again demonstrated his involvement by welcoming to Paris General Jaruzelski from Poland, even though the government of Laurent Fabius knew very little of the visit and Jaruzelski's declaration of martial law in Poland had provoked severe criticism in the West. More importantly, the rather suspicious attitude of France towards Moscow in the 1980s in large part reflected the President's personal attitude.

In an era of conference and summit diplomacy and in a period where communications are so sophisticated, the president can assume responsibilities which were formerly the tasks of ambassadors. A most striking example of personal views and presidential influence was François Mitterrand's forceful speech to the German Bundestag on 20 January 1983, when he advocated the installation of the Pershings and other missiles in German territory.[20] Nor is this an isolated phenomenon. Mitterrand may wield his authority when he calculates it has most effect. At EC Summits in March 1982 in Brussels and in December 1983 in Athens, he virtually overturned the policies of his own ministers, who were dealing with the thorny issue of budgetary compensation for the British. At other times, such as his visit to Morocco in 1984, where the question of a union between Libya and Morocco was the subject, Mitterrand clearly took the initiative.[21]

Another measure of the influence of presidential power is the manner in which Mitterrand employs personal, even unofficial, representatives to act on his behalf. Roland Dumas, a close associate in the Socialist Party, unofficially visited Libya several times in 1983 to raise the important question of French trops in Chad. While Mitterrand might employ the Quai d'Orsay staff, such as Francis Guttman, Secretary-General at the Ministry, and Claude Cheysson, former diplomat and Foreign Minister, he also used personnel outside the Quai, such as Guy Penne from the Elysée, Charles Hernu, former Defence Minister, and General Lacaze, former Chief of the General Staff. Even his brother, Jacques Mitterrand, head of Aérospatiale, a French aircraft firm, can be employed in arms negotiations.[22]

Naturally, given the personal element in the presidency and as no institution comparable to the American National Security Council has developed, the question has arisen as to whether the de Gaulle presidency and its Fifth Republic successors reflect the individualist 'great man theory of history'. If so, then the machinery of policy would hardly have evolved after de Gaulle's reign. In fact, Dorothy Pickles, with some justification, has argued that there has been 'no lasting evolution either of opinion or of machinery, but merely the use of existing machinery by the president for his own ends'. Consequently, her argument concludes that the post-de Gaulle period has witnessed a maintenance of the status quo.[23] Such an argument, however, is largely erroneous. De Gaulle's own life suggested strongly that unless the presidency or ultimate authority was based on

more than the cult of personality, then France was
doomed to slide into oblivion and social dis-
unity.[24] As Cerny has rightly pointed out, de
Gaulle was attempting to go much further through
the process of 'legitimation' of political authority and its 'routinisation' in French society.[25]
By 'routinisation', Cerny is speaking of decision-
making institutions and processes intrinsic to
French society which encourage a degree of consensus on fundamental issues. The 'unspoken assumption' is that de Gaulle's view of French history
necessitated institutions which would ultimately
outlast his personal presence. He viewed the foreign policy traditions of the Third and Fourth Republics as deleterious in the sense that modernisation was achieved through a 'fundamental cleav-
age of the elite' rather than through a cohesive
political elite. De Gaulle, through his ideology,
attempted to shore up the institutionalised authority of foreign policy decision-making. In
effect this was achieved by activating a 'politics
of grandeur' with its cultural and ideological
message to the world, a message which has frequently been misinterpreted from afar as
grandioseness based on aggressive organic nationalism.[26] Rather, his policies were aimed at maintaining French independence in the maelstrom of
bloc and global politics and the nation's position
as a first rank power. Equally importantly, foreign policy, implemented in a more routinised way,
would unite disparate republican elements inside
the country.

Gaullism survived its leader in an institutionalised form. De Gaulle bequeathed to his successors, Pompidou, Giscard d'Estaing and Mitterrand,
not only a certain ideological framework in foreign policy, but also more permanent institutions.
The Elysée staff, headed by a secretary-general of
the presidency, deal largely with those aspects of
policy which the president may view as his own.
The secretary-general, or other members of the
presidential staff, can, at times, rival and even
outstrip the Quai d'Orsay in exerting influence.
This was certainly the case with Régis Debray between 1981 and 1985. Debray, a friend of the revolutionary Che Guevara, was particularly influential in Mitterrand's policies towards the Third
World. Most notably, arms shipments to Nicaragua
in 1982 and a favourable attitude towards El
Salvadorian insurgents were in large part pushed
by Debray. At a broader level he has had a consid-

erable ideological influence on Mitterrand, urging the President towards an active foreign policy.[27]

Other agencies, bureaucrats and ministers can have an important input into policy-making, a process which need not involve the Quai d'Orsay directly. Since de Gaulle's period, such structural changes have been strengthened by the issuing of wider powers in certain foreign policy areas to the Ministries of Industry, Agriculture, Overseas Trade and Defence, among others. Co-ordination of such ministries and the Quai is undertaken by an inter-ministerial commission attached to the premier's office.[28] Weekly meetings, usually chaired by the president, are restricted to those immediately involved. These bureaucrats or ministers are accorded substantial freedom in their dealings, although Mitterrand retains ultimate authority.[29]

This freedom has necessarily curtailed the authority of the Foreign Ministry. For example, since 1958, a counsellor has directly advised the president on former African colonies. While he has links with the Quai (and its Direction Africaine et Malgache), and with the DGSE (military intelligence), he has maintained a function which allows him to bypass even the secretary-general of the Elysée.[30]

The various agencies dealing with defence have also been strengthened. While the position of the chief of the general staff existed in the Third Republic, it was largely subordinated to the Quai and dealt with limited technical matters. However, in a world of interacting global nuclear policy, technical considerations have profound implications for political policy. This has allowed the general staff much more direct access to the president. Given the complexity of defence issues, the Ministry of Defence and the DGSE have much stronger institutionalised authority. The Rainbow Warrior Affair of 1985 was an illustration of the increased status (and perhaps autonomy) of the Ministry. The affair also highlighted the fragmentation which still exists in decision-making. The only immediate link with all ministries and officials is the President of the Republic. No overall co-ordinating body has yet been institutionalised. This leads to the premise that the president must have a 'hands-on' approach at all times. While Mitterrand has certainly relished this approach, less competent or less enthusiastic actors in foreign affairs will find the task of 'synthesising' overwhelming.[31]

Naturally, the recent arrangement of 'cohabitation' between the Right-wing Chirac government and
the President has placed strains on the structures
and administration of foreign policy. Clearly,
Chirac and Mitterrand are jostling for positions.
This has implications for the relationship between
prime minister and president. However, it is
doubtful that Chirac is substantially challenging
the role of the presidency (as distinct from the
person of the president). In the absence of an
overall co-ordinating body the president remains
the essential link. Cohabitation appears to be a
further step in legitimating and routinising authority in Fifth Republic institutions, although
it is a very new development.
  The effect of this has been to encroach upon the
traditional preserve of the Quai d'Orsay. This encroachment is further heightenend by the importance of economic issues in foreign policy.
Indeed, some commentators might argue that foreign
policy is increasingly an extension of industrial,
trade, financial or agricultural policy.[32] Overseas trade objectives directly influence the domestic economy. Moreover, the French state has
adopted a very forward role in financial affairs
and armaments sales. Currently, France is the
third largest exporter of arms, aided by the wish
of Third World clients to remain independent of
either superpower. Moreover, companies such as
Renault, Dassault aviation, the Commissariat à
l'Energie Atomique, Elf-Aquitaine, and Airbus Industrie can contribute considerable input into
foreign policy decision-making.[33] For example,
Elf-Aquitaine, an oil and energy company, has important links with Libya and South Africa. Iraqi
relations are also largely dependent on the inter-
flow of oil and arms, especially since the start
of the war between Iran and Iraq. In such an envi-
ronment, vested business interests are able to
talk with and directly influence members of the
government, a practice strengthened by the fact
that former ministers and officials often sit on
company boards after the cessation of their public
service.

THE QUAI D'ORSAY: PAST AND PRESENT

In the 1980s, the Quai d'Orsay no longer remains
the formulator of policy and no longer acts with
the initiative and independence it possessed in

the Third Republic.³⁴ However, despite this, the
Ministry still plays a very substantial role, especially in the area of administration. This is
chiefly because of the complexity of policy at all
levels, and to a lesser extent, some ongoing
instability in domestic politics. The Elysée has
limitations imposed upon it. Mitterrand's practice
of receiving advice from any relevant source means
that duplication of effort occurs, effort also
hindered by a certain lack of essential knowledge
at the Elysée. Moreover, the staff there numbers
only between forty and fifty, ensuring that they
must rely on other ministries and agencies. The
Quai, however, remains at the centre, dealing
daily with about 5,000 telegrams, of which the
foreign minister might look at fifty and the president about ten.³⁵

While the Quai on occasion has been slow to re-
spond to the challenges of twentieth century intricacies and shifts, it has been nevertheless at
the forefront of reform. In the very early twentieth-century its structure reflected its Eurocen-
tric and traditionalist approach. The Ministry had
a department of political affairs, a department of
economic affairs, a ministerial cabinet and various sub-departments including archives, protocol
and accounts. Before the First World War there was
no secretary-general to co-ordinate the various
branches. The Quai had a rather patronising
approach to the lesser known parts of the world.
It did not fully acknowledge the increased importance of economics in policy-making. Diplomacy was
conducted in a leisurely manner by agents who
formed a club. Through the ritual of the 'thé de
cinq heures' diplomatic agents came to know their
colleagues on a personal basis. Heads of departments could ascertain the mood of the bureaux, the
various sub-divisions of the Ministry. Because the
numbers were relatively restricted, intimate
groupings were formed (such as that of Paul
Cambon), family dynasties were created and paternalism counted for more than any supposed exam.
Aristocrats might still bestride the stage in important posts, where social status and wealth were
at a premium.³⁶

The First World War, and subsequently the Second, shattered such traditionalism. But reform was
not a belated response to these wars. Rather, the
foundations of modern French diplomacy were gradually being laid in an innovative way. As a result
of the crisis over the nature of the Republic in

1877, a definitive transitional period took place. A purging of conservative and aristocratic elements led to the 'bourgeoisification' of the Quai d'Orsay, which has proceeded down to the present day.[37] The Quai began to differentiate itself qualitatively from the thoroughly aristocratic British, German and Russian Foreign Offices. Education and equality of opportunity became the new benchmarks of the 'career', even if there was some very uneven application. The Quai d'Orsay came to depend for its recruits on the Ecole Libre des Sciences Politiques, a private school funded by financial magnates. Between 1899 and 1936, 249 of the 284 individuals who entered the diplomatic corps were products of this school. Here, diplomacy was taught in the positivist strain, where the amateur ceded to the professional, scientific career diplomat.[38] This professionalisation of the service, whereby standards of work and criteria for employment and advancement were established, reflected the prevailing trends after 1871 in the rest of the civil service and in other careers.[39] Indeed it was an integral part of the embourgeoisement of such careers.

The Quai d'Orsay responded in a positive manner before the First World War to some of the new complexities of twentieth-century diplomacy. In 1907 the most thoroughgoing reform in the period eventuated. In essence, the reform joined the departments of political and economic affairs. This was much more than an administrative reshuffle. It was a clear recognition of the economic dimension of modern decision-making.[40] Formal divisions between the diplomatic corps and consular service were abolished. The then Ministry of Commerce became significantly involved in certain policy processes. Commercial attachés were posted overseas. Many of the new positions in the Quai were accorded to men with a high level of economic training and background. France began more aggressively to link financial loans to other countries with industrial orders and political alignments. Along with this went a more farsighted approach to the 'New World', the Middle East, Asia and Africa. The Russo-Japanese War of 1905 profoundly affected the political and economic conditions prevailing in East Asia. The USA, and the Pacific in general, were beginning to be recognised as important areas of concern. As a result some missions in Europe, either obsolete or unusually costly, were terminated, and new missions were created in Paraguay,

Argentina, South Africa, the Congo, Liberia, Egypt, Afghanistan, Japan, Canada and the USA.[41] Such measures, more often than not, reflected the growing importance of financial, industrial and trade links.

The First World War witnessed further substantial changes. In 1914, the office of Secretary of State for Foreign Affairs, filled by a politician and still in existence in the Fifth Republic, was created. The Secretary acts as a liaison officer between parliament and the Quai d'Orsay. Normally, he is given special assignments and acts as a second during the Minister's absence. However, the Secretary has rarely had a central role in decision-making. In the Fifth Republic, the position has not always been filled. Moreover, there are now a number of different Secretaries of State, generally attached to the prime minister or to other ministers. Most are for specific purposes (e.g. the Secretary of State for European Affairs, attached to the Quai d'Orsay). Unlike ministers, they cannot introduce bills into the Chamber of Deputies nor do they usually attend the meetings of the council of minsters.

As more 'open diplomacy' came into vogue after 1918, the Permanent Commission of Foreign Affairs of the Assemblée Nationale, created in 1902, assumed more responsibility. Chiefly, it has reviewed decisions made by the Quai, mostly concerning itself with the daily application of affairs more than overall policy.[42] In the Fourth Republic it came to assume a pre-eminent position. It could invite officials and ministers to sit before it, although such attendance could largely be avoided. Often former prime ministers and foreign ministers who had become members of parliament have sat on its benches. This can sometimes work to the commission's detriment, as former insiders can gain direct access to the Quai's staff, thereby diminishing the institutional importance of the commission.[43] Moreover, lack of information, ill-defined channels of communication between it and the Quai, lack of staff and the divisiveness of party politics ensure that the Quai's role is largely maintained. Indeed, the Assemblée Nationale as a whole has done little to challenge the Quai's authority. Apart from the consensus built up over the Gaullist legacy, there remains a strong tradition inherited from the Third and Fourth Republics that the Quai's power should not be substantively reduced in the area of administration. The Quai still provides continuity and coherence even in the face of the governmental instability which persists to a certain extent in cohabitation. Parliamentarians usually wish to clarify past legislation more than address current problems. Given the regional nature of French interests, the politician is more preoccupied with domestic issues.

Since the First World War, the complexity of international affairs has had major ramifications on the Quai d'Orsay. Conference and summit diplomacy have largely replaced the 'secret diplomacy' of the ambassadorial elite. Because of rapid technological improvements, the head of government and the head of state are able to play a more immediate role, thereby diminishing the importance of the individual diplomat abroad. Such diminution is increased in certain Communist and East European countries, where the ambassador's role is to handle the more technical aspects of cultural, economic and social issues. Moreover, developments in modern international affairs have led to a bureaucratic explosion in the Quai d'Orsay. The number of services has proliferated. Judicial matters, mostly related to the interpretation and application of the various treaties have increased in importance.[44] The question of disarmament has created further specialisation. Supra-national organisations such as the League of Nations, then the United Nations, EC and OECD have swelled the ranks of the Quai.

By 1978, the Ministry had quadrupled the number of staff it had immediately after the Second World War. In all, 6,637 agents, 2,000 of whom were posted to the central administration, worked for the Ministry. Between 1948 and the 1980s the number of diplomatic representatives had risen from 65 to 139 and the number of posts from 213 to 317.[45] The Foreign Ministry, reflecting de Gaulle's notion of grandeur, has attempted to create a world presence on par with the USA. Nevertheless, modern-day terrorism, the hostility existing in certain regions, geographical distance and costly expenses have put a premium on advancement in the central administration. This can be unhealthy, as it may create an administrative elite more entangled with day-to-day politics and less concerned with overall policy and proper representation abroad. While career regulations have largely stopped a clique of 'young Turks' forming inside the Ministry, the fact that the President of the Republic's personal power has grown also means that individual diplomats and bureaucrats can stay in Paris.

THE ORGANISATION OF THE MINISTRY

The complexity of administration is reflected in the internal divisions of the central administration. The Quai d'Orsay has five general directorates (Political Affairs, Economic and Financial Affairs, Cultural Relations, French Abroad, Personnel and General Administration) as well as a number of services (Protocol, Information and the Press, Judicial Affairs, Archives and Documentation) which come under the direct authority of the secretary-general. At the head of the Ministry is the Foreign Minister. Often he has been a rather faceless person subject to changes in government or to the whims of the premier or president. For example, between 1968 and 1980, six different Foreign Ministers held office. They can be brought in from any positions but there is considerable movement from parliament, the Elysée and the Quai. Despite the shifting nature of the post, the Fifth Republic has seen some ministers who have had long tenure and who have wielded considerable authority. R. Couve de Murville, de Gaulle's Foreign Minister between 1958 and 1968, had a substantial input into the formulation and administration of policy.[46] Maurice Schumann (1969-73) also had relatively long tenure, as did Claude Cheysson, a former diplomat, who was particularly influential with France's relations with the Third World between 1981 and 1986.

Since 1920 the Secretary-General has had control over all services of the Ministry. This overall supervision and authority has largely eradicated serious structural defects, such as internal empire-building, excessive ambassadorial independence and duplication of administration. Despite this institutionalisation, the limits as well as the influence of this position have been felt by the incumbents.[47] Outside the Quai, the presidents' own staff have restricted such influence. Inside the Ministry, the Foreign Minister's cabinet, headed by a director, can play an equally restrictive role. The Minister's personal cabinet can be chosen from any source available. Admittedly, a considerable number of career diplomats enter the cabinet but outsiders who have previously had the Minister's confidence, or political allies and friends, can be members with inordinate power. The cabinet deals with relations with parliament, electoral matters, outgoing and ingoing correspondence, liaison with departments, translation and ciphers. While, technically, the ministerial cabinet does not deal with matters of foreign affairs, the unofficial encroachment into policy matters had led to a certain rivalry between it and the diplomats. The director of the cabinet can also have a substantial input in the area of personnel. If the Minister is inexperienced or preoccupied with electoral and parliamentary matters, the consultative role of the director increases considerably.

This potential for competition between the Ministry officials and the Minister's own staff predates the Fifth Republic and has been a constant source of tension since 1871. During the pre-1914 period and even after the war, the Minister's staff were notoriously known as a hotbed of intrigue which threatened to destroy continuity in foreign policy and bring the Quai into disrepute. The paralysis of foreign policy in the 1911 Agadir crisis with Germany was essentially caused by divisions between the ministerial cabinet and the political sub-divisions. Since then, the office of the cabinet has from time to time impeded the effective functioning of the central administration.[48]

Two relatively recent measures have strengthened co-ordination inside the Quai. In 1973 a Centre for Analysis and Planning was created, which acts as a link between the ministerial cabinet and the central services as well as a link between the Elysée and the Quai d'Orsay. Its main aim is to prepare digestible information for the government, analyse it and prepare long-term options.[49] The other measure has been the 'geographisation' of domains since 1976, the organisation of the Quai staff according to regional areas of concern. In part this is a return to the pre-1914 organisation. After 1945 functionalisation of areas created an unnatural division between political, economic and cultural affairs. Understandably, such a separation reflected a notion that foreign policy was more complex and was to be administered by technocrats. Any one country or area, however, could not be viewed in these narrow terms. The return to 'geographisation' after 1976 was a clear recognition that the basis of any sound foreign policy was to view relations with other countries and regions in their entirety. Equally, it was an acknowledgement of the intimate links between political, economic, military and cultural concerns.

'Geographisation' has entailed the creation of mostly autonomous sections dealing with both economic and political issues in designated areas: the Directorate of Europe, Asia and the Pacific, African and Madagascan Affairs, North Africa and the Middle East, and America. Such directorates deal mostly with bilateral affairs. International organisations, multilateral negotiations, atomic questions, and European-Arab relations are handled by the Directorate of Political Affairs. Francophone affairs is a classic example of shifting responsibilities. Until 1981 it was handled by the Directorate of Political Affairs. Mitterrand then created an autonomous Haut Conseil de la Francophonie. In turn, Chirac in 1986 supplanted it with a Secrétariat d'Etat à la Francophonie, which is attached to the prime minister's office. The reorganisation is not finalised as yet, making it very difficult to perceive the exact direction of the central administration.[50]

The next main division in the Ministry is the Directorate of Economic and Financial Affairs, which keeps the minister informed of the economic consequences of political decisions and provides other technical ministries, such as Industry, Transport and Agriculture, with the political and foreign policy ramifications of economic measures.[51] It can be argued that modern foreign policy, if not merely agricultural and economic policy abroad, is increasingly an extension of such domestic issues, and foreign policy is utilised to support the domestic economy, for example, through the sale of arms.[52] Consequently, this directorate has come to assume an increasing share of responsibility and has become entangled with agencies emanating from the Elysée and the European affairs secretariat. Although most of its officials have strong economic backgrounds, it extends its jurisdiction well beyond narrow economic issues. This is largely because, in defending the national interest, it often battles with other ministries which wish to lead negotiations, which see various matters only in terms of financial gains, regional issues and industrial orders, and which can be influenced by special interest lobby groups. In certain areas, such as EC agricultural policy, the Directorate may at times remain sub-

servient to other ministries but constantly pro-
pounds the primacy of politics over economics.
Since the Gaullist legacy has been to employ foreign policy to strengthen political institutions
at home, the Directorate of Economic and Financial
Affairs has maintained its ascendancy with difficulty.

Another major division is the General Directorate of Cultural Relations. This directorate is
broken up into a number of areas: the cultural
exchange services; the service of instruction and
linguistic exchanges, scientific, technical and
development services, which were added after a reorganisation in 1969; administration and technical
services; and a mission of orientation and co-
ordination. This directorate and its agents have
become increasingly more important over the last
forty years. The French, influenced by the idealism of the French Revolution, have had a particularly strong tradition of cultural mission. More
recently, decolonisation has shifted policy towards indirect means, largely cultural, of influencing foreign countries.[53] Indeed roughly 42 per
cent of the directorate's budget goes into providing teachers and education abroad. It also provides technical experts in areas such as health,
justice and industry. Moreover, scholarships are
awarded to overseas students from countries which
cannot maintain sufficient technical and political
education or over which France wishes to retain
some cultural influence.

Despite the Directorate of Cultural Relations'
expansion, growth is sometimes haphazard and the
restrictions on it are evident. For example, Francophone affairs remain the preserve of the political directorate - when the Elysée and Matignon are
not struggling over them. Moreover, where the
president of the Republic shows definite interest
in regions such as Africa and the Middle East, the
Elysée encroaches on the directorate's territory.[54]

The Directorate of the French Abroad, known
before 1981 as the Directorate for Administrative
Conventions and Social Affairs, is by no means as
influential as the previous three. This is largely
because it deals with consulates, presides over
its agents and is concerned with non-political aspects such as services for French people overseas
and foreigners in France. Nevertheless, the directorate does have a certain significance, given the
number of foreigners in France. The consular ser-

vice, for its part, has always been considered somewhat inferior, the épicerie of the Ministry, despite the equivalence in recruiting and administration which resulted after 1945.[55] There are several reasons for this. In no strict sense does a consul represent the national government before a foreign power. His duty is to establish a liaison with fellow nationals and to defend their pecuniary interests. Consuls have tended to complain they are nothing more than a courier service for French products. They contribute little to the overall framework of global policy, even if they provide important information gathering. Even their consular duties have been eroded by the employment of attachés from other ministries and the encroachment of other ministries. In 1961, for example, of the 292 missions in existence only 53 were directly nominated by the Quai d'Orsay.[56] Some of these missions, given the French government's determination to maintain representation abroad, are in distant backwaters of the globe. Extreme temperatures, unsanitary conditions, pestilence and political anarchy have often led to transferral from the consular service to the diplomatic corps or to attempts to establish careers in Paris.

The final major division in the Quai is the Directorate of Personnel and General Administration which has been one of the most controversial departments. While a major function is the routine administration of the Quai d'Orsay itself, its budget, furnishings, property, etc., it has the other function of controlling personnel. Herein has been the central problem. From 1882 standardised personal dossiers were kept on each agent. In 1907 some attempt was made to regulate conditions of service, promotion and career structures. But personnel were attached to the ministerial cabinet, thereby leaving it vulnerable to political influence, nepotism and patronage. Theoretically, the 1907 reforms created a separate Bureau of Personnel, but until the Second World War, interference was rife. During the inter-war period, Berthelot, in particular, fostered the advancement of friends or allies to the detriment of officials who had priority.[57] Only in 1945 did there occur a meaningful examination and only then did the personnel services begin to achieve a measure of independence. Standardisation has evolved gradually. Since 1958 the arrival of the president of the Republic as a major diplomatic actor has led to an

increase in the number of appointments at the top
made from outside.

THE STAFFING OF THE MINISTRY

The general nature of recruitment has changed substantially since the Second World War. The Ecole
Nationale d'Administration (ENA), established in
1946 provides the bulk of recruits, although there
are still recruits from the Ecole des Langues Ori-
entales Vivantes. Its effect was to break the
nexus with the pre-war world. Essentially, those
agents who were the products of the old Ecole des
Sciences Politiques were trained in thoroughly
diplomatic matters. The elitist and statist traditions of the school had a two-fold effect. They
produced a new bourgeois elite convinced of its
own competence to govern. Moreover, they created
an elite conscious of certain notions of the
grandeur and eternity of France, despite the
caprices of politics. In representing the long-
term intangible interests of France, the diplomat
or bureaucrat might deliberately sabotage government policy.

The new elite were considerably different in approach. The standardisation and democratisation of
all civil services made it possible for sons and
daughters of lower income families to enter the
Quai. (Admittedly, many still have strongly upper-
middle class socio-economic backgrounds. Cases of
the working class entering the Quai at the top
level are few.) The new elites' training, moreover, was considerably different. All énarques
(products of the ENA) are given general training
for all the civil services. As a result, a new
technocratic corps has emerged, no longer with the
same strong consciousness of the statist position
and much more prepared ideologically and technically to address more 'mundane' affairs, such as
economic, technological and judicial concerns.
Given that instability remains in the parliamentary system, vested interest groups have tended to
bypass parliament and lobby the bureaucrat, which
has strengthened agents' control over day-to-day
administration.

The training for civil servants is varied. Many
go to the Institut d'Etudes Politiques before taking the ENA entry exam. Some study at a university
or another grande école, or work in administration
and gain admission to ENA by the concours

intérieur. Upon entering the ENA, the applicant is assured of a position in the civil service. The course is diverse. It starts with an initial period of training then a year in a prefecture or overseas, where reports are made on the student's progress. The énarque then spends two months in a private firm, four months of further training in Paris, and finally prepares for a written and oral exam. The options open to candidates depend on their overall aggregate. They may decide on one of the other grands corps, such as the Inspection des Finances or the Cours des Comptes. If the énarque decides on the Quai d'Orsay, then he or she will enter at Category A, the top level.[58]

The consequence of this new system is to break down the vestiges of homogeneity in the Quai d'Orsay. While some follow the steps of their ancestral predecessors, the old closed club mentality and former dynasties have mostly disappeared. This has been reinforced by the impact that the Second World War had on the Ministry. Between 1944-5, new staff from the Free French were introduced. After 1945, administrators, not necessarily from the Quai, were relocated as a result of decolonisation.[59]

CONCLUSION

In sum, the formation of French foreign policy has altered substantially since the turn of the century. The days of the Third Republic where individual bureaucrats and diplomats could exercise independent, even excessive, initiative have gone. The Quai is less involved in formulation of policy than in its execution. This shift has been strengthened by the institutionalised authority of the president of the Republic, as well as the legitimation and routinisation of political structures. The President of the Republic, the Elysée staff, the premier, the Matignon staff, various other government agencies such as the Chamber, the Senate, and other ministries such as defence and finance, provide considerable input into policy-making. Outside vested interest groups such as the press and big business also make substantial contributions. However, given the machinery and personal workings of the presidential system and the intricacies and complexities of global relations, the Quai d'Orsay, through its technocratic expertise and its daily administration of the most complex issues, remains the very focus of modern French policy-making in the Fifth Republic.

NOTES AND REFERENCES

1. P.G. Lauren, Diplomats and Bureaucrats: The First Institutional Responses to Twentieth Century Diplomacy in France and Germany (Stanford University Press, Stanford, 1976), p. 29; F.L. Schuman, War and Diplomacy in the French Republic (Howard Fertig, New York, 1969), pp. 12, 13, 19. For an overview, see also the recent collective work, Les Affaires étrangères et le corps diplomatique (Editions du C.N.R.S., Paris, 1984).

2. H. Leyret, Le Président de la République (Paris, 1973), pp. 31-42, 109-22.

3. R.D. Anderson, France 1870-1914 (Routledge and Kegan Paul, London, 1984), p. 75.

4. See, for example, J.F.V. Keiger, 'Raymond Poincaré and French Foreign Policy, 1912-1914', Ph.D. Thesis (Cambridge University, 1980), and his later published work, France and the Origins of the First World War (Macmillan, London, 1983); also G. Wright, Raymond Poincaré and the French Presidency (Stanford University Press, Stanford, 1942).

5. M.B. Hayne, 'The Quai d'Orsay and French Foreign Policy, 1898-1914', Ph.D. Thesis (University of Sydney, 1985), ch. 9; Poincaré himself noted the diminution of his power in his daily diary (Notes journalières, Bibliothèque Nationale (Nouvelles Acquisitions Françaises 16026) Poincaré Manuscripts.)

6. Between September 1870 and August 1914 thirty men served as Foreign Minister in even more governments. See A. Soulier, L'Instabilité ministérielle sous la Troisième République (Sirey, Paris, 1939).

7. Hayne, 'The Quai d'Orsay', chs 3, 11.

8. G. Dethan, 'The Ministry of Foreign Affairs since the Nineteenth Century', in Z. Steiner (ed.), Times Survey of the Foreign Ministries of the World (The Times, London, 1982), p. 211; R. Pinto, Eléments de droit constitutionnel (Morel et Cordunant, Lille, 1952), p. 328.

9. J.N. Jeanneney, 'Finances, presse et politique: L'Affaire de la Banque industrielle de Chine, 1921-1923', Revue d'historique, Vol. CCLI (1975), pp. 378-81; also G. Kurgan-van-Hentenryk, 'Phillippe Berthelot et les intérêts ferroviares franco-belges en Chine, 1912-1914', Revue d'histoire moderne et contemporaine, Vol. 22 (1975), pp. 272-92.

10. See the chapter on the French Foreign Office in G.A. Craig and F. Gilbert (eds), The Diplomats (Princeton University Press, Princeton, 1972). A revealing book on the

crises in foreign policy before 1940 is J.B. Duroselle, La Décadence (Imprimerie Nationale, Paris, 1979).

11. D. Pickles, 'French Foreign Policy' in F.S. Northedge (ed.), The Foreign Policies of the Powers (Free Press, London, 1968), pp. 195, 196.

12. A. Cobban, A History of France, Vol. 3 (Penguin Books, Harmondsworth, 1965), p. 234.

13. Dethan, 'The Foreign Ministry', pp. 218-9; J.B. Duroselle, 'L'Elaboration de la politique étrangère française', Revue française de science politique, Vol. 6 (1956) p. 418.

14. M. Massigli, Quelques maladies de l'Etat (Plon, Paris, 1958), p. 51; A. Grosser, La IVE République et sa politique extérieure (Armand Colin, Paris, 1961), pp. 55-60.

15. D. Pickles, The Fifth French Republic (London, 1968), ch. 8; also her The Government and Politics of France, Vol. I (Methuen, London, 1972), Appendix H.

16. H. Tint, French Foreign Policy since the Second World War (Weidenfeld and Nicolson, London, 1972), p. 245.

17. N. Waites, 'The Creation of French Foreign Policy', in P. Morris and S. Williams (eds.), France in the World (Association for the Study of Modern and Contemporary France, Nottingham, 1985), p. 1.

18. J.R. Frears, France in the Giscard Presidency (Allen and Unwin, London, 1981), p. 126; P. Cerny, The Politics of Grandeur (Cambridge University Press, Cambridge, 1980), preface.

19. E.A. Kolodziej, 'Socialist France Faces the World', Contemporary French Civilization, Vol. VIII, Nos 1-2 (1983-84), p. 163.

20. F. Mitterrand, Réflexions sur la politique extérieure de la France (Fayard, Paris, 1986), p. 95. For a recent general assessment of Mitterrand's policies and influence, see G. Robin, La Diplomatie de Mitterrand ou le triomphe des apparences (Editions de la Bièvre, Loges-en Josas, 1985).

21. Waites, 'Creation of French Foreign Policy', p. 4.

22. E. Rouleau, 'Diplomatie Secrète', Le Monde, 19 September 1984.

23. D. Pickles, 'French Foreign Policy', p. 197.

24. Charles de Gaulle, Mémoires d'espoir (Plon, Paris, 1970), Vol. 1, p. 7; see also Waites, 'Creation of French Foreign Policy', p. 2.

25. Cerny, The Politics of Grandeur, pp. 100, 119.

26. J.P. Nettl, Political Mobilisation (Faber, London, 1967), pp. 174-5.

27. R. Debray, La Puissance et les rêves (Gallimard, Paris, 1984), pp. 126-32; E. Weisenfeld, 'François Mitterrand: L'Action extérieure', Politique étrangère January 1986), p. 138.

28. Frears, Giscard Presidency, p. 120.

29. Ibid., p. 120. See also S. Cohen, 'Prospective et politique étrangère. Le Centre d'Analyse et de Prévision du Ministère des Relations Extérieures', Revue française de Science politique, December 1982, pp. 1055-74.

30. P. Coste, 'On French Foreign Policy', in Morris and Williams, France in the World, p. 16.

31. Ibid.

32. Dethan, 'The Foreign Ministry', pp. 218-20.

33. Frears, The Giscard Presidency, p. 121; Waites; 'Creation of French Foreign Policy', p. 6; Weisenfeld, 'François Mitterrand', p. 39.

34. See ex-Foreign Minister Claude Cheysson's comments quoted in M.C. Smouts, 'The External Policy of François Mitterrand', International Affairs, Vol. 59 (1983), p. 156.

35. Dethan, 'French Foreign Ministry', p. 212.

36. A.H.J. Mayer, The Persistence of the Old Regime (Croom Helm, London, 1981), p. 309; also Hayne, 'The Quai d'Orsay', ch. 1.

37. On this definite transitional stage, see G. Kreis, 'Frankreichs Republikanische Grossmachtpolitik, 1870-1914', Ph.D. Thesis (University of Basel, 1980).

38. See T.R. Osborne, 'The Recruitment of the Administrative Elite in the Third French Republic, 1870-1905', Ph.D. Thesis (University of Connecticut, 1974).

39. T. Zeldin, France, 1848-1945: Ambition and Love (Oxford University Press, Oxford, 1979), ch. 8.

40. 'Réorganisation de l'administration du Ministère des Affaires Etrangères', Decree of 29 April 1907, Annuaire Diplomatique, 1907.

41. Journal Officiel, Chambre, Report 2015 (1908); 3318 (1914); 6339 (1919); and 2020 (1921).

42. M. Schumann in J. Basdevant (ed.), Les Affaires étrangères (Paris, 1959), pp. 22ff.

43. Tint, French Foreign Policy, p. 242.

44. On the complexity of new legal matters, see K.A. Hamilton, 'The Air in Entente Diplomacy: Great Britain and the International Aerial Navigation Conference of 1910', The International History Review 3 (1981); also C. Parry, 'Foreign Policy and International Law', in F.H. Hinsley (ed.), British Foreign Policy under Sir Edward Grey (Cambridge University Press, Cambridge, 1977), pp. 89-113.

45. Dethan, 'The Foreign Ministry', p. 218.

46. On the views of Couve de Murville, see R. Couve de Murville, Une Politique étrangère, 1958-68 (Paris, 1971).

47. See various memoirs of officials such as H. Alphand, L'Etonnement d'être: Journal, 1939-1973, (Paris, 1977); J. Chauvel, Commentaire, 3 Vols. (Fayard, Paris, 1971-3).

48. Hayne, 'The Quai d'Orsay', pp. 16-17.

49. Cohen, 'Centre d'Analyse et de Prévision', pp. 1055-76.

50. For most recent changes, see the <u>Annuaires Diplomatiques</u> since 1976. The tentative nature of the changes can be seen in the slowness with which they are recognised in the <u>Annuaires</u>.

51. Tint, <u>French Foreign Policy</u>, p. 221.

52. Dethan, 'The Foreign Ministry', p. 217; Coste, 'On French Foreign Policy', p. 16.

53. C. Lebel in Basdevant (ed.), <u>Les Affaires étrangères p</u>. 59.

54. Frears, <u>The Giscard Presidency</u>, p. 123.

55. D. Busk, <u>The Craft of Diplomacy</u> (Pall Mall Press, London, 1967), p. 125.

56. J. Baillou and P. Pelletier, <u>Les Affaires étrangères</u> (Paris, 1962), p. 39.

57. Craig and Gilbert, <u>The Diplomats</u>, chapter on the French Foreign Office.

58. R.C. Macridis, 'The French Administration', in R.C. Macridis and R.E. Ward, <u>Modern Political Systems: Europe</u> (Prentice-Hall, Englewood Cliffs, 1977), p. 280.

59. Tint, <u>French Foreign Policy</u>, p. 234.

INDEX

Index

Maghreb (North Africa)
8-10, 13, 44, 46,
74, 80-1, 85-6, 90-6
passim, 123, 134,
138, 170, 172, 174,
179, 185
Malavoi 177
Mali 9, 77, 89, 94,
106, 109, 123
Malraux, A. 181
Mangin, S. 79
Manigat, L. 175, 190
Mao Tse-Tung 130
Marcellin circular 77
Marquesas 150
Marseille 80, 87
Martinique 148-9, 152-
3, 159-62, 172, 177-
84 passim
Massenet, M. 76
Mater et Magistra 128
Mauritania 77, 103,
106, 109, 123, 176
Mauritius, 9, 123, 174,
175-9 passim, 186
Mauroy, P. 87, 129
Mayotte 123, 149-51,
154-5, 160-2, 164-5
Médecins sans
Frontières 144
media 16, 27, 102, 118,
126-7, 129, 138,
140, 174, 179, 184,
186-7, 194
Mediterranean Sea 44
Melanesians 151, 153,
156, 158, 178
Memmi, A. 102, 181
Mendès-France, P. 65
Messmer, P. 19, 165,
169
Michaux-Chevry, L. 187,
190-1
Middle East 10, 11, 13,
65, 92, 131, 179,
188, 205, 210
migration 74-101, 148,
151-6, 161, 169
military intervention
113-5, 116-7, 123
million Stoléru 78-9

mineral resources 105-
7, 148, 150, 163-4
Ministry of Agriculture
147, 210
Ministry of Commerce
205
Ministry of Co-
operation 5, 110-1,
114, 129, 136, 138,
140, 144, 147, 191
Ministry of Culture 95,
181
Ministry of Defence 5,
111, 202
Ministry of DOM-TOM
148-169
Ministry of Education
147
Ministry of Employment
76
Ministry of External
Relations 98, 147
Ministry of Finance 5,
147
Ministry of Foreign
Affairs 5, 24, 110,
140, 142, 146-7,
191, 202-218
Ministry of Foreign
Trade 95
Ministry of the
Interior 79, 87, 95
Ministry of Social
Affairs 81, 85
Mirage bombers 17-20
missiles, ballistic 17-
21, 25-26
mission civilisatrice
170
Mitterrand, F. 4, 5, 6,
8, 10-16 passim, 20-
1, 23-5, 27-9, 37,
39, 60, 66, 81, 84,
90, 105, 111, 114,
119, 122, 126, 131,
133, 137-41, 147,
173, 186, 188, 190,
199-204, 210
Mitterrand, J. 200
Mitterrand, J.C. 121,
140